A Basketball Story

by

Timothy Brannan

Other Books By Timothy Brannan

Into the Elephant Grass: A Viet-Nam Fable

TEACH [Also Kindle Edition]

Adventures in Another Paradise [Also Kindle Edition]

Manhattan Spiritual [Also Kindle Edition]

Copyright 2008 by Timothy Brannan
ISBN 978-0-9820277-1-4
Published in the United States of America by
Gemini Publishing 2008

Cover design by Debra Walter, ImageMakers Advertising LLC
imdaytona.com

The most amazing characteristic of this NC State team was the ability to conquer adversity in whatever form.

Joe Tiede, *News & Observer*, **March 27, 1974**

Author's Introduction

There was a time when college freshmen could not play on varsity basketball teams. There was a time when the only three-point play in college basketball was a made basket and free throw. There was a time in college basketball when the dunk was not allowed. There was a time in college basketball when only conference champions represented conferences in the NCAA Tournament. This book is an attempt to recreate the story of the 1974 Wolfpack national championship run in those days when freshmen weren't eligible, when there was no three-point shot, when dunks were not allowed, and when only a single team, the conference champion, represented a conference in the NCAA National Championship Tournament.

The focus of this book is, to some small extent, more on David Thompson than most of the other players because of the simple fact that during that time the focus was more on him than on the others. However, in the process of researching this book, I have come to realize that the facts speak very loudly for the final historical focus to be more on the team as a whole as well as on one additional individual player. That player is the one without whom there would never have been an undefeated ACC season in 1973 or a National Championship in 1974 or a 57-1 two year record. The player who was the Most Valuable Player in the ACC Tournament in both 1973 and 1974. The player who faced down and beat all of the most important and impressive big men in the game at that time from Len Elmore of Maryland and Bobby Jones of UNC to Marvin Barnes of Proidence and Bill Walton of UCLA. That player was Tom Burleson. It is evident that it was not David Thompson alone who was an absolutely indispensable ingredient on the 1974 Wolfpack team that was and still remains one of the greatest college basketball teams in the history of the sport. If anyone doubts that conclusion, simply take a look at the results of the following season, when, without Burleson, the Wolfpack did not win the ACC regular season or the tournament.

My observations are in no way intended to impinge upon the superstar stature of David Thompson who is, in my humble estimation, still the single greatest college basketball player of all time, Michael Jordan notwithstanding. I am simply pointing out what I consider, after exhaustive research, to be a glaring historical inequity. For the most part, however, these players comprised a team's team, not a collection of individuals.

This work is **not** a so-called "authorized" biography of any one player or a history of the team. It is a well-researched telling of the team's story using a "dramatic re-enactment" approach that, I hope, reads more like a novel than a straight biography or history.

The basic material facts are true. For example, I rely upon actual scores of games, team win-loss records, basic game descriptions, information about family and friends, and so forth where available. However, dramatic situations may or may not have actually happened the way I have presented them. Norman Sloan or Dean Smith or Al McGuire may or may not have spoken the exact words or thought the exact thoughts attributed to them in this book However, they were involved in the types of scenes depicted and might have acted the way I have written it or said what I have put in their mouths or thought what I might have put in their heads. Sportscasters like Nick Pond and Wally Ausley or Billy Packer and Jim Thacker may or may not have made the actual comments or asked the particular questions attributed to them in this book. Words may have been "put into their mouths" to serve dramatic purposes. Or, a particular press conference that is depicted as taking place just prior to or just after a game may have actually taken place a couple of days before or after the game or there may not have actually been a press conference.

The creation of this work has been a labor of love over many, many years while I continued my career as a political operative and legislative counsel. My hope was to dramatize this extremely significant year in college basketball history, not simply to record the history of that year or to glorify any individual player. I sincerely hope that you enjoy the experience of reading this story as much as I have enjoyed writing it.

Timothy Brannan
Daytona Beach, Florida
2008

Contents

Author's Introduction

1   The House That Case Built

2   Dean's List and The Tar Heels Litmus Test

3   "Tell Walter Cronkite That The Doctor is busy!"

4   Beyond Midnight Madness

5   Reality Sets In

6   On The Rebound

7   Son of Super Sunday and the Tobacco Road to Redemption

8   Overcoming Adversity, Again

9   And The Blind Shall See

10 Maryland and The Preacher Man

11 "Nobody Can Stop Me!"

12 *The Spirit of '76*

13 A Fresh Start, Man

14 David & Goliath

15 Beyond Giants and Wizards

16 At Last, The Ring!

Dedicated Athlete

Three square meals a day
And I'll get plenty of rest.
So when I step out on the court
I'll do my best.
I'm going to run every day and lift weights.
I'm a dedicated athlete and I know what it takes.
I've got to make it for my family
And I've got to make it for myself.
But my dreams will only be fairy tales
If I don't have good health.
God be with me
And lead me to the top.
Help me go
And don't let me stop.

Phil Spence

1
The House That Case Built

> *"[William Neal Reynolds Coliseum] has been called the "House that Case Built," and a case can be made that it has housed as many memorable moments as any college basketball arena in the country."*
> "50 Years of Thrills," *The News & Observer*,
> November 8, 1998

"David!" Monte Towe's voice crackled over the erupting capacity crowd at William Neal Reynolds Coliseum in Raleigh, the capitol city of North Carolina, the home court of the North Carolina State University Wolfpack basketball team, and the site of the 1974 NCAA Eastern Regional Tournament. Back on March 13, 1892 when North Carolina Agricultural & Mechanical College engaged in its very first athletic event—a football game with the Raleigh Male Academy that the College won 12-6—the official school nickname for the team was "Farmers and Mechanics." Later came the "Aggies," the "Techs," and then the popular "Red Terrors." But it wasn't until 1922 that a State fan, disgusted by the football team's 3-3-3 record, told school athletic officials that the team would never be a winner as long as the players "acted like a wolfpack." Once word of the fan's comment got out, State students immediately tagged the football team the "Wolfpack." The name stuck.

"Not since that first game in William Neal Reynolds Coliseum, the House that Case Built, on December 2, 1949 when the Pack prowled past Washington & Lee 67 to 47 has this coliseum been so supercharged, has a crowd been so completely into a game," Wally Ausley, whispered into his microphone. "As Vic Bubbas tells the story, he got the ball on the tip-off in that first game here in William Neal Reynolds Coliseum. He didn't usually take many shots because Dick Dickey and Sammy Ranzino were the Wolfpack scorers in those days. However, Bubbas drove in, shot, and missed. He got the rebound, shot again, and missed. Then, he got the rebound again and made the follow shot. As Vic tells it, he didn't have any intention of passing. 'It was probably the only time in my life I hogged the ball,' he said.

"Coach Case took him out. 'You really wanted that first basket, didn't you?' he asked Vic. Bubbas replied, 'Yeah, I did.' Case just laughed and said, 'Get back out there.'

"The official dedication of the coliseum didn't take place until April 22, 1950, however, at an Ice Capades show. The dedication program read, and I quote: 'It took ten years, three governors, four General Assemblies, four Budget Commissions, two Budget Directors . . . and 3,900,003 North Carolinians to build the William Neal Reynolds Coliseum.' The dedication failed to say: 'And one determined coach,' meaning, of course, the late Everett Case coach of the North Carolina State Wolfpack."

Everett Case was always prepared both on and off the court. Also, just like a Boy Scout, he was thrifty, brave, clean, and reverent. He watched every dollar and invested wisely. He willingly took risks with clever innovations, and he paid attention to detail. He was fastidious regarding the selection of his wardrobe and meticulous in his dress. His reverence, when all was said and done, he reserved for the American game invented by a Canadian physical education instructor in Springfield, Massachusetts.

When James Naismith talked the janitor into nailing peach baskets on opposite walls of the International Young Men's Christian Training College gymnasium in Springfield, Massachusetts, he never envisioned basketball as becoming one of the most popular team sports in the world.

Born in Almonte, Ontario, Naismith was a graduate of McGill University and the Presbyterian Theological College. In 1891, one of the various courses assigned to him at the International Young Men's Christian Training College was physical education. Summer was over and he needed a way to keep a group of bored, trouble-making young men interested in their gym class during the months when they could not get outside. In those days, physical education consisted of calisthenics, gymnastics, and repetitive drills. Naismith, who was a true advocate of the adage, "healthy body, healthy mind", was quite determined to get the young men in his class actively interested in sports by coming up with a new indoor game for them to play.

At first, he tried modifying aspects of soccer, lacrosse, and football but without success. Then, he seriously analyzed what he would like to see in an indoor sport. Since he wanted no out-and-out roughhousing on the hardwood floor, he decided using a large ball about the size of a soccer ball would work. Next, he decided that players could not run with the ball and that an elevated goal made the game that much more challenging.

By December 21, 1891, Naismith had compiled a rough list of thirteen basic rules, posted them on the school bulletin board and with the assistance of the janitor, nailed peach baskets on opposite ends of the gymnasium. He even managed to convince the janitor to climb a ladder and retrieve the ball each time a player successfully landed it in a peach basket.

Students loved the game, and it wasn't long before schools and colleges across the country caught basketball fever and introduced the game to their own institutions. A few of his students suggested that he call the new sport Naismith-ball, but he decided that would never work. Eventually he settled on basketball.

A man of strong religious principles and one who loved sports, James Naismith was eventually inducted into the Springfield Basketball Hall of Fame and received various other accolades for his achievement.

Like Naismith, Everett Case never married because he, more than anything else in life, loved basketball and the players he coached. There seemed to be no room left for a wife and family. He was a man of vision, but he often appeared to be at his happiest off the court when he entertained friends or players or sipped his Early Times in the relaxing atmosphere of his Cameron Village home.

The Old Gray Fox was born in Anderson Indiana June 21, 1900. At as early an age as fifteen, mythology claims that Case coached a Methodist Church team. He graduated in 1919 from Anderson High School, and according to the yearbook; he declared his future occupation as "basketball coach." After graduation, Case went to the University of Illinois to learn from Ralph R. Jones who later became a legend at Purdue.

Although he never played serious competitive basketball, Case became one of the most successful high school coaches in Indiana history. That all started when Frankfort High School selected the twenty-two year old Everett Case from among eighteen applicants for the $1,800 a year job as Frankfort's basketball and track coach. His Frankfort High School teams won four state championships: 1925, 1929, 1936, and 1939. Overall Case compiled a record of 467 victories and only 124 defeats in 23 seasons, beginning at Connersville High when he was only eighteen and still in college.

After enlisting in the Navy in 1941, Case received a commission as a senior-grade lieutenant. He left materials in his desk at Frankfort High School and didn't retrieve them until 1946. The newly commissioned lieutenant reported to Annapolis for a four-week training course. Then off to Chicago for five weeks training and then to Naval Pre-flight school at St. Mary's College in California. He served as Assistant Athletic Director and Director of Basketball. He was also Athletic Director at the Alameda Naval Air Station.

In 1943, DePauw University at Greencastle, Indiana began a naval flight preparatory school and abbreviated the basketball schedule. Case was a Lieutenant Commander by then and Athletic Director of the program.

Upon leaving the Navy in 1946 Case, first, stopped at Frankfort High long enough to clean out the desk he had locked and left six years earlier. Immediately thereafter, he took over as head coach at North Carolina State College. Before the war, Hoosiers had flocked to California to play basketball. After the War, Case brought Hoosiers and Hoosier style basketball to the South.

Media coverage of his arrival at North Carolina State College in July 1946 was limited to page thirteen of the Raleigh *News & Observer*. A proposed fifteen-cent increase in the price of a gallon of ice cream completely overshadowed the six-paragraph story on the sports page. The forty-six-year-old Case stated that he expected to recruit "several tall, rangy lads with plenty of speed" for his first team at State College. The story also reported that many who followed the sport of college basketball closely were predicting that, now, big-time basketball was truly on its way.

Everett Case didn't single-handedly bring great basketball to North Carolina or to North Carolina State. What he did was establish a different style of basketball, a "run 'em gun 'em" fast break kind of basketball. Two of the magical totems he carried in his Indiana gym bag were showmanship and promotion. But, more than anything else in his gym bag full of tricks, Case brought an enduring passion for the sport, one he helped spread throughout the state and region to the level of religious fervor. No one won more converts along Tobacco Road throughout the Bible Belt than Everett Case, not even Billy Graham. You had to eat, sleep, and dream basketball to gain that kind of following. According to longtime assistant Butter Anderson, Case did.

No more walk-it-up, snoozing games for State College. Instead, he recruited some of those "tall, rangy, speedy lads." Many were from Indiana, his home state and thus were nicknamed the "Hoosier Hotshots."

Among them were Dick Dickey and Sammy Ranzino, Vic Bubas, and a tough, headstrong, super-competitive type named Norman Sloan.

The Hotshots ran and ran. Case studied game films, one of the first coaches to do it. He had his players introduced before games with a spotlight. His players cut down the nets after winning championships, a tradition he established in his days as a high school coach in Indiana.

"He was a visionary, a big-picture guy," according to Les Robinson, who played for Case later at State. "He was a great coach, yes, but he was also a great promoter. He was marketing the game in a time when 'market' usually meant the Winn Dixie or the Seven Eleven."

"Case was a salesman of the game," Vic Bubas said, "and he used Reynolds Coliseum to sell it."

His dream for NC State was a large arena overflowing with those as passionate about the sport as he was, a basketball showcase unlike any ever built or imagined in this slice of the South. So, of course, Case saw to it that William Neal Reynolds Coliseum was finished. Construction had begun prior to World War II. Reynolds Coliseum was to have been a replica of Duke Indoor Stadium, now called Cameron. In fact, the blueprints for the two buildings were identical when construction began before World War II. But, Case had his own plans after the war. He demanded that the facility be completed and enlarged. With the steel beams already in place, engineers couldn't widen the building. Railroad tracks prevented expansion to the north. They could only enlarge on the south end of the coliseum, creating a quirky rectangular shape that positioned many seats behind the baskets.

By 1949, he had his new showcase, and soon created the Dixie Classic, which brought the nation's best teams to Reynolds for a Christmas holiday tournament.

In many ways, Reynolds Coliseum not only was a tangible part of Case's legacy but also was the cornerstone of what became the nation's best basketball league. There was Madison Square Garden in New York and William Neal Reynolds Coliseum in Raleigh. The other facilities were gymnasiums.

When the ACC formed in 1953, there was little debate about where the league's postseason tournament would land. Memorial Auditorium in Raleigh had just 3,500 seats and Duke Indoor Stadium 9,000.

"They knew they could sell the most tickets at Reynolds - it was that simple," William Friday, an alumnus of NCSU and president emeritus of the UNC system, recalled. "Money was big then, just as money is big now."

"There wasn't a place in the Southeast as big as Reynolds," opined Marvin "Skeeter" Francis, a former ACC assistant commissioner. "Everett cashed in with Reynolds Coliseum" The ACC and Reynolds Coliseum became synonymous, and the ACC Tournament rapidly gained the reputation as "the best seat in college basketball." The tournament was there every year until 1966, with the State people usually sitting in the same seats every year, the best seats."

The 1950s belonged to the Old Gray Fox and State College. Kids all over the state huddled by their radios to listen to the Wolfpack games. The next day, they were out shooting jump shots on the basketball goals they pleaded with their daddies to put up in driveways or nail to barn doors, kids just like David Thompson and Tommy Burleson.

The Pack won five ACC titles in Reynolds. They felt invincible according to former All-America Vic Molodet.

Carolina, frustrated by a string of losses to the Wolfpack, hired Frank McGuire. Duke, on Case's recommendation, hired Vic Bubas off the State staff. Wake Forest hired Bones McKinney. The race was on, and, in its own way, this race for basketball supremacy along Tobacco Road easily overshadowed the arms race and the race for the moon and outer space. Big Four basketball flourished. Schools built new basketball venues.

But, it went beyond the X's and O's. Case, ever the showman, also conceived an elite eight-team tournament to be played in Reynolds the week after Christmas, inviting schools from all over the country to come and take on the Big Four: State, North Carolina, Duke and Wake Forest. The Dixie Classic, they called it.

"And in the Dixie Classic, not only did you have big-time basketball but you had all the national attention. It was a tournament of the biggest and the best. The environment was incredible," Bubas recalled.

Case knew where the top high-school players chose to attend school. He then would issue Dixie Classic invitations - to Michigan State with "Jumping Johnny "Green, Cincinnati with Oscar Robertson - a few years in advance to ensure strong fields. Until the last one, in 1960, the Classic was the place to be after Christmas.

Vic Bubas, who also coached under Case, characterized the Old Gray Fox as "a tremendous basketball coach, a tremendous salesman of the game. His vision was to use Reynolds Coliseum to promote it.

"At the time, the only thing going in basketball in the South was at Kentucky. But, with Reynolds Coliseum, which was his baby, he began a winning tradition at NC State. He began the Dixie Classic. Because of him, North Carolina got going with Frank McGuire. Wake Forest got going with Bones McKinney. The tie that binds it together is Everett Case and the house that he built—William Neal Reynolds Coliseum. It all started with him."

"When I came along as a player, I didn't understand what a big deal it was," sports commentator and former Wake Forest All-American guard Billy Packer has said. "But the first time you went into Reynolds Coliseum, you realized it was big time. You knew it was the only place in the league that was big time."

In 1964, doctors diagnosed Everett Case with multiple myeloma or Kahler's disease. His mother had died of cancer and his father's suicide was quite possibly due to the same disease.

In failing health and just too sick to go on, the Old Gray Fox stepped down as coach a few games into the 1964-65 season and assistant Press Maravich took over as head coach. During the wildly jubilant moments after the 1965 ACC Tournament championship game when the Pack upset Duke, the players rushed to courtside to a frail Case, lifting him up one final time to cut down the last strands of the net.

"He was a tough son of a gun, but a wonderful guy to play for." Pete Coker, a star on State's 1965 ACC champions, spent afternoons in Case's tiny office analyzing the stock market with his coach. That was at 3 p.m. At 4 p.m., he'd head downstairs to dress for practice. "In his office, he had been all gentle and calm," Coker laughed. "Get dressed, and he was on your butt in practice."

The Old Gray Fox never saw another game in Reynolds. He suffered a slow painful death due to the malignancy that slowly destroys bones in the body while displacing the blood cell producing marrow. He died the next year on April 30, 1966. His estate totaled more than $200,000. He left $1,000 to Frankfort High School, $5,000 to the North Carolina State scholarship fund, and the rest of the estate was distributed among fifty-seven of his former players.

His State teams won 377 games and 10 conference championships. The nets came down often. He was inducted as a member of the Basketball Hall of Fame. But, his impact cannot be measured in mere numbers.

"Because of what Case started, kids wanted to play basketball, and they wanted to stay in North Carolina and play: Charlie Scott, David Thompson, Tommy Burleson, and many others," according to Robinson. "Everett Case built that foundation. That's his legacy."

Monte couldn't catch David's eye the way he or Timmy Stoddard usually did when they lofted an Alley-Oop pass, so he shouted the trigger again. "Go, David!"

Norman Sloan watched his point guard from the sideline as Monte tried to get David Thompson's attention. Just like his mentor the Old Gray Fox, Norm liked his clothes. He was as dapper of dress and as wily on and off the court as his mentor had been. Unlike his mentor, Norman Sloan was a player. Also, unlike his mentor, Norm Sloan saw basketball as a family affair. His wife, Jo Ann, sang the national anthem prior to every home game. His son, Chip, was a student manager for the team. He had found a way to do what his mentor, Everett Case, could not—bring his love of the game into harmony with his love for his family.

Norman Sloan was born June 25, 1926 in Anderson, Indiana. He played guard at Lawrence Central High in Indianapolis where he also lettered in football, baseball, and track. After graduation, he began his career as a student athlete at North Carolina State College in Raleigh where an Indiana coaching legend had just taken on the challenge of establishing a strong basketball program. The teams he played on won three conference championships and they played in the NIT in 1947 and 1948. He also lettered two years in football and one year in track.

Of all the coaches who had influenced him or that he would face this season, Sloan's background as a coach was probably the most unconventional. For, distinct from his mentor, he never coached in high school. And, certainly distinct from most major college coaches, he had, in fact, never coached anywhere before he became head coach at Presbyterian College where he won 69 and lost 36 over four seasons from 1952-1955. With that apprenticeship-by-fire under his belt, he landed an assistant job at Memphis State, his step up to the big time college basketball coaching experience. He remained at Memphis State for one year before taking the head coaching position at The Citadel. His first season there sports writers voted him Southern Conference Coach of the Year. They also selected that first Citadel team as "The Most Improved in the Nation." He stayed at The Citadel for four years and amassed a 57-38 record. Then he moved on to the University of Florida in 1961. In six years as Head Coach, his record was 85-63, and he received Coach of the Year honors in the Southeastern Conference, also in his first season. He came back to North Carolina State as Head Coach in 1966 where he was not able to win Coach of the Year honors in his first season as he had in the Southern and Southeastern conferences, but he had won the award twice in the ACC: 1970 and 1973.

And, that 27-0 team last year won him *Basketball Weekly's* National Coach of the Year and almost won him AP National Coach of the Year honors. If they could've played on and won the National Championship, maybe. So far the best one of his teams had been able to do was make the Eastern Regionals in 1970. Perhaps, with this team, he would be able to improve that finish and bring the championship home to the school that started it all for him and the coach that became his mentor.

But, Norman had a team now that he believed could finally complete the building of the Old Gray Fox's prototype, which he had been a small part of starting as a player, a prototype rooted in the basics of the game as Naismith had created it.

If you looked at his team in that light, Norman didn't have A team, now. He had THE team, and he knew it. It was the ultimate team based upon what Coach Case had believed and how he had recruited his players. THE team needed a quarterback, a small guard who could shot the long jumper, drive the lane and dish. Above all, he had to be heady, smart, like a coach on the court, and run the team. Coach had his Lou Pucillo who developed a super-high-arching jump shot from the top of the key because he believed his team would have to face Wilt Chamberlain and Kansas on their way to the national championship. Norman had his Monte Towe.

Monte Corwin Towe was born September 27, 1953 in Marion, Indiana. He attended Oak Hill High School in Converse, Indiana where he was the starting point guard, a position he monopolized with the Wolfpack varsity over the past two seasons. He also played varsity baseball for NC State. Monte and David Thompson were credited with "inventing" the Alley-Oop in order to get around the no-dunking rule. Towe tossed the ball to Thompson while he was in the air and Thompson gently dropped the ball in the basket without violating the cone created by the rim.

The shooting guard had to be a kid who could dribble and shoot or catch and shoot. He needed to be able to score and, most importantly, that job required a scrappy mentality. Usually these players came from the northeast. Street ball savvy. Over the years, Coach Case had his Sammy Ranzino and his Vic Molodet. Norman had his Mo Rivers.

Morris Rivers, native of New York City, was the ultimate smooth as silk dribble and shoot junior college transfer.

A center with height and ability to catch, turn, and finish within a couple of feet of the basket. Coach had his All-Americans John Richter and Ronnie Shavlik, who broke his wrist on the rim in his final home game. Norman had Tommy Burleson who, listed at 7'4," was the tallest man in college basketball. He could just about dunk the ball—if that were legal—standing on his tiptoes.

Tommy Loren Burleson was born February 24, 1952 in Crossnore, North Carolina. He was a member of the 1972 U.S. Olympic Basketball Team that lost an epic and controversial gold medal game to the Soviet Union. The entire 1972 Olympic Basketball team believed they had been cheated and voted unanimously to not accept the silver. He, along with David Thompson, was also a member of the 1973 World University Games Gold Medal basketball team.

When Burleson was recruited he was officially measured at 7'2.5" tall. The athletic director at North Carolina State decided they would list him at 7'4". They said he would officially be the tallest player in American basketball and it would bring a lot of good exposure to him and the school. Tommy replied that he didn't want to be the tallest player in college basketball. He wanted to be the best player in college basketball.

The strong forward. The tough, wide-body who could make the good pass, take down the offensive rebound when it was important, and occasionally step up and score when necessary. Coach had his George Stephanovich. Norman had his Timmy Stoddard. Both from Indiana. Norm also had depth at this spot. He had Phil Spence who was at least as good as "Greasy George," as Stephanovich was nicknamed by the fans, although not nearly as much fun to watch. And, finally, he had Steve Nuce who would be, at worst, the number two strong forward for most other teams.

Timothy Paul Stoddard was born January 24, 1953 in East Chicago Indiana. The 6'7" Stoddard was the starting power forward for the 1971 East Chicago Washington High School Senators basketball team that many considered the greatest high school team to ever take the floor in Indiana. During their undefeated march to the state championship, they went 29-0 and averaged 94 points a game. Among his teammates was

Pete Trgovich who played at rival UCLA. Tim shared the power forward position with Spence and also lettered in baseball at NC State. He shared the Alley-Oop passing responsibilities with Monte Towe.

Phillip Spence--the poet laureate of this team. He was born in Raleigh, NC on March 13, 1954 and was raised in the south-side of Raleigh as the youngest of four brothers and a sister. He played his high school basketball at Needham B. Broughton, leading the team to the state 4-A tournament as a junior center in 1971. As a senior, he was selected Wake County Player of the Year and earned honors as a Converse All-American. Phillip only lived outside the confines of the capital city for one year, his freshman year at Vincennes University in Indiana where he earned junior college All-America honors. Phil joined the Wolfpack for the '73-'74 season as a sophomore and was a key member of the Wolfpack's run toward the national championship.

The small forward. Well, no one could compare to the fellow Norm had in that slot: David Thompson.

However, what most convinced Coach Norman Sloan that this team was THE team had to be that the players he thought of for Coach Case were on different State teams throughout the Old Gray Fox's career. The players on Norman's team were all getting ready to take the court as a single unit in a specific season, 1973-74, and, soon, against one particularly important foe—UCLA and another Indiana coach, the Wizard of Westwood, John Wooden, and the longest streak of NCAA championships ever.

Yes, twenty-three years in coaching and playing since he could remember told Norman Sloan that this Wolfpack team could very well be THE team Coach Case came so close to in the 1959-60 season. But, they suffered from probation on a recruiting violation just like this team did last season.

Norman smiled, more inside than on the lips. Yet, you could certainly see it in his water blue eyes. Everything he knew, everything he'd experienced in his 47 years told him that, yes, this team of his was one to relish and savor to the last championship drop. It would be his greatest thrill and most profound honor to finish what Coach Case had started with the prototypical Everett Case team.

"Go, David!" Somehow Monte's voice always seemed to be able to penetrate the sounds in the coliseum or any other venue just like that of a football quarterback barking signals, and like a great quarterback he led this team not simply by a matter of his own will but out of general acceptance among the players on the team that he was their leader. He did what was necessary, what he had to do. Shoot the long-range jumper, hit clutch free throws, scorch a pass inside, Alley-Oop passes to David. He was, after all, a very short five-seven no matter how hard he worked at being taller. Nevertheless, that only served to deceive the opposing teams even more, because he sure didn't play like any five seven.

Dick Dickey, Coach Everett Case's first All American, and Norm Sloan's own Father were the ones who told him about Monte Towe. He was from Indiana, too, like his family, like Dickey and almost all of the initial players on Case's teams in the forties and early fifties. "Listen, Norm. This Towe kid is something. Yes, he's small. I'd be surprised if he's actually the five seven they say he is. And, nobody much is recruiting him because of that. I think Bradley and Butler, maybe. Possibly some others, but he's our kind of player. Remember, Norm, I played with you. I know how competitive you are. And, that's exactly my point. This kid's just as competitive as you or I ever was. He's Coach Case's kind of kid. He's our kind of kid."

Monte's lob arched high into the glare of the ceiling lights and the haze that hung around them. For three years those lights had blinded him just after he started the Alley-Oop play for David. Before David, there was no Alley-Oop, unless you considered the caveman cartoon character of the same name or the hero's patented peg shot in the "Ozark Ike" newspaper comic strip. But, Ozark Ike's Alley-Oop was a sling set shot from one end of the court to the other. David's Alley-Oop was the closest thing to a slam-dunk in college basketball without actually illegally dunking the ball. And, they had created it!

Monte couldn't see the basketball just for a moment after he tossed it. When State was recruiting him, the coaches told him they had a kid from North Carolina who was as good as Oscar Robertson. Monte had no idea what that would really look like out on the court until he actually saw him. Then David would appear, flying through the air like the daring young man but without the trapeze or a net. He just kept doing stuff day after day, something new every day that would continue to amaze him. Next, the ball would come back into view just below the lights and smoke. Monte always picked it up just as it entered the dark noisy area near the top of the coliseum known to most people as "the crowd." To Monte Towe, junior guard and floor general of the North Carolina State

Wolfpack, however, that area was where he knew he'd be able to pick up the basketball against that dark backdrop.

He hoped that he'd put enough arch on the lob to give David the time he needed to reach it during flight. He had seen David make hundreds of them at practice and during games, but he was still amazed each time it happened. As David glided from the top of the key toward the rim and the hovering basketball, everything seemed to inevitably shift down into slow motion, then double slow mo.

Number 44's muscular six-four frame hung in the air as if waiting for the three mortal defenders from the University of Pittsburgh surrounding him to drop back to earth so that the round ball would be his alone just like back home on his family's little piece of earth between Shelby and Boiling Springs. The house they had all built from scratch as a family. There were times when he wished that he could go back there for good, sleep in his old room with the plastic covered frame wall, be just David again. But, that wasn't going to happen. It wasn't even possible now. Sometimes he ached for another pickup game with his sister, Precora, just for fun, but she wouldn't play him anymore. She said he blocked too many of her shots now. David figured he could outwait the Pittsburgh defenders just like he used to out-hang the kids by the junk pile back home when his brothers would play and their buddies, Wheat Littles and the McDowell brothers, especially his older brother, Vellie Junior.

Those days were also gone but still so close that David couldn't completely shake them even in the middle of an Alley-Oop in the game for the NCAA Eastern Regional Basketball Championship on their way to the NCAA Final Four to play for the National Championship. A year behind schedule, too, because of the probation. That had hurt everybody on the team and at the school, and he really believed it was his fault. He was the one who played with Coach Biedenbach in that darned pick-up game. He was the one who stayed in that dorm room for free at Coach's camp. Nobody else. Nevertheless, no one, not even the newspapers and magazines and the television stations, expected the NCAA to actually declare State ineligible for postseason play and especially not just before the season started.

They had been so psyched for the National Championship run. It would've been the school's first real chance since the Richter and Pucillo '59 and '60 teams. They received probation, too, because of alleged violations while recruiting Jackie Moreland. The scoring sensation had also been recruited by Adolph Rupp of Kentucky, Everett Case's mortal nemesis and the whistle-blower in that case. This time it was a pick-up game and a rent-free room on campus while attending Coach Sloan's summer basketball camp. Heck, both those things happened after he'd already signed a National Letter of Intent with State. Why would the NCAA care about things like that? But, they were all wrong. The NCAA slammed them with a one-year probation. No NCAA tournament last season, no matter what. So, they went 27-0 and won the ACC Tournament with no chance to even play for the National Championship. Guess not many teams could ever make that claim, but lots of teams can understand "Wait until next year!"

And, *this was* next year.

The All-American Junior forward didn't rely on his jumping ability alone as he glided through the foul lane. He thrust his muscular body far out in front of his trailing right arm as he floated. That arm sneaked toward the path of the descending ball while the Pittsburgh defenders dropped to the floor like ripened apples even as they struggled to tread air like drowning swimmers trying to tread water—only it was a lot harder to tread air. The amber sphere nestled in David's outstretched right hand almost as if it were a homing pigeon coming to roost. My ball, he smiled. No dunks here, either. Have to be careful. The Alley-Oop is a hard call for the refs. He dropped the ball delicately through the sparkling orange rim without violating the imaginary cone above it. Finally, David descended. A Pittsburgh straggler sneaked under David's body, clobbering him pretty good just as his sneakers hit the hardwood. The refs didn't see that? How could they not see that? "Hey, they've been undercutting me for two years, ref. Why can't you call it once in awhile?" Charitably, the referee ignored him.

Monte streaked down court after the shot. Watch out Pitt Panthers, UCLA, everybody! We're finally on our way to a National Championship! He could hardly keep from shouting it at the world, especially after last year going undefeated but still without a national championship. Heck, the freshman eligible rule didn't kick in until after their first year, so they couldn't play varsity until they were sophomores. Then came the probation. It really hadn't seemed fair the way the NCAA kept calling it the David Thompson investigation. Actually, there had been eight violations alleged by the NCAA. Only two were related to David. Duke had also tried too hard to recruit David, according to the NCAA, so they also received probation because an alumnus provided

David with a sport coat to wear to a game. The other six violations dated back to when Tommy was recruited. Sure David felt that they'd all been screwed over by the NCAA for no good reason. They all felt that way. However, he never really complained much although he always seemed to feel a little guilty about it all.

The press and public viewpoint had been expressed repeatedly as it was in an article in *Newsweek*:

> Compared with countless violations that are never even investigated, Thompson's sins would appear inconsequential . . . .

and statements in other media like:

> In all there were eight alleged violations, two involved Thompson and both were picayunish.

The Panther guards brought the ball in and moved up court, Mo Rivers alone challenging the ball. David laid back still eyeing the referee who was still ignoring him. "Come on, David," Mo yelled at him as he followed the ball toward the ten-second line. "You're lagging!"

Suddenly David seemed to become aware of what Mo was saying. He spotted Pittsburgh's Mickey Martin with the ball. His man. David exploded into motion. As he flew across the centerline, he saw Martin preparing to shoot. He knew he was free. Or thought he was. When David hit the top of the foul circle, he left his feet just as the ball left Mickey Martin's hands. The crowd gasped in anticipation of the block. They'd seen David Thompson perform these airborne acrobatics before. They knew the shot was as good as blocked from the moment David steamed into the foul lane and soared like a missile. He had the timing down perfect. And, some critics dared to say anything about his defense.

David's feet tangled around Phil Spence's shoulders, and his usually adroit body lurched in the air like a missile out of control. He cart wheeled head over heels across his teammate's body. His head and neck struck the hardwood with the sickening thud of a shot putt dropping from the scoreboard above the court. His legs twitched. He lay still. The swelling roar of the crowd's near-hysteric anticipation of some new and improved David antics stopped as abruptly as if someone somewhere had pulled the television sound plug.

From just behind press row, that same voice that had called the young David into dinner on those dark winter nights near Shelby sobbed into the silence, "Oh, my God, my baby's dead!"

Phil Spence the junior college All-American saw David's eyes rolling back in his head as he approached his fallen teammate. Phil Spence, team poet-in-residence, gasped, horrified, "And I'm the one who killed him." After all, it was *his* back David's feet had hit on his way up. Team trainer, Herman Bunch, bolted onto the court with smelling salts. Coach Sloan and assistant coach Eddie Biedenbach who signed David and played the infamous pick up game with him hurried close behind. David didn't respond to the smelling salts. "I killed David," Phil muttered to no one in particular. Herman called for the doctors. "I killed David."

Phil just knew that he should've sensed David was coming. They always tried to be aware of where he was on the court and stay out of his way, even in practice, because he was always up in the air, so it seemed.

Monte's stocky legs almost gave way under him, but he was the team leader. He couldn't allow his legs to crumble, no matter how much they tried. He leaped toward the area where David fell. "David's head hit the floor!" He yelled the obvious toward his bench. Each fan in the coliseum held his or her breath as Monte approached the circle. Beyond the growing knot of people, Monte could see his other teammates hanging just at the edges of the circle, and he could hear the rasping whisper of Wally Ausley's voice as if it were coming to him directly through earphones.

"Not in all my 38 years of broadcasting sports have I ever heard such a silence in this coliseum as there is here, right now, folks. It's downright eerie."

"The injured player," C.A. Dillon began over the Public Address system. C.A. had been announcing games at the coliseum since that first game in 1949, but never had he hesitated when he made announcements during the games. Never had such an announcement been as pregnant with portent as this one. "Is number forty-four, David Thompson."

The heels of Doctors James Manley and A.E. Hara and their accompanying nurse echoed throughout the silent coliseum as they dashed across the glistening floor toward the clump of people growing around David.

Monte shoved his way into the knot of bodies. He felt like someone had frozen time in a continuing replay of the fall. "Damn!" Blood oozed from David's ear as he sprawled spread eagle on the glistening hardwood. This fall seemed to be worse than the one in the Maryland game. Ida Thompson's voice still seemed to echo throughout the coliseum: "Oh, my God, my baby's dead!"

"Damn!" David must've blocked hundreds of shots before. How could this have happened? Monte gouged his fists into watering eyes. Just sweat, he thought. "Damn!" he muttered again. Just sweat.

Tim Stoddard blotted out the lights for a moment as he stood over his team leader. "Oh, my God, Monte!" Tim grabbed Coach Sloan's blazer sleeve. "Coach, is David going to be all right?"

"I don't know, Timmy." Sloan motioned toward team trainer Herman Bunch bent over David along with Doctors Hara and Manley. "Herman says he moved when they turned him over."

"Thank God! He's still alive," Monte muttered half-aloud.

"He was trying to get up even though he was out," Herman yelled at the Doctors over the suddenly growing crowd noise. Now, everyone wanted to know what was going on. "He's just about coming around, but he probably won't know what hit him."

"The doctors, Timmy, are calling in a stretcher. We haven't gotten him to quite come around and it's nearly four minutes."

"Let me help, Coach," Monte shoved forward as the stretcher-bearers from the Raleigh Rescue Squad clomped onto the hardwood. Stoddard followed. They came from Indiana together. They played baseball together. They played basketball together. They'd gone to the track meets to watch David do his triple jump thing together. They could do this together also. They could help carry the stretcher bearing their friend and teammate off the court.

"No, you guys have to stay here and play this ballgame. Let the medical people handle this. David'll be all right with them."

Somehow, above the growing din, Monte could still hear that same radio announcer's raspy whispers. "Folks all over this coliseum are crying, many are hysterical at the thought that this good and brilliant young man's career may be at an end as the tragic fall of Maurice Stokes crippled him for life long before his prime was over. We can only hope that is not the case, that David's injuries—and there must be some from such a horrible fall—will be only minor. It's hard, sitting here, watching the rescue squad loading David Thompson onto a stretcher, his body limp rather than leaping, not to be affected yourself by the strong emotional feelings surging through this place right now . . . ." Ausley's voice broke. "The stretcher bearing David Thompson is being taken off the court surrounded by the doctors and the Thompsons who have just made their way to the courtside area.

"On the court the Wolfpack team stands in front of their bench, stunned. Tears are visibly pouring down some cheeks. Others are hiding their faces from fans and cameras."

"God, Coach, I'm sorry," Phil Spence moaned, his strong head bowed as if in prayer as Sloan hustled back to his bench.

"Phillip, it's not your fault. Don't worry."

"I just feel so . . . so . . . .I don't know. I just want to give up . . . to quit."

"I do too, Phillip. Right now, I wish I wasn't even associated with this whole thing, with this game, but David, I know, wants us to win, now more than ever. You know that as well as I do."

"I'm numb too, guys" Monte mumbled, "but we'll beat them numb if that's what it takes. Let's go!"

When Tom Burleson walked up beside you, you knew it. Unless you were somewhere near his 7'4" yourself, you felt his shadow swallow you. Tommy leaned in over the knot of players, his teammates. "Okay, damnit! That scared me. It scared you. But, we can't let Pitt take advantage of this. We're not a one-man team. David says that all the time. We're gonna go out and maul those Panthers for David so when he comes back he'll be coming back . . . ." Tommy turned away to hide his emotions. "He'll be coming back to a team still on its way to the National Championship!" He struggled. "For David!"

"Okay!" Monte yelled, grabbing Tommy's waist.

"Okay!" yelled Stoddard, Moeller, and Spence.

"Okay!" shouted Rivers. He looked up. The clock read 10:00.

"Okay!" chorused the rest of the Wolfpack as they all clumped in a circle, shouting: "For David! For David! For David!" and shaking their fists in the air.

2
Dean's List and
The Tar Heels Litmus Test

In New York City's Madison Square Garden, the entire ACC press contingent covering North Carolina's appearance in the NIT against Purdue abruptly left press row *en mas*. On the Carolina bench, Coach Dean Smith looked up when he sensed the flurry of movement and wondered what was going on. What could have caused the entire press group to leave press row all at the same time right in the middle of the game? His kids were playing sloppy basketball for sure. They had more turnovers in this first half than they usually had in an entire game, and the half wasn't even over yet. But, that bad?

A few moments later someone behind the bench with a portable radio plugged into his left ear whispered to Dean. "It's David Thompson, Coach Smith. He's taken a fall at the Coliseum in Raleigh. Hit his head pretty badly according to the radio announcer."

Dean nodded. "Thanks," he muttered. Now he understood. He also realized that NC State's chance for a championship was surely in question now if David was seriously injured. He certainly hoped not. Yet, a fall from the heights he jumped to? One never knew. One could only hope for the best.

A short while later the ACC press corps struggled back onto press row to watch Carolina and Dean Smith ultimately lose to Purdue 82-71 just as they had lost three times during the regular season to NC State, just as Purdue[*] had lost to that same Wolfpack earlier in the season. and just as Dean had lost to Norm in the David Thompson recruiting wars.

High school. That was when the mythology gestated. So the story went, it all began with the time thirteen year old David Thompson, so excited about being brought up to practice with the varsity, dunked the ball from just inside the foul line the first time he got his hands on it. When Dean Smith was 13, he won the Kansas State table tennis championship in his age group. But, he certainly had not dunked a basketball. He hadn't even thought about such a thing as dunking the basketball.

---

[*] Purdue would eventually emerge as the National Invitational Tournament Champions with a win over Utah 87-81.

One day Dean heard about this kid from Crest High School in Shelby that everybody else was recruiting hard already. Reportedly, he had a true vertical jump of nearly four feet. He'd been beating up regularly on Gardner Webb College varsity players like Artis Gilmore since he was eleven or twelve at the Gardner-Webb basketball camps and during off-season. He could hang in the air, so they said, until he decided he wanted to come down. In other words, he not only defied rationality, he defied gravity.

Coach Smith, born on February 28th, 1931 in Emporia, Kansas, realized later that he had been seduced somewhat by the emerging mythos that surrounded this high school kid from the rural hill country west of Charlotte born on July 13, 1954, just a little more than a year after the ACC was formed. He had, finally, determined to put David Thompson on his list and recruit the young man personally. Soon he came to appreciate that the kid, even at fifteen and sixteen, was better than most any player he'd ever coached or seen, and he was the only player on Dean's list that he had been absolutely sure he was going to sign that year.

Dean also knew that, so far, he had paid a very stiff price for letting that young man get away. To this day, he still couldn't figure out what had happened that summer. He really believed he'd played it right with David. Other coaches cried foul after State had announced signing David Thompson that August. Yet, nothing that ever came out seemed bad enough to have influenced the young man's decision. Certainly, a pick-up game with State Assistant Coach Eddie Biedenbach had not been reason enough for the NCAA to put State on probation for a year and, thus, making them ineligible for last season's national championship. Coach Smith had accepted what David had repeated more than once, that he was just more comfortable at State.

He certainly played as if he was *very* comfortable at State. The true measure for any State player or coach or fan was the Tar Heels Litmus Test. Dean knew that. It was a little like a chemistry litmus paper test to find out if some chemical was acidic or basic. The big difference was that the Tar Heels Litmus Test *had* to come out red. You *had* to beat Carolina, and the only time David Thompson had not beaten Carolina was the first time they played him as a freshman. After one Carolina blue test finish, the rest were NC State red.

No other team in the conference had beaten him at all, as a freshman or as a varsity player. And, that wasn't because the conference didn't have the teams, that was for sure. After all Norm had State at Number 1 or Number 2. Lefty had Maryland in the top five and as high as Number 2, and he had Carolina in the top five pre-season and had been ranked as high as Number 3 and Number 4. So, it wasn't like the Wolfpack didn't have good competition.

In their first meeting and only ACC victory over any David Thompson team, the Carolina Freshmen rallied from a 14-point half time deficit to defeat the State team 95-83 despite David's sensational individual performance.

As Dean recalled, David was so upset over the loss that he banged his head against the door to his locker gashing his forehead. The cut required several stitches. As soon as he heard about the incident, Coach Norman Sloan rushed to the aid of his future superstar.

"Don't worry Coach," Thompson had told Sloan. "I won't let this happen again."

But, David didn't mean the cut on his head. He meant losing, especially losing to Carolina.

Behind him, Smith heard an anonymous voice whispering from the crowd. "Hey, Coach, they just took David off the court on a stretcher. Don't yet know his condition."

Dean Smith nodded, never taking his eyes off of his team on the court in front of him. David had made Dean's List. In fact, he'd been at the head of the list, but Dean had lost him anyway, lost him to a pick-up game, lost him to a school where he felt more at home.

And, so the legend grew.

3
"Tell Walter Cronkite that the Doctor is busy!"

"Get him into that ambulance! Hurry!"
"Hara?" the driver yelled.
"Yeah."
"You in?"
"Yeah."
"The Thompsons?"
"We're in," Ida whispered.
"Hit it!" The ambulance doors slammed shut. Tires skidded across damp pavement away from the side entrance of the coliseum nearest the court. "Dr. Manley? Dr. Jim? Damn. That's who we forgot."

Gus Hara glanced up from his patient who was just coming around. "Jesus!"

The Thompsons winced as if he'd hit them.

"Sorry, folks. Manley will find a way to the hospital. We can't risk turning back now. Not as hard as your son hit that floor."

"What happened? Where am I?" David tried to raise himself up on his elbow. Dr. Hara restrained him. "I want to go back . . . ."

"Oh, thank God, you're alive and awake." Ida began to bawl. "Lordy, boy, we thought you were dead or had broken your neck."

"Praise the Lord," Vellie murmured touching David's brow. "Lay still now like the Doctor wants you to do, David."

"What happened?" David relaxed back onto the stretcher, a little groggy. The back of his head hurt. He reached up toward the pain.

"Don't touch there, David," Dr. Hara warned. That's where your head hit the floor."

"What happened? I can't remember what happened."

"You jumped way up high like you always do to block a shot," Ida whispered while she stroked his hand, "but, then, somehow, you fell." The amazement in her voice was obvious to everyone in the ambulance. "Oh, we were scared for you, son."

David's eyes began to cross and blur. It was becoming increasingly difficult to hold them open. He let his eyelids close. He couldn't really stop them. With the darkness came quiet. The new throbbing in the back of his head seemed to melt away. The ambulance siren squalled as they barreled through the Hillsboro Street main entrance to the North Carolina State University campus.

He loves playing to be the best, don't you, son?" Vellie reached out toward the slack face of his youngest son, the one who played basketball like the verses from that King James Version of *the Holy Bible* sounded when the preachers read them. "Son?"

"It's okay, Mr. Thompson." Dr. Hara gently prevented the Father's hand from actually touching the young athlete's face and possibly disturbing these important moments of rest and quiet. "He's just resting. It's important that he rest now. If there is no major injury, then all the rest he can get is necessary to a quick and complete recovery."

* * * * *

The sun had evaporated into the late fall mountain mists near Shelby, North Carolina almost two hours earlier, yet the dribble of a basketball on clay packed from years of pivoting, dribbling, leaping, and landing again still echoed off those hills. In the growing darkness, a shadow of a figure shifted its dribble toward a beaten-up Chevy, the only thing in the pile of abandoned car bodies near the court that actually worked. The figure reached inside the open window of the Chevy and pulled on a switch. White light glared over the dark clay court and the telephone pole with an aging wood backboard nailed to it. A rusted rim was curl-nailed to the backboard.

The figure glided away from the car still dribbling the ball with the left hand. When the shadow emerged from the darkness into the beams of the headlights, the figure became a child, a young man. This man-child moved to the basket, faking around an imaginary Artis Gilmore. He was only a lanky five nine, but he was as smooth and quiet as the night closing in around him and his one-on-himself pickup game. Picking up his dribble at the point just inside where a regular court would have been marked for the foul line, the young man leaped into the air like a strange bird taking flight. The soiled orange ball slammed through the hoop. The rim rattled with the force of the dunk. The ball hissed through the net, the only thing new about his backyard court.

After three hours of jump shots, lay ups, dribbling and reflex drills, and pretend match-ups with Artis Gilmore and Julius Erving, David was pretty sure that his Daddy was right as usual. He had to go on out there and play the best he could play, all the way, and be thankful for his abilities.

"David? David! Boy, are you coming in to supper tonight or not?"

"Yes, Mama. Be right in." David, the eleventh and last child of Vellie and Ida Thompson, just couldn't resist one last slam-dunk. He hadn't even shown his freshman teammates or Coach Peeler that he could dunk it yet. And, after all the locker room talk about him being a ball hog and such, he wasn't sure he wanted them to know, not yet anyway. Two dribbles. Soar. When you know you can jump more than three feet straight up, then to soar means to dunk even at five nine. His arms stretched high above his head, the ball firmly in the control of his piano-player fingers. Whoosh! It always felt so good. However, it was still against the rules. So, he didn't know if he'd ever get a chance to do it in a game, unless someday he played in the Olympics or in the pros. He could dunk there. No problem.

"Now you come on in here, David O'Neal Thompson! You're gonna run down the battery in your Daddy's car again." Ida ducked back inside the screen door of the green cinderblock home she, Vellie, and the whole family had built. It sure was taking long enough to finish, and they still hadn't done it all. But, it would do. Yes. It was warm with love and caring and Jesus Christ. It would sure enough do. "And you're keeping other children awake in here," she chuckled through the screen as an afterthought. Usually, if she couldn't get David to do something for himself she could coax him into doing it because it would be good or helpful for someone else.

"Okay, Mama." Passing the ball from hand to hand, first in front and then behind his back, David circled the ball around his body as he trotted toward the house. The ball had been last year's Christmas present from his Daddy. It was the first real basketball he'd ever had new and all his own. Before, there were the playground balls or some other kid's pick up ball. Sometimes it wasn't even a basketball at all, just a discarded volleyball and a hoop he'd nailed to a tree until his Daddy had built this one. After awhile, a fellow needed his own ball and a real court to play on.

Up the cinderblock steps, onto the board porch, through the doorway into the warmth of the Thompson's oil-heated living room, Daddy snored in his rocker. Beside him, the table that held the family *Bible*. Each day his Mother opened the book to a different verse, a favorite of someone in the family. Above the *Bible* on the concrete block wall hung a chipped, gold-painted wood framed picture of Jesus. It hung by tobacco twine on the nail behind it. The glow behind the Savior's face—like an aura—seemed to spill into the room, bathing his Daddy and the oil heater in a yellow light. "Is that the children you didn't want me to wake up, Mama?" David chuckled as he tiptoed into the kitchen and dining room.

"Now, don't you be smart with me," Ida chided good-naturedly. "You know your Daddy's not one of the children."

"You could of fooled me," David laughed softly. He spied two thick peanut butter and honey sandwiches and a pitcher of fresh milk and a glass sitting on the table. He could still hear Daddy's snoring. "This for me, Mama?"

Ida's back bent over the sink scrubbing the last of the day's dishes and pots and pans. "Who else," she chuckled.

All day long she scrubbed and cleaned for Shelby High School. Then at night, she had to cook and scrub and clean up for all of them. And, she could still laugh. Someday his basketball was going to make things better for her and for his Daddy. David placed his ball under the table and slumped into the creaking wood chair that always sat in front of his place at the table. He inhaled the sandwiches, washing them down with the pitcher of milk. His swallow seemed to take in about a glass at a time.

Without looking around, Ida knew he was gulping his food again. After eleven children, she just knew that, at David's age, you gulped your food. "David, stop gulping your food."

"Yes, Mama." He gulped the last half of a sandwich and the final two glasses of milk left in the pitcher. "Thanks Mama." He leaped from his chair, wiping his mouth on his soaked sweatshirt sleeve. "Got to study." He snapped the ball off the floor with the toe of his left tennis shoe. Quickly, he slipped the same toe under the ball and flipped it into the air about chest high. There, he caught it, almost on the run.

"Now you keep quiet, David, you hear. Most everybody in this house is asleep by now. And it's plain to see that your Daddy sure enough is."

"Yes, Mama," echoed back at Ida from the hallway.

The next afternoon Coach Peeler stuck his head into the locker room full of the smells of wintergreen and sweat. He genuinely liked locker rooms. But, today he had tournament on his mind, and he knew his team needed a shot in the arm. The smells made his stomach churn around the lunchtime pizza. "David Thompson!" The sounds he yelled almost seemed to be absorbed in the steam of after-practice showers for the Junior Varsity.

"Yes Coach," drifted through the steamy haze.

"Get something on your butt and be in my office in two minutes."

"Okay, Coach."

Peeler extracted his slightly balding head from between the locker room doors, letting them swing closed. He turned and wandered down the hallway beside the gym passing varsity players suited for practice already heading onto the hardwood for a few early shots at the hoop. It was great coaching the kids at this age. They had so much energy and so much desire to play. He stepped over the threshold of the only office on the gym hall, the hardwood door with glass from halfway up to the top stood open as it usually did when the coach was in the area. Peeler walked around his desk and plopped down into his stuffed swivel chair with arms for a quick gulp of relaxation before getting varsity practice going. The tournament for the state championship started in three days. He wanted his team to have their best chance. That was why he had to talk to this ninth grade whiz, David Thompson. He was leading the freshman team in every respect, and they were winning their games too. Maybe he should've been up all season, but David hadn't played organized league-type ball before. He had needed to get the clay out of his sneakers first. Well, he'd sure done that in a real hurry. Maybe he was the shot in the arm the varsity needed . . . . Maybe.

"You wanted to see me, Coach?" David grinned as he stood in the doorway still damp from his shower, barefooted, in his jeans and a T-shirt.

"David. Do come in. Have a seat." Coach Peeler motioned over his metal desk toward a folding chair sitting in front of a short metal bookcase just inside the door.

"Thanks, Coach." David glided to the chair and flopped down all over it more than in it. "Is there something wrong?"

"No, no, David. Nothing like that." How do you approach one like this? His eyes are like a baby deer's, a little evasive, almost frightened. Will this be pressing him? "David. How's your game feeling to you now?"

David grinned again. Basketball was his favorite subject. "I guess I'm coming along Coach. But, I don't know."

"Well I do, son. I do know. And I'd like to have you come up with the varsity and work out from now on." Peeler hesitated. It was hard to read anything on the face of that lowered head. "Who knows, we could probably use your help in the upcoming state tournament. What do you think?"

"Oh gosh. I'm not so sure about that, Coach."

"What do you mean, you're not sure?" Peeler frowned, furrowing his forehead deeply over his gray eyes. "Don't you want to play varsity ball?"

David pouted a little but nodded.

"Then here's your chance, son."

"I don't know, Coach. I've been with my team all year, right?"

"Right?"

"And I'd feel pretty bad about leaving them now, Coach, even though I'd love nothing better than to play varsity even if just a few games." David sat there, his head dangling between slumped shoulders, his dark eyes gazing at the cement floor.

"Well?"

"I just don't know, Coach."

David, again, shrugged. He was only thirteen years old. He hadn't thought very much about what he was going to happen next in his life. He just knew that he wanted to play basketball.

David hedged. "Coach, I just can't do that to my teammates. I hope you can understand."

Peeler smiled through his disappointment. "Better than you'll ever know, young man. Better than you know. But you'll still work out with the varsity. OK?"

"OK, Coach. Gotta get ready for practice, now."

"Go. Go!"

Less than ten minutes later, David didn't see Coach Peeler strolling up from behind with his hands in his pockets as he crossed from the gym doors to the end of the court where one of the team managers retrieved rebounds and tossed balls out to the players to shoot. David felt super. He knew he'd made the right decision to stay with his team. Next year would be plenty of time to become a varsity player. The ball seemed to dribble across the gleaming floor all by itself, leading David along behind. As he approached the foul line of the east glass goal, David suddenly realized it was clear down the lane. He knew as he hurtled his body into flight that he had let himself get too excited. He sailed down the lane, almost against his will, the orange rim glowing in the gym light. David sensed the ball between his hands. His fingers manipulated the sphere into place as his arms swooped from behind his back in a graceful arch toward the basket. The ball sizzled through the net.

For a few seconds, the silence was deafening except for the squeaking of David Thompson's sneakers as he landed safely on the hardwood of the Crest High School Gymnasium.

* * * * *

Now, Rex Hospital loomed in ominous lemony light on a hill overlooking St. Mary's Street not unlike the moonlight back in Shelby. The ambulance raced along the street, careening at the last possible moment off to its left and through the hospital emergency entrance. Brakes slammed, locked up. Tires squalled. The doors flung open. Two attendants had the stretcher up and out of the ambulance before the Thompsons could move. Dr. Hara was right behind them barking orders. "Get it moving . . . to x-ray." To an orderly standing by, Hara screamed: "You! Wait here for Manley . . . Dr. James Manley. He'll be arriving soon. Tell him to scrub up and be ready in Emergency Operating." He paused. "Got that?"

"Yes, Doctor."

"Mr. and Mrs. Thompson. Come with me."

Doctor Jim Manley leaped from North Carolina State Trooper Joe Ellwood's black-over-silver Ford. He raced toward the Emergency Entrance.

Wally Ausley's voice from the Trooper's radio bounced off the still open door into the crisp early evening air. "Ladies and Gentlemen, Tommy Burleson- -NC State's not-so-gentle giant seven-foot-four center—has gone crazy since David Thompson's tragic fall." March madness still continued.

"Burleson- - from the mountain country of Newland, North Carolina- - scored eleven points during the four minutes immediately after play was resumed. He's been a terror on the boards at both ends of the court and has blocked at least three shots that we've counted. All in only a little over four minutes, folks. Amazing! This crowd is still strangely subdued. This Wolfpack team's poise has been unbelievable in the face of not yet knowing what is happening with their beloved teammate, David Thompson, who, right now, is laying on an Emergency Room examining table."

Trooper Ellwood reached across and slammed the door, shaking his head. "Doctors," he muttered. "They think all you got to do is chauffeur them around and close doors after them. We still got a game to listen to."

"Doctor Manley?" The young attendant leered at the graying man in the red sports jacket. "Doctor James Manley?"

"Yes."

"Doctor Hara said to go immediately to Emergency. They went right off to x-ray as soon as they got here, sir."

"Thanks, son." Doctor Jim nodded, patted the attendant on his shoulder as he shoved the glass door open and entered the emergency room without breaking stride.

"Doctor Manley?"

"Jesus, what now?"

"I'm sorry, Doctor."

"Never mind." Doctor Jim continued his brisk pace down the hall toward receiving. "Well, what is it nurse?"

"We've been flooded with calls from all over." She waved her hands wildly over her head. "The switchboard's jammed up most of the time." The nurse sucked in a deep breath. "Now, Walter Cronkite--you know, from CBS. He is on the telephone. He wants to know how David is doing. He wants to talk to the doctor in charge."

Doctor Jim grimaced. Speak to the Doctor in charge at a time like this. Christ Almighty! "Tell Walter Cronkite . . . ." Nevertheless, Dr. Jim also realized that the world wanted to know how David Thompson was doing, so he held his temper. After all, Cronkite was just doing his job just like he was doing *his*. "Tell Walter Cronkite that the Doctor is busy." Doctor Jim pushed through swinging doors of the Emergency Examining Room 2. "And tell Dr. Hara I'm in here," he yelled back through the closing doors at the nurse he left behind with her mouth open between questions.

The same announcer's voice rumbled low from a Zenith transistor radio on a corner table. A nurse stood staring at it as if it were a television. "Towe, Stoddard, Rivers, Burleson, and Spence. The rest of the team still seemed stunned by David's fall. Yet one by one they continue to rise to the occasion . . . to get the basket, grab the rebound, force the turnover needed to keep them just out of reach of the determined Pittsburgh Panthers."

"Nurse?"

She started, cut down the radio so that the well-modulated voice disintegrated into only noise. "Yes, Doctor . . .ah . . . Doctor Manley."

He nodded toward the radio. "Do you know where they have David Thompson now?"

"Yes, Doctor. He's on his way in here from x-ray . . . right now." She coughed behind a smooth tanned hand. "That's why I was listening." The nurse motioned toward the garbled voice of the announcer.

Doctor Jim flashed his twenty-nine-tooth grin that had charmed women, ladies, and girls alike ever since he had twenty-nine or more teeth. "That's all right, nurse . . .ah . . ." He glanced at her nametag. "Nurse Kelly. Turn it up so we can all hear." Doctor Jim moved toward the sink beside Kelly to scrub up before they wheeled David in. "How's he doing, Kelly?"

She shook her head, wonder spreading across her elfin face. "He must be some kind of young man, Doctor Jim. He's wide-eyed. Says he is ready to go back into the game." Her eyes sparkled like pools of oil. "But he does have a nasty gash in the back of his head."

"Probably need some stitching up here and there?"

She nodded, eyed the radio. "The Wolfpack has made it almost to half-time now, Ladies and Gentlemen without their All-Everything forward David Thompson . . . and without knowing how he is." The voice coming from the little black box paused. "We're all waiting for some word . . . . The world waits."

The doors behind Dr. Jim banged open. A stretcher bed rolled through the door. David Thompson lay on his back strapped onto the bed, his head to one side. He smiled when he saw who the doctor was. "Hi, Doctor Jim."

"Hi, David. How are you feeling?" he chuckled as he began checking David over even while the two attendants unstrapped and transferred David to the Examining Room table's fresh white paper.

"Okay, Doctor Jim."

"You sure now, David. It's important." Manley eyed the gash on the back of David's head.

"Well, my head hurt for a little while right after I woke up in the ambulance."

"Right about here?" Doctor Manley touched the area around the gash.

David winced. "Yes, sir."

"That, David is where the cut is. We're going to have to do a little sewing on it, but it'll be fine. Okay?"

"You're the doc, Doctor Jim."

"Nurse Kelly?"

"Yes, Doctor."

"Prepare ten cc's Novocain for a local on David's scalp. Needle and thread," he joked.

"I'll take care of it, Doctor Jim."

"David."

"Yes, Doctor Jim."

"Your pictures came back looking fine." Doctor Gus Hara's grating bass voice interrupted through the doors of the Examining room. "You seem to be suffering from nothing more than a bad cut on your head and a mild concussion." His head stuck part way through an opening between the doors that he was creating with his left arm. "I don't see how you're not dead, David. I swear, your head must be hard as marble." His bald head wagged in disbelief.

"Everything's okay from your end then Gus?"

"Yeah. He's got a clean bill of health from me as long as he's here for a twenty-four-hour observation period over the weekend." Doctor Hara smiled toward David. "Sorry, young man. I do hate to mess up a young man's weekend. But, it can't be helped, I'm afraid. Just like with your knee surgery last spring, we can't take any chances, now, can we?"

David shook his head just slightly. "I guess not, Doctor Hara. I guess not."

"Look, I've got to get back over to the coliseum, Jim. Somebody's got to be there on the bench."

"Then you think David can go back if he really wants to, Gus?"

"No reason why not. Just be easy with it and don't let him overdo like you know he will."

"What you say, Doctor Jim?" David grinned. "What about it?"

"We'll see, David." Doctor Jim nodded at Gus Hara's disappearing head. We'll see after I've finished up here, okay?"

"Doctor Hara, wait!" David lifted up on his left arm. "At least you can deliver a message to the team for me. Okay?"

"Sure, David. Sure. What?"

"Tell the team I'm all right and to just go ahead and win the game."

Gus Hara nodded.

* * * * *

"For Thine is the kingdom, the power, and the glory, for ever and ever. Amen." The circle of players was silent. The locker room echoed from the heels of a videotape cameraman setting himself in place to zoom in on the sweaty faces of each young man in that soggy red-and-white circle. All part of the half-time coverage. The players' heads remained bowed in silence.

The lens zoomed in. As the camera operator heard his announcer reeling off the players and their basic statistics inside his headset, he focused his lens on each face. "Bruce Dayhuff, freshman, 6'2", 175 pounds, from Walkerton, Indiana, John Glenn High School. Also from Indiana, the pride of Carmel High, Freshman center Bill Lake who everyone is looking to replace the big guy, Tommy Burleson, when he graduates after this season. Lake is 6'11" and weighs 192. A pair of freshmen from Ohio: Ken Gehring and Mike Buurma." The camera operator backed off the dimples of Buurma until his lens included Gehring next to him. "Buurma is 6'10" and weighs in at 200 even from Willard. Gehring is 6'9", 203 pounds from Akron."

Mark Moeller's dazzling blond hair matted over his forehead as his head remained bowed in spite of the prodding of the television guy for him to raise his blue eyes until he could see the very small red light on the camera. He was struggling for all he was worth with his beliefs at this moment, and they wanted him to pose for pictures. Well, no thanks. He had more important things to do than that. He had to figure out some things. He had to pray to his God, to find out why something like this could happen. He knew many of the guys would feel the same way.

"Dear Lord," Mark's voice quivered, shattering the eerie near silence of the Wolfpack dressing room. "Be with our teammate and friend in the gravest hour of his need. Be with us, dear Lord, in our time of strife and gnawing doubt about the justice of this world. Forgive us, dear Lord, for our unworthiness of your mercy. In your name we pray." All the voices of the Wolfpack joined him when he whispered, "Amen."

"Okay, fellas," Coach Sloan barked. "Remember how we got here. Remember what we've got to do is win this second half! Remember David!"

4
Beyond Midnight Madness

The NCAA initiated the start practice on October 15 in 1970.

"That means we can start practicing one minute past midnight, so let's get a jump on everybody and do it." With that proposal, Lefty Driesell, head coach of the Maryland Terrapins instituted "Midnight Madness" because he wanted to get a psychological edge on the competition.

By the 1973-74 season, Midnight Madness prepared the way for the eventual March Madness that everyone knew as the NCAA Tournament. Somehow, that seemed appropriate. On October 15, 1973, instead of their traditional midnight jog or intra-squad scrimmage, Lefty Driesell hired a five-foot-three female modern dance instructor to lead his team in slimnastics. He hoped the exercises would reduce overall injuries and that the instructor would teach his big men gracefulness.

Immediately after Midnight Madness came pre-season madness when it seemed that every day was a Red-White game or something like the "David Thompson Day" in Cleveland County one Friday in November. The Wolfpack appeared at a lot of events to help celebrate this day or that day in one part of the state or another. That was how their season really began.

That Friday night the team was scheduled to play in a pre-season intra-squad game between the Wolfpack's Red and White teams. They sneaked into the gym by a side door David knew about from his Crest High School playing days just in time for city and county dignitaries to present a number of plaques to their former Crest High basketball star in appreciation for the recognition that his exploits on the basketball court had brought to Cleveland County. The Shelby Rotary Club, The Shelby Board of Aldermen, and The County Board of Commissioners each presented him a plaque at the ceremony.

"I'm pleased and proud to present this key to the city of Shelby to David Thompson, one of our own who has shown the ACC, the country, and, indeed, the whole world what a kid from Shelby is capable of becoming." Mayor Hubert Plaster beamed as he finally presented David with the key to the city. "But, I'm certain you will never need it, David, because there are no doors in Shelby that would ever be locked to you."

"Thanks, Mayor. I really appreciate this key to the city of Shelby. It means a lot to me. It's a real honor. But," David hesitated and grinned. "But, right now, though, I have a gift of my own to present. You see, I was lucky enough to be selected as the Most Valuable Player in the World University Games held back in August when Tommy and I went to Moscow, Russia, and the Lifesaver Candy Company presented me with this check for $750 as 'The Lifesaver of the Month.' Since I am an amateur, I can't accept the check for myself. Instead, I asked them to make out a check to the Cleveland County Boys Club here in Cleveland County."

David offered the check to the Mayor. "Perhaps, Mayor, in some small way, this check will help some boy to have the same kind of chance I've had."

The Mayor held it up for the crowd to see.

"Well, thank you David. Thank you." See what kinds of things like this would never happen for a place like his Shelby "but for the grace of God."

* * * * *

"Give it to David! Give it to David! Give it to David!" The crowd of more than 1,500 demanded from the Crest High School gym bleachers as the NC State White team brought the ball across the ten second line with a baseball pass from Monte to Tim Stoddard on the right wing. He saw David cut for the basket out of the corner of his left eye. Well, these folks had come to see their hometown boy shoot the basketball and soar like an eagle. So, here goes! "Go, David!" Tim Stoddard lofted a perfectly arched Alley-Oop pass toward the basket.

David left his feet just outside of the lane markings on the left side of the basket. This was no different than if he'd still been practicing over in Moscow with his buddies Quinn Buckner from Indiana and Marvin Barnes from Providence. He met Tim's pass, nestling the ball with the tips of his fingers as he prepared to drop it through the hoop without violating the invisible cone over the basket. What the heck, he'd give them a dunk treat tonight. It would be okay. Just a technical foul in an intra-squad game. After all, it was his home town and his old high school gym. Just three years ago he was practicing and playing on these boards. With both hands, David slammed the ball through the gleaming hoop. The net whooshed just like in his yard at home. His first dunk at this school had been on this very same basket back when he was just a freshman ninth grader.

The crowd leaped to its feet as a single organism, stamping and applauding. The two referees blew their whistles simultaneously, both making "T" shapes with their intersecting right and left hands. The fans booed good-naturedly. David and Tim slapped each other on the back and laughed.

It was late when the Wolfpack finally shuffled back through that side door out of the gym to the waiting bus. David's Whites had ultimately lost the game to Tommy's Reds, but the score didn't matter much except for bragging rights. The main thing was everybody played well. Tim had 20 points. Phil scored 16. Mo got 24. David hit 12 of 30 shots for 29 points to lead the White team and pulled down seven rebounds. Tommy led the Red Team, hitting a fantastic 14-17 from the floor.

They still had four more games left on their road trip of five, and their regular season hadn't even started yet.

* * * * *

Although the December 1 game against the Athletes in Action didn't count in their won-lost record, it was important to them as a team and they all knew it. This was a practice game, for all practical purposes, but it gave them a chance to work together as a team under real game conditions.

The Wolfpack scored 55 points in the first half, but a combination of shaky, uncertain ball handling and a Swiss cheese defense by the Pack resulted in a relatively slim 10-point advantage.

"We didn't move the ball in the first half," State Coach Norm Sloan said later. "We sort of forced things."

State came out looser in the second half and quickly whipped the margin upward. With last year's All-Americans David and Tommy leading the way, the Pack outscored AIA 35-14 in the first 10 minutes to make the count 90-59.

The final score: 119-82.

5
Reality Sets In

AP Poll
1. UCLA 3-0
2. NC State 2-0
3. Indiana 3-0
4. Maryland 1-1
5. N. Carolina 2-0
6. Notre Dame 4-0
7. Marquette 4-0
8. Providence 1-0
9. Louisville 3-1
10. Memphis St. 4-0

UPI Poll
1. UCLA (3-0)
2. NC State (2-0)
3. Indiana (3-0)
4. North Carolina (3-0)
5. Maryland (1-1)
6. Marquette (4-0)
7. Notre Dame (4-0)
8. Providence (1-0)
9. Memphis State (4-0)
10. Louisville (3-0)

A rumor ran rampant among the fraternity houses and the dorms on the East Carolina College campus in Greenville in 1969 and 1970. This gossip overshadowed Clarence Stasavich's resignation as football coach after the 1969 season. It trumped Mike McGee's T-formation offense that replaced ECC's antiquated single wing formation. It was bigger than the Beatles breaking up. And, it gave students and fans something to talk about in line while waiting for campus cops to check for alcohol in carry-in coolers at Ficklen Stadium during another dismal football season.

The rumor was that David Thompson, a country boy at heart, had pretty much decided to play his college basketball in North Carolina, possibly even at ECC. Fans who were usually oblivious to anything relating to sports other than football and water skiing knew that Thompson was probably going to be the best basketball player ever and was fast becoming the primary ACC target in the recruiting wars despite the fact that he was only a junior in high school. He could be their biggest football fan. He would actually *be* their basketball program.

The gossip peaked with the news that David Thompson would attend the East Carolina game against NC State in a few days. So, Pirates fans planned a convoy to William Neal Reynolds Coliseum with a single purpose in mind. They were going to go to that game, find David Thompson, and make him see the East Carolina light even if they had to kidnap him. They would take him down to Atlantic Beach for some sun, surf, shag, and suds. They would make him see the East Carolina light no matter how long that might take.

The ECC basketball team, even with the support of its newly found student activists, lost convincingly by 20. The East Carolina sports subversives never located and kidnapped David Thompson. Rumor had it that some never did make it back to campus but opted for a life of water skiing at the coast. David, ultimately, chose to attend NC State, and the Wolfpack continued to beat the Pirates with regularity.

In the first eight minutes of the first game of the season on the night of December 5, 1973 however, East Carolina seemed to have revenge on their collective minds for that night several seasons earlier as they pushed State around and almost literally shoved the Number 2 rating down the Pack's throat. With 13:03 remaining in the first half and State down 15-9, David took matters into his own hands. He hit from the corner. Mark Moeller guided one in from the key. David hit Alley-Oops on unusual assists from Moeller and Tommy Burleson. Burleson's hook put the Pack ahead 22-21 for good, but David had just begun to warm up.

State led 32-29 when he rebounded for two, stole and drove for another basket, and stole again. This time he fell to the floor and dribbled from a sitting position for several seconds before passing off to Monte Towe who circled back to help out when he saw his teammate slip.

State led at halftime 38-31 but East Carolina, surprisingly, controlled the boards 20-18.

When the Wolfpack came back on the court for the second half, they used a pressure defense to create numerous turnovers that resulted in fast breaks for easy lay ups and turned the Pirates dream of revenge into a nightmare.

Mo Rivers finally relaxed. He was chest-to-chest on defense and stripped the Pirates repeatedly, creating one fast break after another. "I was just anticipating the man. I was following my man, lining him up and anticipating his moves when I made those steals." When Walt Frazier played on television, Rivers was there to see how the N.Y. Knick star did his stuff. "He is the man I watch on defense." Rivers finished the game with 14 points, scoring most of his field goals on lay ups but missing several from outside. He was also in on the play that brought the house down in the second half. With State leading 60-35, Thompson rebounded and was trapped by the end line. He hesitated, wobbled, then passed behind his back to Monte Towe who in turn threw to Rivers down court. A Pirate picked up Rivers, but as he drove to the basket, he did a double-pump scoop shot that left the East Carolina defender looking up at the coliseum ceiling for help.

Once again, the East Carolina College Pirates lost to North Carolina State. This time it was 79-47. This had been the Pack's first real game. Yet, by the second half, it resembled a practice or exhibition about as much as the Athletes in Action game. The big difference? This one counted in the season won-lost record. The Pack was off its blocks, 1-0 and counting.

Post-Game Press

Wally Ausley: "Coach Sloan, when you came back from the World University Games in Moscow last August, you said that you had learned what it was like to have every other team gunning for you because they were all doing it during the games. Does this apply at all to the Wolfpack now?"

Coach Sloan: "You're absolutely right about that observation, and I passed that on to the team here. I believe they understand that they're a target every game, but, for some reason, we just weren't ready to play in the first half. I had the distinct impression that we weren't up for East Carolina, and, that's not a good sign, because when you're ranked high everybody is prepared. Every team you play wants to knock you off."

Ausley: "Your players had a lot of turnovers during the game. Doesn't that concern you, Coach Sloan?"

Coach Sloan: "We're going to make mistakes and we're going to throw the ball away too. We just want to keep those mistakes to a minimum."

Ausley: "And, what about rebounding? Thirty-seven each? East Carolina actually out rebounded your team 20-18 in the first half?"

Coach Sloan: "That was probably mental too. We just weren't ready to play them."

Ausley: "Do you think your guys weren't ready because they were looking ahead to the UCLA game?"

Coach Sloan: "I don't know. But I know we only play one more game before we meet them.

* * * * *

Two days later the Vermont Catamounts played it man-to-man for all they were worth, but all they were worth just wasn't even close to enough against a Number 2 NC State Wolfpack just beginning to feel its oats. Unfortunately, the most noteworthy characteristic of the game was the fact that it was the game after which the State team could, finally, talk about UCLA.

Post-Game Press

Ausley: "Ninety-seven to 42, Coach Sloan. That's more than double the score. Weren't your guys running it up a little out there?"

Coach Sloan: "No, and I'm sure Coach Salzberg knows that. We played 16 kids tonight, and David Thompson sat out more than half the game. We were just finally ready to play after a slow start against East Carolina."

Ausley: "Well, Coach Sloan. December 15 is your next game. What's going on in your mind right now?"

Coach Sloan: "One thing for sure is that we don't have to say that we're not thinking about UCLA anymore. We will focus our minds on two things until December 15: exams and the UCLA game."

* * * * *

Willis Casey was a large, expansive man physically so when he clasped his hands behind his head as he leaned back in his office chair he seemed to occupy two or three times as much space as he actually did. On the other side of the North Carolina State Athletics Director's desk sat Coach Norman Sloan. They had a past that informed and influenced the present. They had both come to State College in 1946, Norman as a player for Everett Case's first team and Willis as the swimming coach. Sloan helped the Old Gray Fox build the foundation for his basketball program that ultimately influenced the entire state, the old Southern Conference, and the Atlantic Coast Conference. Basically, Casey did for the swimming program what Case did for the basketball program.

It was late. Staff was gone for the night. Players were in their dorms. The strikingly ultra-modern Case Center that he had brought into being in 1971 was all but deserted.

"I think it's going to be a fun game, Willis, a lot like going to a football bowl game."

"And it's a big money game, too, Norm, don't forget that. You know, we'll gross about $125,000 for this one game. That's the biggest payday ever for one college basketball game—more than all but the very biggest football games. I think the network is just beginning to realize what this match-up is going to do for college basketball and television. Even more than the Super Sunday games, and we were a part of that too. Along with the C.D. Chesley games, that gives us a pretty good income for the department."

"You're right," Sloan agreed.

"It's also very true that we have a chance to gain immeasurably in national prestige if we can win this one, Norm."

"But if we lose," he shrugged, "so, what? It's not of dire consequences like a conference game loss would be."

"Well, that's true, I guess. But we want to win it, don't we?"

"Oh, hell, Willis. Of course, we want to win it. Can you imagine me not wanting to win a game? Any game? I'm looking forward to this one and our players are, too. They're not uptight. I'm just thinking about the kids. I don't want them to be devastated if they don't win, that's all."

"Okay. Let's call it a night. You have that teleconference with the press tomorrow, don't you?"

"Yes." Sloan stood abruptly.

Willis Casey sat up straight, then got out of his chair also. When he stood, he was of imposing stature. "See you tomorrow, Norm."

"Good night, Willis." Sloan turned and walked through the doorway of the Athletic Director's office into the near darkness of the center named for his own college basketball coach and mentor and the father of the program for which he was now responsible.

* * * * *

"We've been a little slow rounding into playing form," Coach John Wooden responded into the telephone hook-up apparatus the next day. "But, I expected it, really. Replacing two starters presents some problems, especially when one of them started three seasons."

"How about depth, Coach?"

"That hasn't worked out quite as well as I would have liked by now, but I believe depth will come as the season progresses."

"How important a game is this match-up with North Carolina State, and how are your players feeling about the game?"

"Well, it's not a conference game, and winning conference games is how you get to the NCAA tournament. At the same time, we do have a 78-game winning streak going, so we must take any threat to that very seriously." Wooden paused. "As for the players, I'm sure they are eager about it. In a game of such national stature, it would be unnatural if they weren't."

"And what about preparation? What do you know about the NC State team? About David Thompson?"

"We have no information on their team as yet, but we will have by tomorrow. Our players had today off and we'll begin practice tomorrow." The Wizard cleared his throat. "As for David Thompson, I have seen very little of him but have heard a great deal about him. One coach told me Thompson could start for any pro team right now. Another said Thompson was the best player in college basketball, but Walton was the most valuable. I know he must be a tremendous player. But we will be playing a team, not just one player."

"Coach Sloan, should the Wolfpack, maybe, have scheduled tougher opening opponents to get ready for UCLA?" another teleconference reporter asked.

"Possibly if we had inexperienced players that might have helped," Norman Sloan responded into the telephone hook-up receiver. "But I don't see it as any disadvantage for this team. We have been erratic and it has concerned me some. But our guys have been through lots of pressure games."

"What about the Walton-Burleson match-up, Coach? Won't that be a major key to the game for your team?"

"I don't think there is any such thing as specific keys in this game. It's more mental than anything else by the time you get to this level of play. I just want Tommy to be in there contesting Walton constantly. I don't want him out trying to stop a man you can't stop, get into foul trouble, and be on the bench."

* * * * *

"State definitely has a chance," Lefty Driesell drawled. "But I'm not saying who's gonna win. I'm not getting' into all that. I don't want to make anybody mad."

"All right, Coach. Then how can State beat UCLA?"

"Well, they gotta stop them from running. UCLA has a great fast break team. And they've gotta stop them from getting those second and third shots, which they do so well." He shrugged. "We almost did it right."

"What about the Walton-Burleson match-up?"

"It's key," Tom McMillen offered quickly, "because the one who intimidates the other will probably determine victory. And, if Tom gets into foul trouble, State's really in trouble."

"Nobody else wants to say it, but I think UCLA will win by 6 or 8 points," Len Elmore followed, almost off-handedly. "My basis for that is defense. I don't think State can play defense as well. State is reckless. They run and gun. Their defense just isn't as strong. Burleson likes to go up and block shots but he won't overplay Walton to his right and try to deny him the pass to that side, like I did. Instead of playing close, he'll be more conscious of standing behind Walton and trying to block his shot."

* * * * *

"So, David, the big game is coming up on the fifteenth. Have you given UCLA much thought up to now?"

"UCLA is always in the back of your mind. Everywhere you go people are always asking you about them, and there is no chance of forgetting it. But as a team we haven't been talking about UCLA."

The Interviewer laughed. "So are you talking about them now?"

David smiled behind his hands. "I guess so. There's nobody else left to talk about before we play them on Saturday."

"Okay, David, then let's talk about UCLA. How do you and your teammates feel about the upcoming game?"

"I've been waiting, we've been waiting, for a chance to play them since last year. I felt we had a better chance of beating them than any other team.

"We've got enough height, depth, and speed and we've got the desire. There's not much more you need. I've always wanted to be on the Number 1 team."

* * * * *

Unlike fellow Hoosier Everett Case, John Wooden *was* a player. Born in a small town, Martinsville, Oct. 14, 1910, he attended high school there and won All-State prep honors in basketball for three years, leading Martinsville High to the State title in 1927 and the runner-up spot in 1926 and 1928.

In fact, he became a player's player at Purdue University where he won letters in basketball and baseball as a freshman, then went on to win All-American honors as a basketball guard in 1930-31-32. He captained Purdue's great teams in 1931 and 1932, and led the team to two Big Ten titles and, in his senior season, the 1932 National Collegiate Championship. Sports writers voted him College Player of Year. As an English major, he earned a place on Purdue's academic honor roll.

Shortly after graduating from Purdue in 1932, he began a high school teaching career at Dayton, Kentucky High School, where he coached all sports. Two years later, he returned to Indiana where he coached basketball, baseball, and tennis, as well as taught English at South Bend Central High School for nine years. His impressive 11-year prep coaching record was 218 wins and only 42 losses.

World War II interrupted his coaching career. From 1943 to 1946, he served in the U.S. Navy with rank of full lieutenant. Following his discharge in 1946, he went to Indiana State Teacher's College (now Indiana State University) to become their athletic director and to coach their basketball and baseball teams for two seasons from 1946 to 1948, guiding the team to a 47-14 win-loss record while Everett Case was coaching his first NC State College Wolfpack teams on which another Hoosier, Norman Sloan, was a player.

"The Wizard of Westwood" had served as head basketball coach at the University of California at Los Angeles (UCLA) since 1948. He led UCLA teams to nine NCAA basketball titles (1964-65, 67-73), more championships than any coach in history. He was the first person elected to the Basketball Hall of Fame as both a player (1961) and a coach (1972).

He was the only coach to compile four undefeated seasons of 30-0, and his teams also had captured 16 conference championships, all at UCLA.

The Wizard's star, Bill Walton, scoured the St. Louis Arena basketball court as well as the seats that surrounded it. The arena was filling quickly with college basketball fans from UCLA, NC State, the St. Louis area, and all over the country, even the world. The NC State folks all seemed to wear the same red-and-white garb along with straw hats. He had noticed them in the lobby of the Chase Park Plaza where the two teams were staying. Despite their costumes, he realized that today's game was not going to be a Grateful Dead concert. It was going to be sports event warfare witnessed throughout America thanks to that technological wonder called television, that commercial wonder called networks, and that ethical wonder called greed.

Walton rose to national prominence by leading UCLA to NCAA championships in the two previous seasons. He'd been selected as *The Sporting News* College Player of the Year in 1972, '73, and, again, this season. The red head also held NCAA Tournament records for highest field-goal percentage in one year (76.3 in 1973). Now, he was shooting for a career record percentage as well.

At 6'11" Big Red, as the press he seldom talked to often referred to him, could see over just about everybody. Sometimes he thought that the way he viewed life was also like being 6'11". The inscrutability of life intrigued him most. How could he be so competitive that he practically lusted after victory yet eschewed red meat, ate raw fruits and vegetables, meditated, and—most mysteriously—chased after the Grateful Dead from concert to concert like just another "Deadhead?" He realized that many viewed him as some latter day hippie type or simply as trouble laying in wait. He knew that the press thought him to be arrogant, distant, and unapproachable. He was, for sure, distant from them and definitely as unapproachable as he could make himself. Hell, even when it came to basketball, all the press really seemed to care about was generating a quote or something that would incite and titillate. He certainly knew about that sort of thing first hand.

"We've heard rumors of marijuana use at Grateful Dead concerts?"

"Well, I've been to a lot of those concerts and I'd have to say that such rumors are probably not ill-founded."

"Are you saying that you smoked marijuana?"

"I didn't say that I did or that I didn't. What I said was that it's a pretty good bet there is some marijuana use at Grateful Dead concerts." Bill Walton scowled directly at the reporter. "You see, this is exactly why I don't like talking to you people at all." He stood abruptly to his full 6'11" height and turned toward The Wizard. "Coach, I'm done here." He turned and walked away from the table and the bank of microphones leaving the Wizard and the rest of the team to fend for themselves with the barracudas of the press.

On the court, they would always be able to count on him, just like now. Nevertheless, off the court, with the press, no way could they count on him. No way. Those barracudas were called the press because that's all they ever did . . . press! It was worse than a great full court pressing defense. The vultures wanted too much out of you about all the wrong things for all the wrong reasons.

"Does transcendental meditation interfere with playing basketball, Bill?"

Jesus, what an imbecile, Walton remembered thinking at the time. If the fool who asked that question had ever meditated, he would have realized the complete ignorance his question revealed.

So, intellectually demanding of the press? Yes. Arrogant? He thought not.

The arena din was growing louder as basketball fans continued to fill the seats.

"Is it true that you circulated petitions among your coaches and teammates calling for the impeachment of President Nixon?"

What did his political views and activities have to do with his ability to play the game or with UCLA's ability to win them?

This David Thompson dude, he talked to the press. In fact, the press seemed to like him, even idolize him, yet he seemed to have his head on straight about that and about other stuff. One of his teammates—maybe it was Mo Rivers—said that Thompson was the best thing ever for race relations in North Carolina. That was cool. From his comments, Thompson seemed to have the whole money or school thing in perspective. Money didn't seem to drive him either. That could make him truly dangerous on the court: a pure player playing purely for the love of the game. After all, that was what it was all about, wasn't it?

Walton canned one last short jumper off the glass as the horn sounded. He was ready now, ready for the big time media hype contest that was about to begin between them and North Carolina State, between Number 1 and Number 2. David and Goliath some were calling it. Well, he was going to prove that analogy wrong, because he came to play and no David or anybody else was going to bring him down with some slingshot. On the court, amidst the battle, that was all that mattered. That was his mantra. That had always been his mantra. He came to play.

"This is Jim Simpson along with Billy Packer here at St. Louis Sports Arena."

The lights dimmed as players returned to stand in front of their respective benches and equipment managers collected the last basketballs. Suddenly, a white spotlight illuminated the center circle.

"Good evening, ladies and gentlemen, and welcome to the St. Louis Sports Arena where, this evening, we are pleased to present the

Wolfpack of North Carolina State University versus the Bruins of UCLA."

"Here we go, Billy. The first time these two have faced off and each with a long winning streak to protect. The Wolfpack's 29th straight and the Bruin's 78th in a row."

"And, now, for tonight's line ups. First, for the North Carolina State University Wolfpack: At guard, a five foot seven junior from Converse, Indiana, Monte Towe. At the other guard, a six foot one junior from Brooklyn, New York, Mo Rivers. At Center, a seven foot four senior from Newland, North Carolina, Tom Burleson. At forward, a six foot seven junior from Hammond, Indiana, Tim Stoddard. And, at the other forward, a six foot four junior from Shelby, North Carolina, David Thompson. The Wolfpack is coached by Norman Sloan."

"And, for the UCLA Bruins. At guard, a senior from Tallahassee, Florida, Tommy Curtis; at the other guard, a senior from Reseda, California, Greg Lee; at forward, a junior from La Habra, California, Dave Meyers; also at forward, a senior from Ventura, California, Keith Wilkes; and at center, a senior from La Mesa, California, Bill Walton. The Bruins are coached by John Wooden."

"Yes, Jim. The match ups will probably look something like this: NC State's Tom Burleson will go up against UCLA's Bill Walton; Keith Wilkes and David Thompson will go at each other; State's Tim Stoddard against UCLA's Dave Meyers; Mo Rivers against Greg Lee; and Monte Towe versus Tommy Curtis."

"Well, Billy, history says nobody beats Bill Walton."

"But, Jim, history also says that nobody beats David Thompson."

"Which way will history go today? We'll be back with the tip off after these messages."

The Wizard of Westwood clutched a small silver cross in his left hand. The Wolfpack missed its first five shots. Then, they made one and missed six more. Wooden clung to the silver cross, but Walton picked up two fouls in the first 2 minutes. A third at five minutes. Wooden chastised the eastern official, Fred Hickel. With 11 minutes left in the first half, Thompson tried to drive on Walton who committed his fourth foul although he seemed to have position on the play. The Wizard pleaded with the Western official, Louis Soriano, on a first-name basis.

The score was 15-10 Bruins. Coach Wooden benched Walton.

At 20-17, Burleson picked up his third personal in 13 minutes. He also went to the bench. "Two of his fouls when he went up for rebounds were very questionable," Simpson offered.

State went ahead for the first time after baskets by Spence, Towe, and Nuce made it 19-20, 21-20, then 23-20.

Then Wilkes went on a tear, hitting seven points in a row.

UCLA remained in front until Mo Rivers scored twice in the last minute to make it 33-32 State at half time.

"This is the first time since last season against Stanford that UCLA has been behind at the half, Jim."

In the locker room, Walton begged Coach Wooden to let him start the second half in spite of his four fouls. "I can play with four fouls, Coach!"

The Wizard knew better than to take such a chance with his star. "Bill, I know you're ready, and I'm confident you'll be ready when the time is right. But the time is not right yet."

To start the second half, Dave Meyers quickly put UCLA up with three baskets in a row and the Bruins built a 7-point lead.

Baskets by Burleson and Towe cut the lead back to two with 11:15 remaining.

Still up by two with 9:54 remaining, UCLA finally brought Bill Walton back into the game. The score was UCLA 54 and NC State 52. Steve Nuce stuck a 15-foot jumper to tie the game at 54 all.

Walton scored the first time he touched the ball back down the court, the first of nine straight points. UCLA was off on a 19-2 run in the next four minutes.

Finally, Monte hit a 20-footer for the Pack, but UCLA came back with eight more.

At 5:20 left, the score was 71-56.

Walton blocked three straight Burleson attempts underneath the basket. After the third slam block, he smirked and pointed at the other end of the court, laughing all the way to the UCLA goal.

"We're Number 1! We're Number 1! We're Number 1!" the UCLA fans chorused again and again.

The Wizard released his life-line-like grasp on the small silver cross in his left hand, finally dropping it into his left trouser pocket.

When the clock reached zero, the score was 84-66 Bruins. Their fans' chants echoed off the arena walls and ceiling. "We're Number 1! We're Number 1! We're Number 1!"

Coach Norm Sloan had a glazed looked in his eyes as he stumbled down the hallway toward the NC State dressing room. His jacket and trousers were, uncharacteristically, rumpled. He seemed unable to speak as he avoided the growing swarm of reporters.

The players followed close behind their coach. "David? What happened out there this afternoon?" a reporter tossed at the fabled Number 44.

"I haven't got time to talk." David Thompson brushed by reporters almost seeming to hide at the side of Tom Burleson.

"What about it, Tommy? You guys got beat pretty bad?"

"Where's the bus?" big Tom asked Chip Sloan, completely ignoring the reporters clumping around them as they continued to press toward the safety of their locker room.

"You gotta shower and change first, Tommy. But, I'll have to ask Coach. He handles that," Chip volunteered as he pushed passed the two trapped players and helped to clear a path to the locker room door with his white canvas towel bin on wheels.

A semi-recovered and somewhat defiant Norm Sloan stopped reporters at the slightly ajar Wolfpack locker room door. "Their team just beat our team, in the last 10 minutes, soundly." He paused and mustered a twisted smile. "So, our kids need some recovery time. I hope you'll all understand. No locker room interviews this time." With that, the protégé of Everett Case, the coach of his prototype team, the bearer of the Case torch, and the keeper of his coaching secrets stepped inside the locker room and closed the door.

Post-Game Press

"A crowd of 18, 461 plus a national television audience saw this game tonight. UCLA shot 49%. State ended up with 43.7% even with their problems. Both teams handled the other team's press pretty well with State committing 17 turnovers to UCLA's 12." Billy Packer was speaking with Coach Wooden just outside the Bruins' dressing room.

"Dave Meyers and Keith Wilkes really carried the game for us while Walton was on the bench. Wilkes did a fine job on Thompson, who wound up with only 17 points, while Wilkes had 27. Meyers added 15 and Walton 11.

"Thompson couldn't hit from outside. He was seven for 20. Towe scored 14 and Burleson 11" Packer continued. "And, rebounding was dead even with 42 each. Burleson grabbed 15 and Thompson 13 for the

Pack. Meyers had 10 and Walton 11 for the Bruins. So what was the big difference, Coach?"

"Bill Walton was the big difference. When he came back in with nine plus minutes left in the second half, the entire complexion of the game changed. He then proceeded to dominate with nine of his 11 points over the next couple of minutes or so. That broke State's spirit, I believe."

Long after the game was over, the UCLA dancing pom-pom girls still performed to the accompaniment of the school band.

"Do you do this if UCLA loses?" a disgruntled passerby wearing a North Carolina State sweat shirt and straw hat asked the band director.

"I can't remember," the band director responded.

6
On The Rebound

AP Poll
1. UCLA 4-0
2. Maryland 2-1
3. Notre Dame 5-1
4. North Carolina 4-0
5. NC State 2-1
6. Marquette 5-0
7. Indiana 4-1
8. Louisville 3-1
9. Providence 3-1
10. Alabama 3-0

UPI Poll
1. UCLA (4-0)
2. North Carolina (5-0)
3. Notre Dame (5-0)
4. Marquette (5-0)
5. Maryland (2-1)
6. NC State (2-1)
7. Indiana (4-1)
8. Providence (3-1)
9. Louisville (4-1)
10. Southern Cal. (4-1)

This was no David and Goliath match-up by any stretch of the imagination. It was more like that *being-fed-to-the-lions* kind of feeling for the University of Georgia when they took the court in William Neal Reynolds Coliseum on the night of December 18. Only in this case it was actually being fed to the wolves.

"Tonight at 8 o'clock in Reynolds Coliseum The Wolfpack entertains Georgia," Wally Ausley opened. "NC State hopes to begin recovering some of the ground lost in Saturday's 84-66 loss to UCLA. Coach Norm Sloan's club carried a Number 2 ranking into Saturday's game in St. Louis. Today, they have slipped to Number 5.

"Georgia is a surprising young team picked for a low second-division Southeastern Conference finish but is unbeaten to date. The Bulldogs, led by former South Carolina player junior Ed Peterson (18 ppg), stopped Louisiana State-New Orleans (94-63) and Louisiana College (63-53) so far this season.

"Junior Bill Magarity (12.5 ppg) and senior Charlie Anderson (10.5 ppg) have assisted Peterson with the early-season offensive burden. Six-nine junior Steve Waxsman (7 ppg) and 6-7 freshman James Johnson share center position duties. Johnson also leads the team in rebounding with 11 per game.

"State's top scorer is all-American David Thompson (21.3 ppg) despite an off day against the Bruins in St. Louis. Guards Mo Rivers and Monte Towe follow at 12.7 and 11 ppg respectively. Surprisingly, Towe is the team's leading shooter from the floor with 16-22 or 73%. Tommy Burleson tops Wolfpack rebounding with 13 retrieves per game.

"State's two chief rivals for the ACC title Maryland and North Carolina reaped immediate profits from the Wolfpack's late-game collapse against UCLA. Maryland, which lost only by a single point to the same UCLA team in their season opener, took over the Number 2 spot while Carolina, unbeaten in four games, moved up one spot to fourth."

State dropped behind 2-0 at the outset, but baskets by Towe and Thompson enabled the Wolfpack to take the lead 4-2 and keep it for the remainder of the blow out that materialized despite David still being as arctic cold with his jump shot in the first half as he had been in St. Louis, scoring only eight points on four of 10 shots.

The Wolfpack foundered until the second part of the opening half. In the first 10 minutes of the period the Pack hit only seven of 20 field goals and committed nine turnovers. In the remainder of the half, however, they threw the ball away just once and hit with enough regularity to boost the count to 43-27 at intermission. The margin could have been larger, but Spence in his enthusiasm to control the boards accidentally tapped in two baskets for Georgia off missed free throws.

David connected on nine of 15 in the second half, however, eliciting roars of approval repeatedly from the 8,100 coliseum fans.

Tom Burleson had 15, Towe 14 and Spence (who came in as sub for Tim Stoddard and played 29 minutes, hauling down a game-high 15 rebounds) scored 11.

"Phil gives us more quickness and board strength," Coach Sloan explained. "I was generally pleased with the team's play. It's tough coming back after that loss on Saturday. These kids aren't used to losing. But, we just haven't played well all season. However, we did some things tonight that have been lacking. We went to the boards better, and we were tougher on defense. I really liked our press."

The full court press applied by the Pack resulted in a whopping 32 turnovers for Georgia.

"We caught State at a bad time when they wanted to bounce back from that loss," Coach John Guthrie stated. "But I did think we'd handle their press better than we did."

Ed Peterson, junior transfer from South Carolina, a 6-4 guard was the Georgia star, hitting 10-14 shots, all in the 15-30 foot range, and finished with 22 points. "He was absolutely uncanny with his shooting," Sloan observed, "but I still thought Mo Rivers did a good job on him defensively."

"Next high scorer for Georgia was Dave Lucey with six.

"The Pack, now 3-1, doesn't play again until the Sugar Bowl tournament in New Orleans December 28-29."

Post-Game Press

David was somber despite the 94-60 rout of Georgia. "We've been guilty of overrating ourselves. There may have been a tendency for us to just naturally assume that this team would start off as good as last year's team finished. If we did, it has cost us and I think we'll straighten ourselves out again.

"Who knows, losing may even help us in the long run. I think it taught us some lessons, and we'll have to remember them.

"We have more talent on this year's team than we did last year but, right now, we just aren't as good a team. We have some new people in the line-up and, we haven't adjusted to each other as quick as we should have. It's a matter of getting it all together and I'm still sure we'll do it."

"Phil Spence is the bright spot for us right now," Coach Sloan commented. "We'll play him more and more. He's a fine athlete and is remarkably quick at getting up and down the floor. He can help us at both ends of the court on the same play and that's unusual for a guy his size."

"My biggest problem," Spence said, "is not so much changing from Vincennes Junior College to State, but it's changing positions. I've never really faced the basket all that much. Coach Ed McLean at Broughton used to have me work facing the basket a little each practice, just in case. Basically, I've always been a center and have had my back to the basket.

"To play forward, I've got to get my short jumper going. I'm working on it every day in practice, but I'm not pushing myself to take that shot because we have a team of great jump-shooters. I think I can add a lot to the defense and the offensive rebounding, particularly."

"We've made a little progress out there," Sloan added. "I saw signs of jelling. I just hate that we have to take a few days off. But at least I can rest a little easier now."

"This was the best we've played," David admitted. "But I don't think there's a guy on the team who will say that he is pleased yet, though."

After the Georgia game, they all knew how important the two upcoming tournaments would be to reestablishing their confidence as a team and their reputation as winners. It would not be easy, but they were determined to a man to win every game they played until they got the chance to meet UCLA again . . . for keeps!

Sugar Bowl Tournament

State's basketball team left Wednesday night for New Orleans and a Friday night date with Villanova in the Sugar Bowl Tournament. Three days after Christmas, it was a little tough to think basketball. It was even tougher to think about "comeback" basketball. And, it was the toughest to deal with all that in the Big Easy. Villanova, however, was to be a little more sweets for my sweet, sugar bowl for my heartache to the Wolfpack.

9:30 p.m. central standard time. Villanova was an old and respected opponent on the basketball court. Over the years, State and Villanova had tangled on the hardwood a total of 25 times with the Wildcats owning an edge in the series 14-11. The two clubs last met in 1961 with Villanova taking the decision 72-63.

"Villanova always fields a top-flight basketball team, Wally," Coach Sloan remarked. "Although their record this year is only 3-3, I'm sure they'll be ready for us. It seems like everybody is gunning to knock us off."

"The Wolfpack bounced back from its loss to UCLA by trouncing Georgia. In that game a new State star was born, sophomore Phil Spence from Raleigh's Broughton High School and junior college All-American at Vincennes."

"Phil certainly was impressive, and there's a strong possibility we may use him as a starter against Villanova. He was even named Rookie of the Week in the ACC this past week. We feel that he has tremendous potential."

Six eight Larry Herron leads Villanova, which starts four freshmen and a senior, with a 19.4 average and guard Chubby Cox at 10.4.

It's not that Coach Norm Sloan was greedy. He just thought NC State should have looked better in its 97-82 victory over Villanova Friday night. The game was never in doubt and the Wolfpack led by as much as 20 points in the second half in running its record to 4-1. Still it wasn't enough.

"We just can't get it going," moaned Sloan. "We'll look pretty good in spurts and then have a lapse and act like we don't know what the game's about.

"This is not to criticize our effort," he added hastily. "We need to relax. Maybe we're trying too hard."

Thompson made difficult plays look easy, poured in 26 points and pulled down 8 rebounds before fouling out with just over five minutes to play. In an impromptu tribute to his smooth individual performance, much of the crowd of 4,500 began filing out when Thompson left the game.

Tommy Burleson dropped in 20 and grabbed 12 rebounds and blocked a half dozen shots although Sloan said the big man, "just couldn't get it in gear for some reason."

Larry Herron paced Villanova, now 3-4, with 20 points.

* * * * *

The next day David Thompson was at his dazzling best as State's Wolfpack swept to the Sugar Bowl championship with a victory over Memphis State. Seeming to finally shake off his UCLA cold hand, the junior from Shelby had his finest game of the season, a 34-point effort that paved the way for a 98-83 State victory over Memphis State.

Thompson got 19 of his points in the first half and that's when the Pack did its building job for the tourney trophy. Thompson and Towe triggered an eight-point spurt that put State ahead for keeps, 16-8. Memphis State, despite a 33-point production by 6-5 guard Bill Cook, never got closer than six points the rest of the way.

Center Tom Burleson after a slow start came on to score 20 points and add 15 rebounds. Mo Rivers had 16 points and Towe 14 as the Pack lifted its record to 5-1.

While State's early cushion held up all the way, it was needed as Burleson, Tim Stoddard, and Phil Spence all picked up four personals by midway the second half. Spence, Stoddard, and Steve Nuce ended up fouling out.

Thompson did equal damage inside and out. He also pulled down 11 rebounds. His play enabled the Pack to get off to a fast start. He scored 12 of his team's first 24 points as it opened an 11-point lead.

The score was 8-8 when his two baskets sandwiched around a pair of 25-footers by Towe gave the Wolfpack a working margin.

Memphis State, now 8-3, ran a guard-oriented offense in an attempt to use a height advantage by Cook and 6-3 Dexter Reed over Towe and Rivers. Cook and Reed did most of the shooting. Reed was second high scorer with 13 points and Bill Laurie, another guard, was next with 10.

State had probably its smoothest game of the year offensively, executing sharp passing and accurate shooting most of the game.

Memphis State's best opportunity to close the gap came in the middle portions. They rallied just before the end of the half to reduce the margin from 11 to six, 49-43. However, Steve Nuce sank two free throws with 3 seconds left, making it 51-43 at the half.

The margin stayed between six and eight in the early minutes of the second period. With the score 71-65, a technical foul against the Tigers helped State go ahead by ten.

A tip by Nuce and two foul shots by Thompson made it 81-67, just about sealing the outcome with eight minutes left. Memphis rallied once more, cutting it to eight, but that was as close as it got. State went to a delay game in the last five minutes to preserve the victory.

State's next game: Carolina on the following Friday in the opening round of the Big Four Tournament in Greensboro.

All Tournament Team

Tom Burleson dominated the boards. David Thompson led all scorers. And, Monte Towe was the crowd favorite as the three North Carolina State starters captured all-tournament honors in the Sugar Bowl Classic.

Burleson finished the two-day tournament with 40 points and 27 rebounds, but Thompson was the hottest shooter for the Pack with 60 points, including 34 in the Championship game, and 19 rebounds. He was also named the tournament MVP.

Towe's cool style and team leadership as well as his smooth ball handling captured the hearts of the fans.

Memphis State's Bill Cook hit a career high 33 points in the championship game to land a spot on the all-tournament team. He had 54 points in the two games.

Freshman Warren Booker exploded for 30 points in the consolation game to lead Louisiana State-New Orleans (a victim earlier in the season of Georgia) to an 81-80 overtime win against Villanova. He rounded out the all-tourney team.

Big Four Tournament

"As of Sunday, December 23, and for the first time in its four-year history, the Big Four basketball tournament, to be held January 4 and 5 in Greensboro Coliseum, is sold out. Seating capacity is 14,885 for the Big Four event," Frank Weedon, Assistant Athletic Director at North Carolina State University and tournament manager, announced today.

"All four universities and the Greensboro Coliseum are out of tickets and each has had to return unfilled orders.

"Individual sessions have been sold out in other years, but never in advance of the tournament. Pairings for this year match fourth-ranked North Carolina and fifth-ranked North Carolina State in the opening game at 7 p.m. while Wake Forest meets Duke at 9 p.m. on Friday, January 4. Winners meet for the championship at 9 p.m. on Saturday, with the third-place game at 7 p.m.

"The tournament will not be televised."

* * * * *

On this fourth day of the New Year, Dean Smith knew well what he was facing in their first conference opponent of the season. Regardless of the fact that the game was a part of the Big Four Tournament and didn't count toward the conference standings, it *was* big. His kids had been playing really well so far. They were the only unbeaten team in the conference at 7-0 and ranked fourth in both AP and UPI polls. Higher than State at Number 5, and that did surprise him.

So, this game was like Bruce Phillips wrote in the *News and Observer* that morning. "If the Big Four tournament results don't mean anything, then the Greensboro Coliseum is a trinket." Guess you would have to have a pretty large neck or wrist to wear that coliseum dangling from it, Dean chuckled. So, yes, it must mean something. His boys certainly had not yet arrived. They played well at times and at times not so well. They had been too inconsistent so far, and no one had truly tested them the way they would be tested tonight. It meant something to them—to play well for forty minutes. It meant something to them to turn the litmus paper Carolina blue.

State and Carolina dashed up and down the Greensboro Coliseum floor for the full 40 minutes, and when it was over there was only one point separating them. With fans of both teams trying to provide the loudest support, first one team and then another seized control of the game. Nevertheless, it was always temporary. State, down 42-39 at the half, ran off ten straight points early in the second half and that cushion kept the Wolfpack in command for some 15 minutes. With a four-point lead, 69-65, State went to an old UNC weapon, the Four Corners control game. It didn't work.

Baskets by Elston and Walter Davis with a free throw by Burleson in between sliced the margin to a point, 70-69. Morris Rivers hit from the floor with 3:12 left, but Elston countered 20 seconds later. Rivers and Elston exchanged baskets again, but with the Pack in front 74-73, Carolina blocked a shot under the basket. Elston who seemed to be everywhere during the closing minutes came out with the ball. Tar Heel fans then erupted as Stahl hit a 15-footer to put their team ahead 75-74.

With 1:03 left, State committed a traveling violation, and Carolina had a chance to wrap it up. However, pressure near mid court forced a bad pass, and Rivers drove full speed for the basket. Elston blocked his shot, but State retained possession.

Burleson scored underneath with 42 seconds left, and Mitch Kupchak fouled him. Tommy missed the foul shot, but State still led 76-75.

On Carolina's next possession, Davis attempted a twisting bank shot, but it rolled off the rim. Burleson snatched the rebound and tossed the outlet pass to Monte Towe. Elston immediately fouled him.

After a time out, Monte quickly swished both free throws without touching the rim, giving the Wolfpack a 78-75 lead with 18 seconds left.

Stahl scored with seven seconds left and the Tar Heels immediately got the ball back. The ball went back to the hot Ed Stahl. But Tommy Burleson loomed in front of the 6-11 Stahl like one of those mountains he was raised in. The UNC junior tried a last ditch jump shot from 15 feet. The ball rimmed. The referee called a jump after a scramble for the ball, but time had run out.

The Wolfpack won it 78-77. It was the fifth straight State victory over Carolina dating back to the last game of the 1971-72 season.

They dominated the backboards throughout the fast-paced game 40-22. Burleson grabbed 14 of those rebounds. But the Tar Heels hit 55% to State's 50%, although Burleson also took scoring honors with 22 points while David Thompson, making nine of 12 from the floor, accounted for 20 points and 7 assists.

Elston with a nine for 13 performance contributed 18 points for Carolina. Davis was next with 12.

"The lead changed hands 10 times in the first half alone with both teams pressing and running and few fouls being called. Carolina didn't make a foul shot in the entire period, and it had only two attempts. State was three for four," Bill Jackson commented in his wrap up.

"The Tar Heels led by five on one occasion, but they needed a spurt by their swift-passing reserve unit, the Blue team, to take the halftime lead.

"With the score 47-44, State went on its streak of 10 points early in the second half. Ray Harrison retaliated with two quick ones for the Tar Heels and the margin stayed between one and seven points until the finish.

"Bobby Jones fouled out with 3:49 left, but Stahl came in to give UNC a strong replacement.

"Phil Spence came off the bench for State to supply ten points and seven rebounds in another fine performance. Burleson was a big factor defensively, making it difficult for Carolina to operate its normal inside game. Consequently, UNC's guards outscored the big men, something that usually did not happen."

"Good game, Tommy," Smith commented almost out of the side of his mouth, as he passed the 7-4 center in the hall on the way to the locker rooms. "That's the best I've ever seen you."

"Thanks, Coach Smith, we always get fired up for you guys."

Post-Game Press

It didn't matter that a sell-out Greensboro Coliseum crowd screamed and cheered like the national championship was at stake. It didn't matter that his players whooped and hollered as if they had clinched their second straight Atlantic Coast Conference title. Moreover, if you believed Coach Norm Sloan, it didn't matter that the Wolfpack beat Carolina for the fifth straight time 78-77 in the first game of the Big Four Tournament Friday night.

Sloan, dapper and debonair as usual, brushed off the victory as if he were whisking a piece of lint off his red-and-white plaid sports coat. "I've said it before--that game didn't determine or decide anything," he contended in a brief post-game press conference. "It was just a matter of what the officials called and which way the ball bounced in the last minute. Fortunately, it bounced our way.

"I think we can play better and they can play better," said Norm, cool as a bowl of gazpacho. "As I said, the game didn't mean anything. Now we can look ahead to two games with Carolina that do count."

Norm was right, of course. The game didn't even count in the ACC standings. However, that was about the only place it didn't count.

Sloan did learn a few things, though. He found out that Carolina is "a great team with more overall board strength than any team we've played, including UCLA." He learned that the Wolfpack's "tease" game was ineffective and nearly cost them the game. "It didn't work too well. We were too cautious with it. Morris was the only one who took it in there."

Sloan lauded his players. Burleson, he said, "did an outstanding job" with his 22 points, 14 rebounds, and 4 blocked shots. Spence, Towe, Thompson, and Rivers all received strong praise from the coach.

Sloan refused to allow reporters into the State dressing room again after the game. "So that they can get back to Raleigh and get some rest," a team spokesperson gave as the reason for the locked doors. The spokesperson didn't think to add that they still had another game tomorrow night back here in Greensboro against either Wake Forest or Duke.

* * * * *

In a game during his high school playing days, so the story goes, a referee whistled Horace Albert "Bones" McKinney for a foul. When the official turned his back, the young McKinney fell to his knees and acted as if he were pleading for mercy. When the crowd roared with laughter, the referee wheeled around only to find Bones innocently tying his shoe.

After high school in Durham, Bones played basketball at NC State for two years prior to the days of the Old Gray Fox before the Army drafted him into World War II. He played Army basketball for four years, and his jersey was retired at Fort Bragg. By 1946 when Everett Case began his triumphant years at NC State and Bones resumed his college career, he was playing for North Carolina State's arch rival University of North Carolina. After graduation came six NBA seasons.

Bones served as head coach at Wake Forest from 1958-1965 where he had a lifetime contract with school president Dr. Harold Tribble. "Then Dr. Tribble called one day, pronounced me dead, and fired me," Bones used to joke.

He was an ordained Baptist minister who lived a full, rich life, but never took it so seriously that he couldn't find the humor, and he's the only man many have ever known who could tell the same stories year after year at public appearances and still draw belly laughs from the audience. He drew from some mysterious well of boundless energy, and his punch-line delivery was flawless.

A magazine article about him many years later carried the headline: "Bones McKinney -- Magnificent Screwball." Not a bad summation. He was 6-foot-6 and gangly, but that was not how Horace Albert McKinney got his nickname. It came from a performance in a school play when he portrayed a character named Beau Brummel Bones. "People started calling me 'Bones' and I just kept it," he said once. "Besides, I always thought Horace sounded too much like 'Horrors.' "

His antics as a coach were legendary. His artistry with a towel made the later Jerry Tarkanian look as sedate as Dean Smith in a blowout. He kept a bucket of water and a dipper underneath his bench seat, ladling sips to quench his thirst when he wasn't leaping and gyrating to inspire his players or bait officials. He often accidentally knocked the bucket over, curiously at times when Wake Forest might need a free time out.

Red socks and assorted bow ties were good luck charms. He could shed his sport coat, flourish it like a matador's cape, and then fling it into the stands in a fit of excitement. He could slam a clipboard so hard it sounded like a rifle shot.

"I never meant to do stuff like that," he often said. "A lot of people thought it was an act, but if I could act that good, I'd have been in Hollywood. I just wanted to win."

He used to tell a story about a preacher who was walking in the woods and came upon a hungry bear. Frightened, the preacher began to run. The bear began to chase. The preacher leaped over logs, crashed through bushes and ran as hard as he could, but the bear kept gaining ground. Finally, the exhausted preacher dropped to his knees and began to pray. "Lord," he wailed, "please let this bear see the light of Christian values." The bear, only a few feet away, suddenly dropped down and raised its front paws in a prayerful pose. The amazed preacher listened as the bear spoke: "Lord, thank you for your many gifts, and bless this meal to the nourishment of my body."

Bones McKinney's shadow loomed large over the coliseum floor peering over the shoulder of Coach Carl Tacy with that special intensity only a Bones McKinney stare contained. He was what Tacy and anyone else taking on the gold and black Demon Deacons basketball challenge had to live up to. He was the only coach ever to take Wake Forest to the final four, and he was one of only five who had both played in and coached in the NCAA semi-finals. That list included two other ACC coaches, Vic Bubas and Dean Smith. Bones was, in effect, much like an Everett Case for Wake Forest University.

The Deacons looked more eager than the Wolfpack at the start. In the opening minutes of the first half, they seized eight-point leads on three occasions as they zipped in eight straight points after an opening basket by Thompson. With guard Tony Byers and center Cal Stamp striking consistently, they moved out to a 12-4 lead before State cut it to 14-12. Another flurry by the Deacons raised it to 22-14, then 24-16 as a large part of the crowd shouted its approval.

Then came a State counter attack. Rivers and Towe harassed the Deacons with steals and a very fast conversion from defense to offense. The turnovers they generated broke the game open in the first half. The Wolfpack ran off 12 straight points, eight of them by Rivers, to go ahead 28-24. After the Deacons tied the score at 28, State put in seven more points in a row, four of them by reserve forward Phil Spence. The Deacons switched to a zone, but this didn't stop the Pack either. During the rally over the last 11 minutes of the period, State outscored Wake 35 points to nine. Tommy Burleson and Thompson led another surge that lifted the half-time margin to 51-33.

Thompson provided much of the entertainment with his unique soaring into the stratosphere, accompanied by his deft scoring touch. He got three baskets by fielding high passes above the rim and gently dropping the ball through the rim. On another occasion, he switched the ball behind his back in midair while driving for the basket and laid it through in one continuous motion. There was little doubt about the eventual outcome as nearly half the crowd of 15,095 departed by half time.

State's margin through the second half varied between 15 and 25 points. The result was a 91-73 State victory over the Deacons in a game minus the suspense of Friday's opening squeaker with Carolina.

State finished at 54.6% compared to Wake's 46.7%.

Thompson was 10-14 from the floor. Fourteen of his 20 points came in the first half. Yet, Burleson was high man with 23. Rivers added 17 and Towe scored only 8 but added 5 assists.

Rebounding was nearly even as Lee Foye and Mike Parrish gave the Deacons a boost in this department with ten each. State, with Burleson getting nine and Spence eight, had just a 35-34 edge.

Tony Byers led the Deacons with 18 points. Parrish and Stamp each had 14.

It was the third Big Four Tournament championship in four tries for Norm Sloan's Wolfpack. State had made the finals all four years.

Post-Game Press

"I felt our defensive play really came together. We knew all along that we had fine defensive talent. However, we hadn't been able to bring it together as a unit. Then, we had this one great defensive spurt. Defensive pressure and turnovers changed the rhythm, gave us a cushion, and sort of turned it around," analyzed Norm Sloan. "Also I had been concerned about our board play. But now I feel comfortable that we can hold our own with Carolina and Maryland."

Wake coach Carl Tacy concurred: "Things began falling apart when their pressure defense got several turnovers. They got several easy ones. Then they started with their inside game, and that is very difficult to stop. We had hoped to be close by the end of the first half and then make some adjustments."

One man who helped turn the tide was Mo Rivers. He came up with a couple of key steals that got the Pack running. "I saw our team was starting to slow down," the State guard explained. "We were trailing by 8 at that point, so I knew we needed someone to spark us to get us going." Steals weren't all that Mo did. He also collected 17 points.

"We came in a little overconfident," added David Thompson. "They took it to us at first, but I knew we had to go out and play our best ball." Thompson did just that, hitting 10-14 from the floor.

"After last night, we felt a little tired," confessed Tommy Burleson, who dumped in 23 points and grabbed nine rebounds. "We didn't play as well as we did against Carolina.

"Personally, I didn't feel quite as alert and as quick as I did last night, but you always get up for a Big Four team, no matter what."

All-Tournament Team

David Thompson unanimous choice of 64 sports writers. Tommy Burleson with 60 votes. Darrell Elston (UNC) 54 votes. Tony Byers (Wake) 52 votes. Bob Fleischer (Duke).

7
Son of Super Sunday
and the Tobacco Road to Redemption

AP Poll	UPI Poll
1.UCLA (42) 8-0 840	1.UCLA (28) (8-0) 280
2.Notre Dame 7-0 646	2.Notre Dame (7-0) 207
3.Maryland 6-1 633	3.Maryland (6-1) 187
4.N. Carolina 7-0 603	4.North Carolina (7-0) 183
5.NC State 5-1 510	5.N. Carolina State (5-1) 170
6.Marquette 9-0 509	6.Marquette (9-0) 165
7.Alabama 6-1 500	7.S. California (9-1) 79
8.Indiana 7-2 364	8.Indiana (7-2) 47
9.Long Beach State 3-1 262	9.New Mexico (10-0) 35
10. Vanderbilt 8-0 176	10.Alabama (6-1) 34

There has always been an understanding among the ACC teams, even among the fans. In fact, this understanding might be one of the very few things that competing ACC teams and fans have, over the years, consistently agreed on. That understanding goes something like this: It *ain't easy to travel Tobacco Road and come away unstained.* Or, in other words, Going *undefeated in the ACC just isn't going to happen very often.* This principle is not one of mere intellectual conjecture. It is rooted in empirical knowledge gleaned from twenty plus years of experience as a conference. Only four times had teams gone undefeated in conference play until 1974. The 32-0 '57 Heels, the '68 Blue Devils, '70 Gamecocks of South Carolina, and the previous year's 27-0 Wolfpack.

* * * * *

"Coach Driesell, after your team's big win against Wake Forest 72-59 to push your team's record to 9-1, what about the Son of Super Sunday coming up next on January 13 with your Terps ranked Number 3 against fifth ranked NC State?"

"I haven't even thought about State. We'll practice tomorrow in Raleigh after the State-Clemson game at noon, but I don't expect it'll be much of a practice. There ain't really much you can do at this point but play good.

"And, I'm pretty sure State ain't been thinking much about us, either, with Clemson to play first."

"What do some of your players have to say about the upcoming game with State? John? John Lucas?"

"They beat us three times last year, including Super Sunday, so they're better going into this game. So, we've got a lot to prove in Raleigh on Sunday. That game last year was the worst loss we had all year, including the ACC finals and Providence in the NCAA playoffs.

"It was the toughest loss I've ever been associated with and I'll never forget it, no matter what. We've been living with last year's three losses for a year now, and I want State more than I wanted UCLA. We'll beat them."

"Tom Roy? You're getting the David Thompson assignment, according to Coach Driesell. Did you know that?"

"Hummm. Coach said that, huh?"

"Yes, he did, Tom."

"Well, I never guarded him before. I guess I'd play a step off of him. Yeah, that's what I'll do. You can't get too close to Thompson outside because, if you do, he's so quick that he'll drive on you."

"But, Tom, wouldn't playing off of him a step leave the jump shot open?"

"I got the size on him, so maybe I can get a hand in his face on the way up. I guess it's the lesser of two evils, you know. Jump shots or drives." Tom Roy seemed to reflect for a moment on what he had just said. "Really, though, I don't think there's any way that one man can stop a player like Thompson. I know UCLA did to some extent, but Keith Wilkes is a great defensive player and Thompson was a little off that day.

"We just have to beat State as a team and not Thompson as an individual.

"And, I believe it would be a mistake to get too worked up about it. Sometimes you get so fired up that you lose direction and over react on the court. I want to try to keep my cool and play a business-like game."

* * * * *

David could feel the elbows, the shoves in the small of his back. For some reason, the officials were allowing Clemson forward Jeff Reisinger to have his way with him on defense. He kept flashing on the state finals his senior year at Crest. In that game, the guy who was guarding him kept crowding him, shoving him. Finally, when he just couldn't take any more, he shoved the defender back, and he shoved really hard. Sure, he got a foul, but the guy laid off him after that.

Reisinger jabbed his right elbow into David's left side as he tried to prevent him from driving to the basket. The sharp elbow was bruising his ribs. He could feel it. He glanced up at the clock. 4:09 left in the half. He'd been taking this crap for almost 16 minutes. Why the refs didn't call something was beyond him, but he had to protect himself and his team. He always felt that if he'd shoved the guy back sooner in that high school championship game maybe he and his Crest High team could have been state champs. So, he had promised himself then that he was never going to take that kind of chance again. When somebody pushed him too far on the court, he had to retaliate, even if it was not what his nature told him to do.

David put the ball on the floor and started to drive Reisinger's left side. The ball flew off David's leg as he nearly fell from the concussion of Reisinger's elbow against the side of his head.

"Damn it!" he muttered in a voice not really audible or understandable except to himself. He looked Reisinger directly in the eyes as his hands balled up into fists. "That's it!" he yelled at his tormentor and struck quickly, hitting Reisinger in the jaw with a roundhouse left.

Whistles blew.

The opposing player's knees partly buckled under him, but he didn't quite fall to the floor.

"Flagrant foul on white number 44!"

David smiled inside. He dared not smile openly. The refs might think he was being a smart-ass or something and hit him with a technical. In fact, he was surprised they had called only a personal on him. Heck, he was surprised that he was still in the game after he nearly decked an opposing team player. He figured that the refs must have realized how much Reisinger had been beating him up all half, how much they had been letting the Clemson player get away with.

Reisinger wobbled in place staring off into the coliseum lights as if he were in some kind of trance and then crumpled to the hardwood.

At 2:03 left in the half, Reisinger hit the floor again, this time along with Burleson as they scrambled for a loose ball. When Burleson's hands finally snatched the ball from Reisinger and cradled it to his chest, Reisinger seemed to snap. He started swinging at the 7-4 center as he stood up. Tommy, not wanting to get a foul himself, backed away while fending off the wild swings by the Clemson forward.

Whistles blew from every direction it seemed.

A referee stepped between them. He grabbed Reisinger and held his arms while his teammates restrained him. Then the referee backed away forming a T with his two hands and blowing his whistle. He pointed to Reisinger, and jerked his thumb toward the locker rooms.

It was the twelfth of January not the twelfth of never, but it never really was much of a game after that. State played nearly everybody on the team and rested starters a lot in the second half as they breezed to a 96-68 win.

With only a few minutes left in the game, Lefty Driesell left his seat on Press Row and shuffled off to the coliseum dressing rooms where his team was already getting ready for their Son of Super Sunday practice. That way he could avoid the gaggle of reporters he would have been susceptible to once the final whistle had blown, and he could make sure that his players hit the coliseum floor on time.

Post-Game Press

"Coach Locke, what in the world was going on out there with Jeff Reisinger and David Thompson?"

"It was a rough game physically."

"Coach Sloan?"

"Yes, I agree, Wally. It was awfully rough out there. I understand that the Carolina game at Clemson was extremely physical also. But, let's face it, physical is part of the game too."

"But, Coach Locke, Coach Sloan, come on now. David Thompson cold cocked Jeff Reisinger with 4:09 to go in the first half. And, what's even more bizarre, the refs didn't throw him out of the game. No, they waited and threw Reisinger out after he got into it with Tom Burleson with about two minutes left in the half. What do either of you have to say about all that?"

"Well, I can't speak for Tates, but I can tell you that we aren't going to get into all that kind of stuff about individual players. It was a rough game with some very tough defense played all the way around."

"Norm is right. The game was a rough one all around and pointing to individuals just won't serve any good purpose."

"And let me say something about all this so-called rough play," Norm Sloan continued almost as if he'd never stopped. "It certainly didn't hurt us. In fact, I thought our team played its best game of the year, and our defense is getting better and better. Also, a couple of our players had their best games of the season: Tim Stoddard and Steve Nuce."

"Okay, Coach Locke, let's take a different subject. What about tomorrow's Super Sunday match-up between the Number 3 Maryland Terps and this same NC State Wolfpack. Who's going to win it tomorrow, Coach?"

"Look, I don't mean to not answer your question, but I'd rather not get into that. We have to play them both again this season."

"Well, what about you Coach Sloan?"

"Maryland is one of the great teams in the country. This is one of the strongest boarding teams around, and Lefty says he has the quickest guards in the conference.

"Their defense is awfully good too. It's not a coincidence they are holding teams down like they are. What is it? I think something like 59 points per game average. Heck, they held UCLA to 65 points and only lost by one. That's better than we did. They held Wake's Tony Byers to just 14. They must be playing good defense."

"I think you're right, Coach, and a big part of that defense is the Terps' 6-9 pivot man, Len Elmore, a great shot blocker and leading rebounder in the conference. What do you think about Elmore, Tommy?"

"He's definitely better than last year. He's lost a lot of weight and is just playing really well."

"But, it's their guard play, John Lucas of Durham averaging 19 points a game and the league's top freshman guard, Mo Howard, that keep the offense steady and generate most of the turnovers on defense," Coach Sloan volunteered.

"And, don't forget Tom McMillen," Tim Stoddard added. "I mean, he just broke Gene Shue's individual scoring record at Maryland a week or so ago. He can score some points and play some defense too."

"David, how do you assess the Terps now?"

"Since that game with UCLA they have been playing real well. They've been playing with a lot more confidence."

"With confidence and experience." Burleson added. "Last year they were a young team, but now they seem to be getting everything smoothed out."

"How do you guys think you stack up? David?"

"Well, we have some pretty good material ourselves," he chuckled. "But, we're just now getting used to each other. We're really just beginning to jell and are playing better overall."

* * * * *

Lefty Driesell had seen Reynolds Coliseum for the first time on a recruiting trip to the NC State campus when he was a senior in high school. That trip also provided Lefty with his first plane rides. And, he had the opportunity of scrimmaging with players like State three-time All-Americans Dick Dickey and Sammy Ranzino. Ultimately he decided on Duke. Lefty grew into a 6'4", 190 lb. Education Major and Forward, Number 25 for Duke University from 1952-1954. But, Lefty even admitted at times over the years that he would sometimes sneak back over to Raleigh to see the Pack play in the coliseum.

After serving as Head Coach at Davidson College from 1960 to 1969 and being named Southern Conference Coach of the Year four times, he had returned again to the coliseum as the Maryland Head Coach.

The place and some of the people were familiar. He felt, somehow, oddly at home in this house of the enemy. "How ya doin', John?"

"Doin' good, Coach." John Baker, a Raleigh Policeman and former football star, laughed as he always did when Lefty Driesell showed up. John served as guard and greeter at the teams' entrance at the south end of the coliseum. "We're going to kick your butt today, Coach, just like always."

"Actually, we had pretty good luck here, John, until you guys snuck in that David Thompson fellow and put a varsity uniform on him," Lefty chuckled. "There must be some way," he muttered more to himself than to John as he walked passed John Baker toward the locker rooms.

"Did you say something, Coach?" John laughed with his entire huge former lineman body.

"Not yet, John." Lefty looked back at him and winked. "Wait 'til after the game. Maybe I'll have something to say then," he chortled.

They called him "Senator." It set him apart because, in his own way, he was apart from the rest of the Maryland team just as much as he was a part of the Maryland team. He had been awarded a Rhodes Scholarship last week, but that had not helped him in deciding his future, either short-term or long-term. The scholarship had only complicated things more, in a good way, of course.

"All I know right now is that I have a Rhodes Scholarship," the 6-11 forward for the second-ranked Maryland Terrapins said. "I don't know what I'm going to do, but I don't think money will make a difference."

Tom McMillen carried a 20.3 point scoring average to go along with his 3.8 scholastic average, but he was not ready to commit himself on the future until he at least got an idea of how pro teams might value his services.

"That would lead to a clarification of goals," he said. "But it would be presumptuous of me to make basketball plans now."

McMillen, a senior pre-med student, was active in various student affairs and devoted many hours to charity and off-campus community activities. He served as a member of President Nixon's council on Physical Fitness and Sports.

He conceded he would study politics, philosophy, and economics at Oxford University in England should he decide to accept the Rhodes. "I thought about a Rhodes Scholarship since I was a freshman. I always said I wanted more than one option when I graduated. At the moment, though, I guess my professional school plans will have to be postponed."

McMillen said while he "spends 25-30 hours a week on basketball," he didn't think it unusual to excel in sports and academics. "I'm not a resident genius. I think anybody can get an A in almost any course if they put the time in. It all depends on what you want to achieve."

While participating in the rigorous competition for the scholarship, McMillen said he told Coach Lefty Driesell, "I'd rather play UCLA any day of the week than go through this."

The day after his father's funeral, McMillen scored 17 points against Richmond College to raise his career total to 1,405 points breaking Gene Shue's scoring record of 1,397. "My appreciation of the record would have been greater had my father been here." His father had died four days earlier. Dr. James McMillen was his most ardent and biggest fan despite his quiet and dignified manner. For three years, he had traveled five hours each way from Mansfield, Pennsylvania to College Park, Maryland to watch his son play basketball. He rarely missed a game until this season. The tall, gray-haired retired dentist who sat quietly during his son's games occasionally nodding his approval was confined to his bed the previous Thanksgiving. Tom flew home that weekend and his father told him it was the greatest thing to happen to the family in 200 years. "What happened 200 years ago?" Tom asked.

His father laughed. Even in the bleakest of times, they had that. He could always make his dad laugh.

"My father was probably the most influential person in my going to Maryland," Tom stated even though his brother, Jay, had a highly successful basketball career at Maryland. "I think a big reason I went there is because my father wanted so much to see me play.

"You couldn't hope for a better fan."

On Sunday January 13, 1974, church pews were packed for the early services throughout Raleigh and the Triangle area according to local ministers like Reverend Albert G. Edwards, minister of First Presbyterian Church in downtown Raleigh. "There were a few late comers this morning that didn't look quite encouraged about the hour of the day," Edwards commented. "The faces of the loyal early risers are familiar, and I had a good idea why the others were there."

Other ministers from Reverend John W. Cobb at Holy Trinity Lutheran Church to Reverend Johnny J. Smith of Calvary Baptist talked about the increased early service attendance. Smith even announced from the pulpit that they would try and finish the service in time to get home for the game.

He made it home in time for the second half himself.

It was high noon. All the cards were on the table. All the marbles were inside the ring. All of the eggs were in one basket. All the TV sets were tuned to ABC. The Terps and the Wolfpack were going at it for the second year in a row as the warm-up act for the Super Bowl. Only thing was, last year they sort of stole the show with a super clash that the Pack ultimately won 87-85 on a Stoddard to Thompson Alley-Oop. Today, both teams had only one loss, to the same UCLA they each ached to meet again. Both teams knew, very well, that in order to meet UCLA again this season this was step one. And, both teams knew that there could be as many as three games between them before all was said and done.

The Wolfpack sizzled in the beginning minutes of Son of Super Sunday, running up a 13-6 lead. Nevertheless, the Terps, unbeaten since a one-point loss on UCLA's home court in December, began cutting away at that margin to, finally, go ahead by one point.

With 8:50 left in the half, Maryland guard and floor leader John Lucas committed his third foul. Coach Driesell started to send in a sub, but John waved his hand defiantly. Lefty sent the sub in anyway, and Lucas came to the bench because that was what the coach ordered. However, he goaded his coach incessantly to get back onto the floor. He had come to play, not spectate.

With Lucas on the bench, the Pack jumped out to a seven-point lead, mostly on Thompson's shooting. So, with less than three minutes remaining, Lefty was forced to send his floor leader back into the game. Lefty needed a first half miracle, and Lucas nearly delivered by single-handedly engineering a Maryland comeback to within four points of the Pack as the half ended at 45-41.

Early in the second half, Maryland ignited to take a 50-49 lead.

Then, State threatened to break it open. Thompson guided in a high pass from Towe and rebounded a Burleson shot for another two. With the score 55-52, the Pack knocked in 10 straight, four each by Thompson and Towe and two by Mo Rivers.

Down by 13, Maryland called time, but the score reached 68-53 before the Terps were able to mount their final assault. The Senator, Tom McMillen, and Lucas combined for an eleven point flurry, and suddenly the margin dropped to 72-64.

With 4:54 left and the score 76-70, State went to a spread offense that obviously displeased the partisan crowd of 12,400. A Wolfpack missed shot and a traveling violation were followed by Mo Howard and Lucas baskets that made it 76-74.

At that point, Len Elmore fouled Burleson who hit twice at the line with 1:52 remaining. Maryland threw the ball away 20 seconds later, and Thompson drove the lane for one last spectacular Alley-Oop to seal the outcome.

"Super Sunday or David Thompson Day, Billy Packer? Fans at William Neal Reynolds Coliseum and watching on national television couldn't be sure which it was this afternoon at William Neal Reynolds Coliseum. When the noise died and the final horn blew, David Thompson had 41 points, a career high, and Maryland had seen its nine-game winning streak come to an end, 80-74.

"It was almost a repeat of last year's first Super Sunday game at Maryland when Thompson scored 37 points in an 87-85 victory. Action was fast and furious in the great Everett Case style even though both teams trailed off in their shooting after a red-hot opening ten minutes.

"This time, however, the Wolfpack didn't have to come from behind. It led virtually the entire game in its second ACC test in as many days."

"That's right, Jim Simpson. And, David Thompson who was 14-20 from the field and 13-17 from the line led the Wolfpack. Monte Towe hit five from around the 25-foot mark and finished with 12 points. Tom Burleson had 13, but he was three for 19 from the floor, which must have been his worst percentage ever."

"Remarkably, both teams shot 42%, but State had a 39-31 rebounding edge, primarily thanks to Burleson."

"Also, Billy, it is worth noting that Maryland was handicapped by foul trouble in the first half. Roy, Lucas, and Howard all sustained three during the first 15 minutes of play."

"Their next meeting at Cole Field House should prove to be very interesting, Jim."

Post-Game Press

"I think David was sort of waiting for this game," State Coach Norman Sloan commented after the noon showdown. "I think he was awfully disappointed in his play in St. Louis against UCLA. I know we were disappointed as a team and we wanted to show what kind of team we have."

"David, you outscored the three men guarding you by a combined margin of 39 points. You shot so many baskets over Tom Roy that the 6-9 junior might be suffering from a stiff neck by now. Even with a hand in your face, you were putting the ball in the basket?"

David shrugged. "It's hard for a 6-9 guy to guard somebody 6-4."

"You're probably closer to David than anyone else. Have you ever seen him play better, Monte?"

"Have I ever seen David play better? Only in my dreams. Look I practice with the guy every day, and I haven't seen all he can do yet. You watch game films and he's like a guy dropping down out of heaven over the basket.

"Words can't describe him," Monte mumbled behind his towel. "I know you writer guys struggle to find new adjectives for him. He just does it all better than anyone else."

"I was just playing my regular game," David Thompson insisted, brushing aside the theory that TV or Maryland affected his performance. "I didn't play very well against UCLA. I felt if I could do well against

Maryland, it would help make up for that. Plus, I read in the paper that Maryland players said they thought their game against UCLA was bigger than this one. And, I read where John Lucas said they were going to win the game.

"All this plus it was Maryland. They were ranked Number 3 and we were ranked Number 4. It's just easy to get 'up' for a game like this. It was a conference game, and they ranked higher in the polls. But I really don't get that psyched up for a game."

"Does this win sort of make up for the earlier UCLA loss?"

"Sure, I won't deny that I think this win makes up a little bit for the UCLA defeat. But, I really hadn't thought about UCLA that much. I tried to get it out of my mind."

"We wanted to make him shoot from the outside like he did, but he just made them," Maryland Coach Lefty Driesell shrugged. "Plus he fouled out one of my boys, Tom Roy, and nearly fouled out Owen Brown and Jay Trimble."

"John Lucas, you showed once again how much you thrive on pressure basketball. Ignoring the boisterous crowd, you scored 24 points, but even that wasn't quite enough. What went wrong?"

"It's really hard to put your finger on why this happened. Missed free throws hurt us and we went through one stretch where we couldn't get anything going.

"Honestly, I figured we would take them today. And, I was planning to personally see to it down the stretch. I really wanted to take the last two or three shots," continued the Durham native.

"But they double teamed me and I had to pass off. When I got into foul trouble though, I had to change my game some. And, Monte Towe played pretty good, too. He kept stinging us outside.

"But, I can promise you we'll be back."

"We did one heck of a job coming back," Driesell drawled. "We came from 65-52 to within two points in the closing minutes.

"Our free throw shooting (24-36) hurt us a lot. And, there was one period when we lost our discipline on offense and State outscored us 16-2. We forced some shots then. Also, they got too many second shots.

"But we didn't give up. I'm certainly not discouraged with our play. John Lucas and Tom McMillen played real well.

"Like the young man said, we'll be back."

Then the Preacher Man opened up the Maryland locker room. Terrapin players dressed and talked quietly. There was disappointment but no tears, no sense of ultimate defeat. This was just one game. They would play again, and next time it would be in Cole Field House.

Tom Roy knew that on this Super Sunday his assignment was one that any mere mortal would have had trouble handling--guarding David Thompson. "There was nothing you could do to stop him," the big fellow said softly. "It was like he had a homing pigeon on his shots. I put a hand in his face. But, he was making them anyway. He was hitting shots from the pro three point line."

Owen Brown and Jay Trimble, who also shadowed Thompson, had no luck either. It was like trying to catch a shooting star.

"He's too good, too quick," Trimble added. "He can just hurt you too many ways. He's almost the perfect player--tall enough to take you inside and a great outside shooter."

"But, they gotta come to our place now. I can't wait. I'm really looking forward to it. I want to guard him the next time we play them. He can be stopped. I know he can," Roy concluded.

"Sure, he can be stopped," an unusually gracious Driesell agreed. "No one is unstoppable, not even Thompson.

"No zone. We'll play man-for-man defense the next time, too. I don't know whether I'll change the assignments or not. I've got a long time to think about that, but I doubt we'll do much different.

"Heck," he snorted. "We came within two points of catching them at the end of the game despite the problems we had with Thompson and our lousy free throw shooting.

"Besides, there ain't much you can do about Thompson. You just got to outscore him and we didn't."

"What about your match up with Burleson, Len?"

"You can go tell that dude that, win or lose, I'm still the Number 1 center in this league," Len Elmore muttered as he draped a towel over his head and shoved his locker door shut. The banging of the metal resounded throughout the otherwise quiet locker room.

It was as wintry as it gets in Raleigh, short of the occasional snowstorm. Regardless of the bone chilling weather, several hundred kids and their parents waited patiently for their hero. As David, Dwight Johnson, and Mo Rivers stepped into the early evening chill, kids and their parents huddled next to the door and along the coliseum wall to avoid the wind that swept the cold air across the parking lot. Teeth chattering and knees knocking, nonetheless, they cheered and clapped as the players closed the door behind them and began to walk toward the parking lot which they had to cross in order to get to Sullivan dorm.

A small boy extended his program booklet with David's picture on the cover from behind his Mother's overcoat. "Can I have your autograph, David? Please?"

David stopped in his tracks. He turned and saw the program booklet almost seeming to float in the air. It trembled in the boy's hand. "Sure, you can." David reached out and took the program. "Got a pen?" he mumbled to Dwight and Mo.

Both began searching their pockets. "Here, David." Dwight Johnson offered him a Bic black ink pen.

David took the pen. "What's your name, buddy?"

"Davey. Just like you."

David signed *To Davey, All the best from your buddy with the same first name, David Thompson*. He returned the program to the trembling hand.

"Thank you, David."

"Thank you, David," Davey's Mother whispered. "We've been waiting since the game was over."

"We all have," a Father chimed in behind her. "All these kids have been waiting," he continued, waving his right arm toward the crowd against the coliseum wall.

"No problem," David responded. "Just line all the kids up and try to keep warm," he chuckled. He turned to Mo and Dwight. "You guys go ahead. Guess I'm going to be awhile."

"Man, what are you doing?" Mo answered.

"It must be twenty degrees out here, David. You could get a cold or worse."

"It's okay, Dwight, Mo."

"But why?" they chimed in together.

The children and their parents lined up for David so he could begin autographing programs.

"Mo. Dwight. What if you had stood in line for Julius Irving's autograph or something and didn't get it. You can imagine how disappointed you'd be, right?"

"Yeah."

"Well, it's the same for these kids. You know, I can really imagine how I would have felt if I had waited forty-five minutes in the cold to get an autograph from Charlie Scott or Doctor J and they never showed and only to learn later that they slipped out the back door?"

The two teammates looked at each other and shook their heads. That was David. "We'll wait for you," they chorused.

David nodded and turned to the first young lady in line. "Hi. What's your name?"

"My name's Marsha." Her flushed cheeks seemed to glow as she spoke, her pale blue eyes glued to David's face as he took her program in hand and dashed off: *Marsha, have a great life, David Thompson.*

"Can't write too many of those books, David," Dwight chuckled.

"Yeah, your hand'll cramp up," Mo chortled.

"Thank you David." Marsha accepted her program back from her hero. "Thank you so much." Marsha's Father extended his gloved hand. David accepted his handshake. "You're welcome, sir. I was once a child myself. So, I know how much autographs mean to some of these little kids."

* * * * *

Four nights later, cat calls and boo's filled the University of Virginia gym as the announcer introduced the Wolfpack.

"At guard, from Brooklyn, New York, number 10, 6 foot 1 Morris Rivers!"

Banners waved aloft by UVA students for benefit of the regional television cameras read:

"Got a headache, Mo?"
"Aspirin Thief!"

A hail of aspirins hit the floor as Rivers trotted onto the floor under the glare of the spotlight and a chorus of boo's.

"What is that?" Jim Thacker asked Billy Packer sitting next to him on press row.

"My goodness, Jim, it looks like some spectators are throwing aspirins onto the court. I've never seen anything quite like this before, have you?"

"No, Billy, I sure haven't, but by way of explanation to the viewing audience, it was just two days ago, January 15, that Morris Rivers—Mo to his NC State Wolfpack teammates—was arrested and charged with shoplifting a thirty-five-cent bottle of aspirin at a Mission Valley drug store. He was arraigned in Wake County District Court according to District Attorney Burley B. Mitchell, Jr. The story has obviously already gotten around, and it has not been lost on the Cavaliers fans here tonight."

* * * * *

After State's lopsided 90-70 win over UVA at Charlottesville, UNC-Charlotte's coach Bill Foster knew what kind of a mess he was getting into on the evening of January 19.

"The Wolfpack players are slapping each others' palms as each player is introduced. Now the starting five is charging to the center circle, and they are so supercharged that they have all but stomped through the floor here," Wally Ausley observed. "It's almost as if they're trying to stamp out the cat calls and boos from spectators directed at Wolfpack guard Morris Rivers who was just recently arrested for allegedly shoplifting a thirty-five cent bottle of aspirin."

"Good Lord," Coach Foster moaned on the UNC-Charlotte bench. "They're actually up for us!"

He just didn't think it would be a 104-80 mess.

Post-Game Press

"I thought we might catch them a little down, Wally. But did you see them during player introductions?" Bill Foster queried incredulously.

"Yes, I did, Coach, and after what Norm Sloan told his charges before the game, I can understand why. According to my sources, Coach Sloan harkened back to an interview we had months ago when he compared the U.S. World University Games team to the NC State team this season.

"He told me, then, that he felt his Wolfpack might be the same kind of target every game, for every team they play, as the U.S. World University Games team—starring both Tom Burleson and David Thompson--was last summer.

"Coach Sloan told his team that they had to keep that in mind. They had to go out on that court tonight and be ready to play because UNC Charlotte coach Bill Foster would sure as the devil have his team ready to play.

"So, when the Pack came out for player introductions, they were sky high according to Assistant Coach Eddie Biedenbach."

* * * * *

"Bill Jackson, Voice of the Wolfpack, died of cancer earlier today, the twenty-second of January, 1974, at Duke Hospital in Durham. North Carolina State Chancellor John T. Caldwell issued a statement that 'Bill Jackson was part of the family at NC State for almost a quarter of a century. We admired his tremendous professional skill and we loved his personal integrity and charm.' Thank you, Chancellor Caldwell, for those kind words. He was my partner. We always seemed to know when the other one wanted to talk. I guess now it's my turn. I will miss him. The Wolfpack will miss him. WPTF will miss him. I will miss him.

"This is Wally Ausley for the Wolfpack Sports Network. I'll be back with tonight's game from Carmichael Auditorium right after these messages."

Courtside while the players for both teams warmed up, a last-minute television interview was underway.

"Coach Sloan, tip-off is only moments away. How do you feel about playing here at Carmichael tonight?"

"Billy, I think it's the toughest place to win at in the league. That's not to say that winning in Cole Field House at College Park is easy. It's not at all. In fact, winning anywhere in the ACC is tough, but Carmichael is the toughest, I think."

"And, it sure doesn't help matters any that Bobby Jones just got Player of the Week in the ACC for the second time this season, does it, Coach?"

"No, Billy, it doesn't. You can bet he'll be ready to play us."

"Even though your guys won the last contest with Carolina 78-77 in the Big Four Tournament and have won the last five in a row going all the way back to an 85-84 win at William Neal Reynolds Coliseum late in the 1971-72 season, the odds makers have your Wolfpack as two-point underdogs, Coach. If Carolina wins, they take over the ACC lead and probably your number three ranking in the polls. If State wins, you take over as the undisputed ACC leader and keep or increase your national ranking. This is an important game, so how does this place really effect State?"

"Well, when we won at Maryland, for instance, there was a great deal of room around the court, separating the players from the fans. At most of the gyms in the league, there are press rows and other buffer areas. This cuts down on the impact of home advantage. But, at North Carolina, the building is smaller and the fans are closer. I think it's a definite advantage for them. Is it worth two points?"

The horn sounded. Players for both teams tossed their last practice shots toward the baskets.

Sloan shrugged. "I guess we're about to find out."

Equipment managers collected the balls and stored them on long metal ball racks on wheels.

"Thank you Coach Sloan."

The lights went down in Carmichael Auditorium.

From the tip-off, both teams shot the eyes out of the basket. Then, Burleson missed a free throw. The ball bounded to the top of the backboard, came back down to bounce once on the rim, and UNC's Bobby Jones waited to haul down the rebound. David waited until the last possible moment then leaped and, with his extraordinary sense of timing, reached over Jones and gently nudged the ball in for two points.

Carolina scored only one basket in the next seven minutes while 15-footers by Mo Rivers and Monte Towe began an 18-5 run. The Pack built an 11-point lead by 4:43 of the first half.

As the second half got underway, Carolina's Mitch Kupchak pulled in a rebound and looked for the outlet pass. While he was looking, Thompson stripped the ball from his hands and dropped it in for two.

Carolina was, again, on fire from the floor, however, making shot after shot. Despite State answering more than it didn't, Carolina was able to cut the lead to 60-57 midway of the second half. Momentum seemed to be shifting their way.

Then, David leaped over two defenders to score an Alley-Oop and was fouled. He sank the free throw, and the lead was, suddenly, doubled.

The Wolfpack went to their spread offense with a five-point lead and just under five minutes left as the two teams continued to trade baskets. Elston made a 20-foot jump shot to get the Heels back within four at 82-78. Elston immediately picked up a loose ball and drove the length of the court only to miss the lay-up.

At 1:04 left, Monte missed a free throw. After the rebound, Elston scored again on a 10-footer with 50 seconds remaining.

82-80.

Monte dribbled up court in a frenzy of dodges and pivots and evasive changes in direction. Carolina players were nearly falling down trying to steal the ball from him. With 25 seconds left, Dean finally signaled his team to foul immediately. They hadn't been able to steal it from Towe, so they had to put somebody on the line.

It took another 14 seconds before Ray Hite finally fouled David with 11 seconds left. David went to the line and hit the first one. He rimmed the second. Carolina rebounded and called time to set up a play.

83-80.

Carolina Guard Ray Harrison accepted the ball from the referee who immediately began to count. One thousand one. Nobody was open yet. One thousand two. Still couldn't get a clear pass to anybody close. One thousand three. Mitch and Bobby seemed to have the basket at the other end sealed off. One thousand four. Harrison heaved the pass the length of the court toward Kupchak and Jones. One thousand five. Too late Harrison saw Burleson who leaped into the air and brought the ball down and, with it, the final hopes of the Tar Heels.

Post-Game Press

"It's not the end of the season for us, but if State plays like they did tonight for the rest of the year they may go undefeated in the conference again," Dean Smith responded into the cameras.

"Let me tell you, we tried everything possible, but State was just the better team. I don't know how Norm feels about it, but I don't think two teams can play any harder. I know we gave it all we had."

"What about Monte Towe?"

"Monte Towe is an amazing story. I think he must have been trying to impress the Carolina Cougars or something here tonight. He went through our press as if it wasn't there and threw up those 40-footers like they were lay-ups. What a player!"

"And, then, there's David Thompson? What about him, Bobby Jones?"

"Towe played great. No doubt. But, it's really a one-man thing. It's Thompson. He just will not let them lose. I don't care what it is, if State needs it, Thompson will get it for them. I can't explain his greatness, it's just there. He's just the best I've ever been around and that's all I know to say about it."

"You guarded him Darrell Elston. Not an enviable task. What do you think of David Thompson? Can he alone keep you guys from ever beating them?"

"David is the best player I've ever guarded, but we've got one more shot at them, maybe two, and I think we can beat them. We'll have to play them man-to-man to have a chance. We came extremely close in Raleigh last year and I think we'll probably play better on the road."

"Dean. You recruited him?"

"Yes, and you can see why. David Thompson was just fantastic against us tonight. He proved that he is the most dominating player in college basketball with the exception of Bill Walton, I guess."

"We played against Julius Erving and he didn't dominate play the way Thompson does. There is simply no comparison between the two at this stage of Thompson's career."

There were no yells of triumph or tears of joy, no throwing coaches into the shower in the Wolfpack locker room. Once you'd tasted defeat in any form you realized that celebrating victory until it was final and absolute was a waste of time and energy and fraught with the potential for grave disappointment. There would be time enough to celebrate after March Madness was complete and they finally had that National Championship banner hanging from the rafters of William Neal Reynolds Coliseum. In the meantime, there would be other hunters at their den door within days. The Pack feared one of those hunters the most: The Preacher man's boys from College Park. However, even before that, would be the Big Ten leaders, Purdue.

"We have self confidence, now," Monte explained to Billy Packer. "It's not a cocky kind of attitude or anything like that. I mean we feel we're going to win but I'd never tell you that we are never going to lose again. That would be stupid."

"Yeah, but we just got to keep winning," Tommy Burleson interjected as he came up beside Monte, his 7-4 frame nearly eclipsing the smaller player. "Keep winning them all, one by one."

Packer turned to their coach. "What about this win, Coach Sloan?"

"This was an extremely big game for both clubs. We both had some fantastic players out there. Monte, here, did a fantastic job. David Thompson is just, well, David's just one of the finest players around anywhere." The inheritor of the Everett Case legacy controlled his nearly erupting smile to just a glimmer of a smile, although that was difficult. "He's just the best. But, as I said in Greensboro, the games that count are the ones in March."

"And, then there *is* David Thompson?" Billy Packer turned toward David who stood beside his coach. "You *were* the best again tonight,

David. Twenty-six points, 10 rebounds, and 3 assists. You always seem to be ready to play these big games? Especially Carolina?" He stuck the microphone in front of the young forward's face.

"It's just a lot easier to get up for ACC games than for non-conference games. That's all." David hesitated and smiled. "And, well, Carolina *is* Carolina."

8

Overcoming Adversity, Again

AP Poll	UPI Poll
1. Notre Dame 36 10-0 990	1. Notre Dame (21)(10-0) 334
2. UCLA 15 13-1 944	2. UCLA (14) (13-1) 329
3. NC State 11-17 82	3. NC State (1) (11-1) 272
4. North Carolina 12-1 651	4. Maryland (11-2) 212
5. Maryland 10-2 649	5. North Carolina (12-1) 198
6. Marquette 14-1 510	6. Marquette (14-1) 178
7. Vanderbilt 12-1 423	7. Providence (13-2) 85
8. Providence 13-2 375	8. Vanderbilt (12-1) 76
9. Alabama 10-2 334	9. Long Beach St. (12-1) 37
10. Long Beach St. 12-1 285	10. Alabama (10-2) 31

    Coach Norman Sloan was finally at his wits end on the cold Indiana evening of January 26. He had watched his Wolfpack miss its first three shots of the game in sold-out Mackey Arena and turn the ball over on its fourth possession. He fumed as Purdue calmly rolled up a 7-0 advantage on baskets by Dave Luke, John Garrett, and a three-point play by Frank Kendrick. He breathed a slight sigh of relief when Burleson finally broke the ice for the Wolfpack, driving for two and drawing a foul on the play. Tommy converted the three-point play.

    However, it was 6-11 Boilermaker center John Garrett who, moving like he was 6-5, dominated the first half, making nearly everything he put up. He seemed to beat Burleson to the proverbial spot every time while Burleson just sort of stood around being 7-4 and not much else. He just couldn't seem to make it register that this non-conference game *did* matter. He just couldn't seem to get it through his head that they were on the verge of losing again, something they had all promised themselves would not happen again this season. Once to UCLA had been more than enough.

    Jerry Nichols, David's shadow, wore a mask to protect his broken nose making him look more like a goalie or something out of *Star Wars* than a basketball player. He stalked David relentlessly and effectively. David hadn't even scored in the first half until there was just over four minutes left.

Coach Fred Schaus knew the history. There wasn't much. The only time they had played previously, State beat them in '72 under former Purdue Coach and now Athletic Director George King, 84-71. He also knew that he hadn't been very happy about changing the game from December 5 to the middle of the conference schedule. It was simply too big a game to stick in the middle of all the conference games that they had to win in order to win the Big Ten Conference championship and get to the dance. However, he'd been with the Lakers. He knew about money driving basketball, so he realized that his objections didn't stand much of a chance against a nationally televised game between UCLA and North Carolina State and all the money that would be generated from the match up. The game had certainly not turned out like anyone had imagined except maybe Wooden. He'd been all-American and player of the year right here at Purdue. He knew about national championships as a player as well as a coach.

Now, midway in the second half, State was down by 15 at 56-41. Norman Sloan knew the history too. He also knew that he needed to do something to infuse some energy, some sense of urgency in his team. Something. That was what coaches did—successful coaches anyway—as far as he was concerned. Sure they continued to drill in fundamentals, but it wasn't those drills any more than it was their play calling or precious systems that made championship teams. It was knowing when to do something and figuring out what that something needed to be, then doing it.

Coach Norman Sloan, inheritor of the Case duffel bag of tricks, glanced down his bench. Greg Hawkins was staring at him, his eyes sparkling, his jaw set. He seemed eager to get into the game. That was what Norm needed out there. That was the something, somebody who really wanted to be out there on the court. And, the time was now. He waved Greg to him.

Hawkins leaped from his chair to his coach's side seemingly in one smooth movement. "Yes, Coach."

"Greg. You're a senior, son. And, seniors have maturity and drive, right?"

"That's right, Coach. Comes with the territory, so they say."

"Okay, then, Greg. Let's get out there and give this darned team some maturity and drive. Okay, son?"

A whistle blew.

"Okay, Coach."

There was a break in play. He slapped his young player lightly on the back. "Get in there! Stir things up some, son!"

Hawk hadn't played a lot during the season although he was a senior, so he almost forgot to report to the scorer's table before going into the game. He got himself positioned just as Purdue tossed the ball in bounds from behind their basket. Mo Rivers popped the in bounds pass loose from Kendrick's outstretched hands. Hawk dove headfirst for the ball as it squirted across the gleaming hardwood like a greased pig. He had it in his grip but was falling. If he hit the floor, he'd be traveling. He spotted David breaking away from the crowd of players around the ball and flipped the round ball high in his direction. David took the pass on the run and dribbled for the basket at the other end of the court. No one was near him, so he took it all the way and laid it in off the glass.

Norm leaped from his seat. "That's it, Hawk!" he yelled. "Stir things up, son! Just keep stirring things up!"

As Purdue crossed the mid court line with less than three-and-a-half minutes to play, Rivers stole the ball and drove half the length of the court, making an awkward lay-up in order to draw a foul. By completing the three-point play with 3:19 left, Mo pulled his team into an 81-81 tie. That was the first time State had been even with Purdue since the opening tip-off.

With three minutes remaining, Kendrick drove the lane for the lay-up. Burleson rejected the shot. The ball caromed off the glass back into the State center's hands. Next time Purdue brought the ball down and drove the baseline. Again, the pivot man from Newland put pressure on the shooter who missed the short jumper. On Purdue's third possession after State pulled into the tie, they again tried to go right at Burleson. This time he blocked an attempted lay-up with such determination that the sound of his hands against the leather of the ball clapped like thunder throughout the Boilermakers Mackey Arena.

"What a block by Burleson!" Ausley screamed, uncharacteristically. "He's been a real factor in stopping Purdue's John Garrett in this second half. Garrett worked his way around and over Burleson for 18 points in the first half, but he has managed just six here in the second period.

"While Garrett has been limited, however, Frank Kendrick has taken up the slack. The 6-6 senior has hauled down 17 rebounds and scored 17 points in the game, mostly in this half.

"However, after taking a 73-65 lead on Bruce Parkinson's three point play, the Boilermakers have not made another field goal. Purdue has been virtually without an offense in the last several minutes. State's pressure tactics, which bothered the Boilermakers only slightly most of the game, are finally paying off.

"All eight of Purdue's last points have come from the charity stripe. However, from the 4:31 mark on, the Wolfpack defense has held them scoreless."

With 1:39 left, Thompson gave the Wolfpack its first lead on a running jumper from six feet out. They held the lead until the horn sounded. The final score: 86-81.

"Thompson came on strong to score 18 of his game-high 26 points in the last 10 minutes of the contest, including one stretch of 10 straight points.

"Monte Towe, keyed up for this game in his home state, wasn't as sharp as usual, but he sure awed many of these 14,123 fans jammed into Mackey Arena by hitting a number of long-range jump shots. He finished with 18 points."

Post-Game Press

Coach Sloan: "Purdue was extremely well prepared for us and came out playing hard. They played the best first half against us that has been played against us all season, including UCLA, Maryland, and North Carolina. We were just lucky we had a big time spark off the bench today.

Ausley: "Who was that spark, Coach?"

Coach Sloan: "Greg Hawkins, our senior forward from Huntington, West Virginia. You may remember that he transferred here from Tennessee a couple of years ago, and we've always been able to count on Greg to give us everything he's got. That's all a coach can really ask of a player. But, today, Greg made his greatest individual contribution to this team since he's been here with his aggressive and hustling play. I asked him to go in and stir things up, and he sure did. Greg truly made a big difference today.

"David wasn't sharp today, but he played good at the right time—along with Tommy. They made the crucial plays at the end, and I believe the Hawk and our shut-'em-down defense in the last ten minutes or so motivated them and the rest of the team. That's why we won this one."

"I agree with Coach Sloan that David Thompson wasn't totally sharp today." Purdue Coach Fred Shaus followed Sloan's remarks. "But, 26 points, 18 in the second half when his team really needed them most. I still say that he is one of the ten best basketball players in the world, including the pros."

* * * * *

Time Changed
The North Carolina State-Maryland basketball game has been shifted from 9 p.m. to 7:05 p.m. on Wednesday to avoid a conflict with President Nixon's State of the Union address, which will follow at 9 p.m.

"Celebrate Here!" a College Park motel sign seemed to shout.
"Victory drinks inside," another sign announced.
"Sack the Pack" T-shirts covered the backs and fronts of the crowds as they pushed their way into Cole Field House long before 7:05 p.m.
The Raleigh *News and Observer* headline earlier in the day had read:

**(N.C.) State of the Union
hopes to upstage President**

But competing with the President of the United States for television air time certainly was not something that Norman Sloan, his staff, or the members of the Wolfpack team had ever intended to do any more than they had meant for Super Sunday to compete with church services. Neither was playing Maryland twice in one month. In fact, they might have preferred to compete with President Nixon for airtime than to play The Preacher Man and his boys twice in the same month. But, they just didn't have much choice about the date of this return engagement in College Park on the next-to-last day of January. That was how the conference schedule had been put together, so that was how they played them. In addition, playing Maryland after the Terps just had a tough loss to Carolina made them even more dangerous than usual. They did, however, have some control over the time, so they agreed to bump the game up in order not to force people to make a choice between the State-Maryland "State of the Conference" game and President Nixon's "State of the Union" address.

"Good evening, basketball fans. This is Jim Thacker along with Billy Packer. It's ACC Basketball, brought to you by Pilot Life. Tonight we have a shoot out at Cole Field House as Maryland hosts North Carolina State."

"Yes, Jim. State goes after number 23 in a row against ACC opponents, and Maryland looks to keep itself in contention for first place in the ACC. After losing to Carolina at Carmichael, this game tonight is a must win for Maryland to remain in contention for the top spot in the ACC and that coveted first round bye."

"That's right, Billy. And we're coming to you a little early this evening so the game won't conflict with the President's State of the Union address at 9 p.m. But, with these two teams, you never know. One or more overtimes is always a distinct possibility."

"It has certainly happened before, " Billy Packer interjected, "and if that happens tonight, I'm betting there won't be many basketball fans watching the President's speech."

The 14,500 fans crammed into Cole Field House practically tore the roof off while their Terrapins were being introduced.

As half time approached, Monte Towe hit another jumper from downtown giving the Wolfpack the lead 36-35 just before the horn sounded.

"Isn't that Towe's third straight basket, Billy Packer?"

"Yes, it is, Jim Thacker, but that's about all either of these two teams has to crow about in this first half of play. They certainly haven't played like the nation's Number 2 and Number 5 teams. Both teams shot poorly. State shot 43.2% and Maryland: 41.7%. There were lots of turnovers by both clubs. And, during one five-minute stretch midway in the half, the two teams managed only one basket each."

With 9:04 remaining in an equally unspectacular second half, Maryland completed its surge to an eight-point lead at 67-59.

"A-A-men. A-A-men. A-A-men. A-men. A-men," the capacity crowd sang as the referees called an official commercial time out after Len Elmore's fourth block in a row.

In the loose huddle in front of their bench area, Pack players, determined looks on their faces, stared at each other. "Feel that energy, guys? Take that crowd's negative energy and use it," Coach Sloan urged.

"It *is* sort of a catchy song, isn't it?" Monte joked. "Come on, David, sing along with me," he jibed. Then, Monte started to sing softly, almost whispering, fighting laughter as he struggled to get the words out without calling attention to himself from the refs, the Maryland team, or the crowd.

"A-A-men. A-A-men. A-A-men. A-men. A-men."

David hesitated and then began to whisper the words along with Monte, grinning self-consciously. Tim Stoddard and Mo Rivers joined in. Then Tommy Burleson draped his arms around the circle of players and boomed in his own whispered "A-A-men. Let's finish this, guys!"

As they came back onto the floor chanting together, the horn sounded. "Okay, guys, let's get the A-A-men out of here with a win. What you say?" Monte shouted over the crowd.

They all tried to answer: "A-A-men." However, they could only laugh.

On the Maryland bench, Coach Charles Lefty Driesell was left to wonder why, when they were eight points down and Elmore was cleaning their pumps with his blocks, the Wolfpack players were all of a sudden laughing as they came back onto the court to resume play.

"Okay, David," Monte whispered as he readied to toss the ball in bounds. "It's about time for you to find that phone booth of yours." He faked the pass in to David who was too well covered, so David streaked off toward their basket as Monte tossed a high line drive pass to Stoddard just on the other side of the mid-court line. He immediately turned, sighted David's direction, and tossed a high-arching Alley-Oop pass. David leaped and gathered the pass on the tips of his fingers just in time to drop it through the hoop.

The crowd's A-A-men's ceased.

"Somebody get the hell on him!" Lefty shouted urgently at a bewildered Tom McMillen while pointing at David Thompson. State had been on a 10-2 tear ever since they came off their last time out laughing, regaining the lead 70-69. Time remaining: 6:26.

Tom looked back at his coach blankly. They'd tried everything. Roy had even tapped him on the forehead when he took jump shots. He hit them anyway and sometimes Roy fouled him. Len stalked him like a predator. David slithered past. Owen Brown yelled. Tom, himself, clapped. Coach Driesell stomped. The fans waved and the cheerleaders leaped. The stands shook and the state of Maryland screamed "unfair!"

David Thompson simply ignored them all, and there was absolutely nothing that "the Senator" Tom McMillen--All-Conference, All-American, All-Academic, Rhodes Scholar, advisor to the President--

could do about it. Except to keep on trying as hard as he could. If they couldn't stop David, then he'd just have to put more points on the board himself. He wanted this game. He wanted the ACC Tournament Championship. He wanted UCLA again! Tom took the pass down low from John Lucas. He had Stoddard moving toward the baseline, so he pivoted in the other direction and hooked a shot toward the basket. It swished putting the Terps back up 71-70. "We got 'em now, guys. Come on!" the Senator shouted at his teammates.

But, David connected on a driving jump shot with 5:43 left to regain lead. He then came down court and blocked a Maurice Howard shot into the hands of Rivers. David zoomed down court to complete a fast break with a backhanded lay-up over the out-stretched hands of Len Elmore.

At 4:45, the Wolfpack went into its "tease" offense and gradually pulled ahead to a more comfortable 79-73 advantage with 3:44 left.

However, like strikes from a cobra, first, Tom McMillen struck again. Then, John Lucas. Next, Mo Howard sank a free throw cutting the margin to 79-78 with 1:19 remaining.

Suddenly, David slipped by Len Elmore. Playing catch up, Elmore hurtled himself toward David and the backboard in an attempt to still block David's shot, slamming the ball against the glass and David Thompson to the floor. The ball bounced around on the gleaming orange rim, then fell off as whistles sounded.

"David Thompson hit the floor hard, Billy, and he isn't moving."

"No, Jim, he's laying motionless on the floor. Monte Towe is by his side, leaning over him."

"This is terrible, Billy."

"We can only hope that David's okay, Jim. Coach Sloan has left the bench and gone onto the floor."

"But, wait a minute. He's moving now, a little gingerly, but he's gathering himself. Monte and Tim Stoddard are helping him to his feet."

"Thank goodness, he's moving toward the free throw line. He seems to be okay."

David's head was whirling but not as much as it had been only moments before. He could barely hear the referee through the ringing in his heaad when he announced: "Two shots."

David focused his eyes on the foul line. He stood behind it and received the ball from the official. He took his time, bounced the ball a couple of times, but shoved the first shot, aiming it because he couldn't see the rim very well yet. He drew front iron and missed.

By the time the ball was in his hands again, his head was clear, the ringing had stopped, and his vision was no longer blurred. He could hear the referee's: "One shot left." He stroked the free throw. Nothing but net. 80-78.

Moments later, after a Monte Towe steal, David faked past Elmore again for an easy lay in and an 82-78 lead.

The Terps scored once more with five seconds remaining.

"There are three seconds on the clock, Billy, and Monte Towe is headed for the free throw line again."

"If the game's not already out of reach, Jim, Monte Towe can put it out of reach with one or more of these free throws."

Monte took the ball from the referee, quickly bounced the ball once, and then sank one of his quickest-free-throws-in-the-NCAA. Nothing but net. The second was a repeat of the first. Then, he stole the Maryland in bounds pass and sank a 20-footer at the buzzer for the final 86-80 score.

Post-Game Press

"I am so very, very, very, very damn disappointed to have lost this one," Lefty moaned into the microphones. "It was embarrassing." Coach Lefty Driesell looked down at the page of stats on the table in front of him. He crunched it into his meaty hand.

"I apologize to everyone who supports our program here. We should never lose in Cole Field House. I'm burned up about it!" Then, he stood up and stalked out of the press conference, mumbling to reporters as he stormed out of the room, "We apologize. We really do apologize."

Tom McMillen tried to make light of the situation. With a wry smile, the Rhodes Scholar and friend of President Nixon noted: "Well, they don't have Maryland to kick around any more."

"David, of course, was tremendous," Norm Sloan stated as he opened the NC State portion of the press conference. "A little slow getting out of the gate, but in the second half he was unstoppable. Just ask Roy, Brown, and McMillen. Twelve for 15 from the floor. Seven of ten from the line. Thirty-one points in 20 minutes.

"But, Monte Towe was the man. Three baskets at the end of the first half to give us a 36-35 lead, and two free throws and a steal and basket to finish this one off and put the game out of reach and into the win column for us. He was just great.

"And we needed this game, believe me. It moved us another game closer to the regular season championship and that first-round bye. I think this year the bye has a tremendous value. This league is so strong, that it would be nice to go to Greensboro on Thursday and just sit and watch the rest of them battle. And you'd be pretty sure that the Number 2 and Number 3 teams would have to play in the semi-finals."

"David, do you have anything to add?"

"I agree with Coach Sloan. Monte was great today at a time when we really needed him. And, you know, we were 15 points down to Purdue Saturday and we won. We were eight points down tonight and we won. That's a challenge. I want the team to win. We all want to win. Winning is the challenge."

Paul Attner of *the Washington Post* described the situation appropriately:

> "Driesell quickly called time but he had nothing but mortals around to cover Thompson. They were not enough."

* * * * *

February 2, 1974 wasn't "Tim Stoddard Day" at William Neal Reynolds Coliseum, but it was Tim Stoddard's day. He shot with a deft touch. He attacked the boards with abandon. In the end, it looked as if he had won his season-long fight with frustration.

For most of State's players, however, getting up for a team they had just waxed 90-70 a few weeks earlier in their house was a difficult assignment. For the first 15 minutes, the Pack lolled around in a lethargic state and Virginia managed to stay in the lead. Virginia led by as many as seven points in the opening minutes and held four and six point leads frequently. However, once the Pack got going there wasn't much the Cavaliers could do. UVA held lead at 37-32 with 4:10 left in the half. Pack getting some steals from Mo Rivers and a flurry of points from Thompson put in 17 points to six for Virginia in the next four minutes. State went ahead on two free throws by Thompson at 1:38 left which made it 43-41.

The half ended 49-43 Wolfpack.

At the beginning of second half, the Pack picked up where they left off. Stoddard hit two quick ones, and a 16-4 burst moved the lead to 18 points within the first 5 minutes.

The score was 96-72 when Sloan cleared his bench with 5:16 remaining. The widest Pack margin was 26-point lead in second half, and the final score was NC State 105-University of Virginia 93.

"Gus Gerard, making some nifty moves underneath and drilling in several line drive 15-footers, led the Cavaliers with 20 points, Billy. He also had 12 rebounds."

"Yes, Jim, and the Cavaliers shot 54% from the floor to State's 50.5%, but the Wolfpack won the board battle 51-39 as Burleson took down 13 and Thompson 11. "Thompson and Towe had six assists each. However, Towe waited a long time before scoring his only basket, which came on a stationary lay-up."

"The Coliseum crowd of 12,100 was a little slow warming up, Billy, but it was turned on by the fast-breaking Pack in the middle stages of the game. That Mo Rivers looks like he's jet-fueled when he heads for the basket. He made some brilliant plays and Number 44, as always, had a few dazzlers to offer us."

"But, the standout of the day was NC State forward Tim Stoddard."

Post-Game Press

"I've got my confidence back now," smiled Stoddard, "I found out what I was doing wrong on my shot. And, today, I felt I was moving better on offense and getting open a lot more."

It was, in the words of Coach Norm Sloan, "Timmy's best performance of the year. He pumped in 8 of 14 shots, several from long range, grabbed 8 rebounds, scored a season-high 16 points, and hustled on defense."

And, as teammate Monte Towe said: "It was the Timmy Stoddard of 1973 out there."

"I didn't know I was going to start until just before we went up for pre-game warm ups. But, the main thing is I just want to play. I know if I go hard when I'm in there, he'll let me play."

"It's no secret that the season has been an uphill struggle for you, Tim. You came into the game with a 3.7 scoring average and 3.3 rebounds per game. To begin with, you reported to pre-season camp weighing 250, about 30 pounds over your present size. Then, to complicate matters, you had some physical problems including a bad wisdom tooth and a sprained ankle."

"Excuses, excuses," needled Monte Towe, a fellow baseball player, eavesdropping on the interview. Stoddard, off the court as friendly as a Saint Bernard puppy, shook Monte off with a little chuckle.

"No, at the beginning of the year, I was playing real poorly," Tim continued. "But the last three or four games I've been working hard. And, if you work hard, good things will start to happen. Also, I have a history of coming on late."

It was better late than never. The Wolfpack was glad to have the old Timmy Stoddard from 1973 back Saturday afternoon against Virginia.

"Virginia came out playing the best basketball I've seen them play, but we were not sharp mentally and were not ready to play at the start," said Coach Norm Sloan. "I could sense it before the game, but I couldn't do anything about it. But we went to work, anyway, and played extremely well until we started substituting a lot late in the game."

The Cavaliers, victimized by Towe's long bombs in their first meeting, pestered the darting dwarf most of the afternoon. Monte took only five shots and scored a mere two points. Nevertheless, he dished off six assists, and he was, as usual, most definitely in charge.

"It doesn't bother me at all about not scoring," the feisty 5-7 guard said. "When teams cover me, it gives us more of an advantage. Other people can go one-on-one more often."

In Virginia's locker room, Coach Bill Gibson allowed that State's swift tempo trapped his Cavaliers. "The game was more fast-paced than we're used to," he lamented. "And we got caught up in it. The last four and a half minutes of the first half and the first 6 minutes of the second were crucial. But State is great. When David wants to score, he scores.

"I believe he got something like 23 points, 11 rebounds, six assists, and unofficially a dozen or so ooooohs and aaaaahs."

* * * * *

February 4 the Wolfpack continued to howl 92-78 over Duke in Durham.

9
And The Blind Shall See

AP Poll
1. UCLA (49) 18-1 998
2. NC State 17-1 893
3. Notre Dame (1) 18-1 797
4. N. Carolina 17-2 642
5. Vanderbilt 18-1 576
6. Maryland 15-4 431
7. Pittsburgh 19-1 386
8. Alabama 16-3 331
9. Marquette 18-3 302
10. Long Beach State 18-2 299

UPI Poll
1. UCLA (30) (18-1) 318
2. NC State (2) (17-1) 278
3. Notre Dame (18-1) 244
4. North Carolina (17-2) 210
5. Vanderbilt (18-1) 150
6. Maryland (15-4) 114
7. Marquette (18-3) 71
8. Pittsburgh (19-1) 62
9. Indiana (14-3) 50
10. Long Beach St. (18-2) 49

North South Doubleheader

On February 8, the Wolfpack faced Georgia Tech. The Yellow Jackets were 7 and 10 versus NC State. The two schools had most recently played in the North South Doubleheader the previous year. State won that contest 118-94.

NC State won their first contest of this North South Doubleheader in Charlotte by a margin the size of David's jersey number, 98-54.

* * * * *

The most memorable event during the Pack's 111-91 win over Furman in their second game of the North South Doubleheader on February 9 was the following exchange.

"Towe pulls the trigger on the free throw. It's good. And, boy, is he fast, Billy."

"Jim, our viewers might be interested in knowing that a reporter timed him in yesterday's game with Georgia Tech. From the time the referee handed Monte Towe the ball until he shot it was 0.9 seconds. By comparison, Furman's Clyde Mayes used up 9.7 seconds on one occasion and 7.9 seconds on another. Towe's teammate David Thompson is quick with the free throw trigger himself, firing once at 1.8 seconds but another at 3.3."

* * * * *

Lefty Driesell's former team was doing well without him but not as well as the team he now coached. It was fitting, as NC State went up against Lefty's old team, that he was the only one who had voted State number one. After the Wolfpack beat Maryland in College Park a couple of weeks earlier, Lefty had said he would cast his vote in the weekly coaches poll for State, and he did.

"Any team that can beat us and North Carolina on our home courts has to be number one," Lefty commented in explaining his vote.

Nevertheless, that was the only first place vote for State.

The following week, however, Dean Smith said that he would keep Lefty company. "My vote tomorrow will have to be for NC State," Smith said Saturday night in Charlotte after the second round of the North South Double Header. "They've really been playing that well the last month or so.

"You're supposed to vote for the team that you think is number one at this time and that's the way I feel.

"They beat Maryland at Maryland and I was surprised, then they beat Carolina at Carolina and I was . . . depressed."

In the Coliseum Wednesday night the Wolfpack hit its first six shots against the Davidson Wildcats, and Monte Towe sank his first seven. He hit four of those from 25 feet or more. Tim Stoddard knocked in four more from 20 feet, but Tommy Burleson picked up three fouls fast, barely breaking a sweat before sitting down.

The Wolfpack pulled steadily ahead 13-7, 22-15, 36-21 as they built a 50-33 lead by half time, popping a blistering 67.6% from the floor.

"Thompson gobbles up the defensive rebound but hits the floor. On his back he fires the ball three quarters of the length of the court to Towe. Monte lays it in.

"Davidson in bounds with a long pass down court. Rivers comes out of nowhere and snatches the ball. He whips a behind-the-back pass to Towe near midcourt. Towe immediately tosses it blind behind his back to Thompson underneath. Number 44 lays it in and is fouled on the play.

"My goodness," Wally Ausley enthused. "That's some kind of fancy playmaking! These Wolfpack players are really putting on a show for this sellout Coliseum crowd of 11,300 in the waning moments of this game."

The second-ranked Wolfpack rolled to its 17th straight victory, 105-78. It was the 23rd home court win in a row, matching a school record.

Post-Game Press

Coach Norm Sloan praised the play of Rivers, junior college transfer who hit a personal high for the season. Rivers was nine for 16 and six for seven at the line.

State hit 61.4% for the game. Towe, whose first miss was a 25-footer that barely spun out, was eight for ten. Towe added 17 points and David Thompson 16 as the Wolfpack placed all five starters in double figures.

Davidson seldom taking the ball inside, hit 40 % from the field. Greg Dunn, 6-5 junior scored 19 points and 6-8 Sheldon Parker added 15.

The Wildcats, now 14-8, led only once, 2-0.

Biggest margin in the second half was 30 points, 84-54.

State did some different things on offense, running a 1-4 instead of the two-guard offense they had used all season. Towe usually played the point, with Rivers taking over when Monte was out of there.

State's regulars stayed in until the last three minutes although the game was never close in the second half.

It was the 300th victory in the Coliseum, and it left the Pack 19-1 for the year.

Davidson's Terry Holland, whose team lost to third-ranked Notre Dame 95-84, said State was "the best team we've played, particularly when they shoot that well from the perimeter.

"Our plan was to make them shoot from the outside." Terry Holland shrugged and nearly smiled. "So much for that plan. If they shoot that well, they're going to be tough for anybody."

* * * * *

"Look, I'm not trying to prove anything at all," Monte Towe responded after the game. "I like to play basketball and have a lot of fun doing it. I really don't think that much about being short."

Towe played as if he was just as tall as anyone on the court. He hit shots from beyond the pro three-point range more regularly than most pro guards did.

"I scored a lot in the first half--fifteen, I think--but in the second half I concentrated on other things besides scoring. When I'm shooting that much our offense isn't functioning as it should.

"We should be a much more potent team inside than outside. I know the percentage is a lot better for David and Tommy to shoot a lay-up than for me to shoot from outside."

Many people felt Towe threw up his seemingly radar-controlled barrages indiscriminately. That wasn't the case according to head Coach Norm Sloan.

"If I hadn't seen our people make those kind of shots before, I'd be concerned about our taking them," Sloan noted. "Monte is our leading percentage shooter at 56.7 percent and he knows when to quit shooting them. He'll stop when he starts missing."

"I never shoot from over 25 feet," Towe said to the giggles of all that were listening. "No, now seriously, I just don't shoot from far out.

"I never practice shooting long shots. Oh, I might go out and try some hooks from mid-court or something just fooling around, but I never go out and practice shooting extra long shots."

In fact, Towe insisted he has never practiced anything to compensate for his lack of height in a tall man's game. "Naw, I just go out and play," he said. "I've never worked on anything special because I am smaller."

"Fans--especially short ones--picture you knocking down three-pointers in the ABA, Monte. What about that?"

"I don't really want to play professional basketball," he said, much to the disappointment of short people everywhere. "If I get an offer, I'll probably turn it down. There are many things I'd rather do than play professional basketball. I might like to play in Europe because I've never seen Europe, but I don't think I want to play basketball for a living."

"I did think about coaching, but I talked to Coach Sloan and Coach Waters and they say I'd be crazy to go into coaching. They say everybody is your friend when you're winning but not when you're losing. I don't need that."

"Guard Mo Rivers had another fine game, contributing 24 points to lead all scorers. He hit a number of medium range jumpers in addition to leading several fast breaks. Authorities arrested him and charged him with shoplifting January 15 in Wake County District Court. But, District Attorney Burley B. Mitchell, Jr. said he decided to drop the charges of stealing the 35 cent bottle of aspirin from the Mission Valley Food Mart because 'I felt the state simply could not prove any intent to commit larceny. Rivers said he left the store with the aspirin in his hand,' Mitchell explained. 'His girlfriend would have testified that he had it in his hand when he asked her for 35 cents to pay for it because he didn't have any change. At that point, the private security guard came up.

"'My feeling is that his evidence, together with the fact that as a member of the team he can get aspirin from the trainer any time without charge, would tend to make a jury have more than' reasonable doubt about intent to commit larceny.'

"Mitchell said the warrant under which Rivers was charged was also defective and would have to have been changed by the court. 'Under these circumstances, I decided to *nol pros* the case,' Mitchell concluded.

"Regardless, to countless anti-State fans he was guilty, is guilty, and will forever be guilty no matter what the evidence shows or doesn't show."

Rivers nodded. "It was really rough. It was really bad. I felt like it was a bum rap but it stayed in the back of my mind."

Rivers was having a tough time adjusting to the ACC's large crowds before the incident. After it, pre-game introductions were to be feared rather than relished.

"I have never played before more than about 4,000 people," said the Brooklyn native. "Suddenly, here I am in front of 12,000 people either really pulling for me or really strongly against me.

"It was hard for me to adjust at first. It was so different. It just took some getting used to."

Rivers had been in the spotlight before his arrest. He had hit crucial buckets against North Carolina in the Big Four Tournament and had won repeated praise for his defensive work. Nevertheless, to many people, Rivers was the other guard.

After his arrest, Rivers became the focal point for every State opponent. On the road, banners flew, spectators showered him with aspirin, and chants rang in his ears. Rivers remained quiet other than saying he was innocent.

"I knew it was giving me a bad reputation," he said. "People who know me knew that I wasn't guilty but a lot of people went ahead and just judged me anyway.

"I wanted to come out and just tell everybody exactly what happened. I thought that if I did that though then someone would deny it and I would have to repeat it and it would just keep being drug around."

"The real story about the 35 cent bottle of aspirin will probably remain unknown. However, there has long been a rumor of new player initiations at NC State and at other schools. That initiation is usually simple and daring, just like an initiation into a tree house club when you were a kid or a fraternity or sorority. At some institutions, it's a panty raid. At others, streaking down the hall of a girls dorm. At State, the rumor is a new player must steal something other than the basketball or the spotlight. The thing was, most times, nobody got caught.

"Now used to the crowds and with his day in court behind him, Rivers hopes his nine of 16 gunnery against Davidson becomes the rule instead of the exception.

"Sure it was in the back of my mind most of the time. It was a pretty big thing. I tried to block it out but I really couldn't."

Rivers adjusted to more than large crowds and a court case this year. Simply running up court without dribbling a basketball was a major change. "I had always been a point guard. In practice, I'd just toss the ball over to Monte and go on up court. It took a little getting used to, not being the boss."

Head Coach Norm Sloan has been pleased with the progress of Rivers. "He's played well all along," Sloan said. "He's now getting his timing down better on his shooting and is handling the ball and the club a little better."

"People are just realizing now that I can handle the ball, because the team has only needed me to handle the ball more recently," Rivers observed. "I feel like I haven't played as well as I can yet. I'm still learning the ropes. It's a hard league to break into, and this aspirin thing hasn't helped."

* * * * *

Saturday, February 16, State and Wake Forest traded baskets so fast at the Coliseum in Raleigh that a casual viewer--if there is such a thing in basketball--might have actually missed some.

"A win almost assures the Number 2 Wolfpack of the Number 1 ranking in the national polls this week since top-ranked UCLA lost twice over the weekend, falling to Oregon State 61-57 Friday night and to Oregon 56-49 Saturday," Billy Packer said to his co-anchor Jim Thacker.

Wake Forest led by the super quick freshman Skip Brown trailed by only five at half time, 58-53 while Burleson sat on the bench with foul trouble. Wake surprised the crowd of 11,600 by cutting the margin to three points late in the period after State had zoomed in front by 15 in the opening six minutes.

Trailing 23-8, the Deacons dropped their man-to-man defense and went to a 2-3 zone. It was 36-20 when they began cutting away at the lead, helped by the fact that Burleson was on the bench with his second foul.

With the score 50-39, the Deacons got eight points in a row, four each from Cal Stamp and Skip Brown.

State built its lead to nine again but buckets by Brown and Jerry Schellenberg cut the lead to five at the buzzer. They just wouldn't give up. Old Bones would have been proud.

However, at the start of the second half, the Wolfpack steadily padded its advantage as Burleson enabled the Pack to pull ahead early in the second half with a flurry of moves to the basket. He picked up his fourth personal with 10:30 remaining but the score was already 87-69.

"We're Number 1! We're Number 1! We're Number 1!" the Coliseum crowd chanted, many waving signs with the same message. The clock had almost run down now, and they had been waiting patiently since the UCLA debacle to finally be able to scream it at the top of their lungs. One small North Carolina State fan wearing his own treasured Number 44 jersey waved his Wolpack pennant and screamed, "We're Number 1!" as loud as he could even though he wasn't able to see much beyond a few inches from his courtside chair. His mother described every detail of what was happening to him as it happened. She had been doing that for most of her son's nine years. However, at least for the Wolfpack basketball games, she had the help of Wally Ausley's play-by-play.

"Thompson takes the ball out of bounds and prepares to make the in bounds play. There are just a few seconds left in this one."

"David has the ball just off to your right, honey," the little fan's Mother yelled in his ear over the noise. "He's getting ready to pass it in to one of the other players."

David glanced at the slender boy wearing number 44 and squinting in his direction. Somehow, he seemed familiar.

The referee glanced at the scorers' table before starting the in bounds five-second count. Someone signaled to him. "Okay," the referee muttered. "TV time out!"

David tossed the ball to the referee and took a couple of steps toward the slight young boy who was still squinting at him. "Hey, man. Are you Marvin?"

"Yes, sir."

"I'm David Thompson. Glad to meet you."

"Me too, David."

David knelt by the boy's chair and touched his right hand. It was so very small and delicate just like the boy. He remembered receiving several letters from Marvin written with his Mother's help because he couldn't see more than a few inches from his face.

"After the game's over, Marvin, I've got a surprise for you, okay?"

"Okay." Marvin could hear Wally Ausley in his earplug describing him and David together courtside to the entire Tobacco Sports Network audience. "What is it?"

David smiled as he turned and headed toward the Wolfpack bench. "If I told you now, Marvin, you wouldn't be surprised, now would you?" he laughed over his shoulder.

"David Thomson was just kneeling by a young boy who is sitting just to the right of the NC State basket. He was talking with the boy before he left for the bench after the referee called a TV time out. We have no idea what went on down there, but both David and the boy were smiling and laughing. We'll try to find out what story is behind this little scenario as soon as we can. For now, let's take a break. This is Wally Ausley for the Tobacco Sports Network. We'll be back shortly with the final moments of the second half."

"Ladies and gentlemen. This is Jim Thacker along with Billy Packer. After the time out, it's Mo Rivers making the in bounds pass for the Wolfpack. He gets it in to Monte Towe. Monte dribbles up court, across the ten-second line. "There's a fireball of a pass to Stoddard and . . . it's an Alley-Oop to Thompson. David soars and drops it through without violating the invisible cone that extends up from the rim. The horn sounds, and, that's it for this one. The final score: the NC State Wolfpack 111-the Wake Forest Demon Deacons 96."

David fielded the ball after it bounced on the floor. Instead of tossing it to the official as he might usually have done at the end of a game, he asked one of the officials if he could have the ball. After hearing David's reason, he waved him toward the other end of the court. David carried the ball toward where young 44 Marvin stood alongside his Mother cheering: "We're Number 1! We're Number 1!"

Marvin's Mother spotted him as he approached. She leaned toward her only child, a boy who could never see to hit a baseball or shoot a basket, touching him on his left shoulder to gain his attention. "Honey, look whose right here. David Thompson."

David leaned down and placed the ball in Marvin's petite hands. "Can you hold this, buddy, while I put you up on my shoulders?"

Marvin beamed. "You bet, David." He hugged the ball to his chest as his hero lifted him onto his broad, strong shoulders and trotted out onto the court of William Neal Reynolds Coliseum. Marvin thought his heart would burst.

"Feel that, Marvin? Can you feel the vibes out here on the court?"

"Yeah, David. I think I really can feel something out here."

"Look up now, Marvin, and get up close and personal with the basketball rim. Just put your hands up a little and drop the ball through."

Marvin could see the orange of the rim but not the rim itself that clearly. He could feel the coarse net and cool metal of the rim against his fingers as he pushed the ball over the orange of the rim and heard it plop into the net. "Wow, man, that's cool!" he shouted gleefully as David snatched the ball when it dropped through the net.

Post-Game Press

"They had too much height for us," Wake coach Carl Tacy observed. "It made us hesitate to work inside. Their inside game was the key, but they have very good balance outside and inside."

"The Deacons shot 54.3 % in the first half and most of their baskets came from 15-20 feet and they really made a run at your team late in the first half?"

"I thought we were playing as well as we could," Coach Norm Sloan mused. "We weren't playing bad defense when Wake made their run. They just have some great shooters and a lot of times you can't do anything about it."

"You heard the crowd toward the end of the game, Coach Sloan, I'm sure."

"Yes, I did, Jim."

"Do you agree with the Reynolds Coliseum crowd? Should your Wolfpack be ranked Number 1, now, Coach Sloan?"

"I do agree with our fans. Yes, I sure do. It's going to be interesting for me to see what the people who vote in the polls do. We've beaten nationally ranked teams on their home courts and that should carry some weight in the voting.

"We weren't thinking about that at the start of this game, but it would mean a lot to the team and to me to be Number 1. I'd like to see us have it."

Monte Towe, State's articulate court leader, said he felt the Wolfpack should have been Number 1 all season. "We lost to UCLA in December and that hurt," he noted, and quickly added: "But we're a different team than we were in December. I think we're playing better now."

Towe said State was not trying to go out and stomp Wake Forest unmercifully simply to look good for the pollsters. However, he admitted they did think some about the rankings. "We thought if we went out and played real well, it would enhance our chances of being Number 1 some."

"David, who was that young boy you carried out onto the court on your shoulders after the game?"

David shuffled his feet, his head lowering somewhat automatically. "Well, he's a little fan who writes me letters all the time. His name is Marvin, and he can't see more than a couple of feet away, so we got him seats under the basket for him and his Mom. When I saw him squinting up at me in those last few seconds, I just had to go over and say something, do something for him."

"I'll bet he was thrilled?"

"Yeah, he seemed to really like it when I took him out there and let him dunk one."

"Does Marvin think you guys are Number 1?"

"I think so," David smiled. "Yeah, I really think so."

"And what about David Thompson? Would you be disappointed if you guys aren't voted Number 1 now?"

"I won't be real disappointed. Being Number 1 doesn't mean that much. The main thing is the NCAA tournament, and you still have to go out and prove your ranking.

"But, yeah sure, it would be a good feeling," he said. "And I think we're playing as well as anyone. I think we are better than we were in December."

"Wake's a good basketball team," Towe commented. They are such great shooters. Skip Brown is probably the fastest player I've ever played against. It didn't surprise me though, because I knew he was very quick. He's doing a great job for a freshman."

"We tried hard to get him at State," noted Sloan. "He's fast and a tremendous shooter, a really great player."

As far as his own squad was concerned, Sloan cited the play of all five starters--Thompson with 31 points and 12 rebounds; Burleson with 26 points and 12 rebounds; Mo Rivers with 19 points; Towe with 11 points; and Tim Stoddard with 11 points and seven rebounds.

"Timmy Stoddard played superbly again," the Wolfpack coach added. "He has a history of being a slow starter and he is really coming around. He gets better and better."

"So, if you attain the Number 1 ranking next week, will all of your goals be accomplished?"

"Nothing is over yet," Sloan warned. "We have four conference games left and they are all big. You saw what happened to Maryland today. They almost lost to Clemson."

"It will be a dog fight all the way, and I don't think we will get caught flat in any of our games from here on in. Maryland is still in it. Carolina is still in it. We're still in it. They both want it. We want it."

* * * * *

Streaking Wolfpack Voted No. 1 in AP Poll

"We must make some changes," Coach John Wooden declared to the Southern California Basketball Writers. The press corps had just informed him that the streaking North Carolina State Wolfpack had knocked his UCLA Bruins out of the top spot in college basketball. They had not lost a game since their December loss to UCLA. "We must make some sort of line up changes to make our players a little more hungry, but I won't go any further on that."

"Are there too many outside distractions, Coach Wooden, like the big money professional offers that are likely for Walton and Wilkes?"

"That's possibly true, but I really can't see where that would have much effect on them. Both men have told me more than once that they do not want to meet any pro scouts until the end of the collegiate season.

"Let's just say, I'm not particularly happy with our play at this time."

* * * * *

"Where we really want to be is Number 1 in March, first in the ACC tournament and then in the NCAA tournament," Coach Norm Sloan commented to the handful of reporters hanging out at practice. "But, for now, I'm pleased and proud that this team is at the top in this week's AP poll. We're a vastly improved team from last December.

"The two new starters on the team have come a long way. Morris Rivers is playing beautifully now, and Tim Stoddard at the big forward spot is getting over a slow start.

"Defensively, we're coming together much better, particularly on our press. We've beaten two of the top five teams on their home courts. We beat Purdue at Mackey Arena when they were leading the Big Ten."

Sloan stopped and turned back toward the court where his newly ranked number one Wolfpack was practicing. "Hey, guys, hold up a minute. I've got an real important announcement to make."

Everyone stopped what they were doing and gathered around their Head Coach. He didn't stop practice for much, so it had to be important. "The AP Poll results are in. And, guess what, guys? We're Number 1!"

They smiled. They high-fived each other and clapped each other on the back. A few let controlled shouts rip. They even posed for a photograph. Then they went back to practice as if nothing had happened.

"Hey, it's not that we're not enthused," explained Tom Burleson. "It's just that we have a lot of other things on our minds, like four more ACC conference games including one with Carolina next week."

* * * * *

"NC State tries out its national Number 1 ranking for the first time in 15 years in tonight's 8 o'clock meeting with Duke at William Neal Reynolds. However, according to Coach Norm Sloan, he and the relentless Wolfpack don't intend to let up.

"The last time the Wolfpack was ranked number one it was short-lived. The late Everett Case's 1958-59 club won the top spot in both the UPI and AP polls on a Monday and lost to North Carolina here the following Wednesday. Coach Sloan anticipates his players will last a little longer in that position."

"Yes, Jim, and the Pack is driving toward an unprecedented second straight unbeaten season in the ACC. They were 12-0 last season in conference play. This year, so far, they are 8-0, looking for number nine tonight."

"That's right, Billy. And just two weeks ago in Durham, State blasted Duke on February 4th in Cameron Indoor Stadium, 95-78."

"Entering tonight's contest, the Pack has averaged 103 points per game in each of its last six outings and has gone over 100 points in three straight.

"David Thompson leads the Wolfpack scoring with a 25 point average, followed by Tom Burleson at 17, Monte Towe at 13.4, and Morris Rivers--who seems to improve with each bounce of the basketball--at 12.9.

"Duke, 10-11 overall, defeated Georgia Tech in its last outing. Junior Pete Kramer sparked the win with a career high 20 points."

Duke started with a man-to-man defense but dropped it after the first sixty seconds. State then went to work on the Blue Devil's zone, knocking in 11 straight points to go ahead 15-4.

Thompson took a high pass on a fast break and scored when it didn't look as if he would even catch up to the ball. Coach Sloan came off the bench applauding.

The high pass was a potent weapon for the Wolfpack. Thompson converted most of them, but Burleson and Spence also shared in putting down some high pass baskets. Guards Monte Towe and Mo Rivers had seven and four assists, respectively.

The Wolfpack charged to a 60-43 half time lead.

The Pack maintained the furious pace throughout the second half as well until Coach Sloan cleared his bench with 5:51 to go. It was 99-70 at that point.

Post-Game Press

"Unlike the last time the Wolfpack was ranked Number 1, back in 1958-59, the team did not lose its ranking within three days. This time they played as if they were determined to justify their new ranking. And, justify it they did with a decisive 113-87 victory over the Duke Blue Devils."

"Jim, it was also the highest point total of the season for the Pack, it's nineteenth straight victory since a December loss to UCLA, and its 27th conference win in a row."

"And, Billy, I guess you'd have to say that David Thompson's play defied description. He ended up with 40 points, several of them coming on plays that seemed to be impossible until we actually saw David do them. He seemed to be in a world of his own out there tonight."

"And, you know, Jim, Duke didn't really play that badly either. There just wasn't much they--or probably anyone else for that matter--could have done about NC State tonight.

"Notre Dame's coach Digger Phelps says his team should be number one, not NC State, because they've beaten UCLA. Your Blue Devils have played them both, Coach McGeachy. What do you think?"

"We lost to Notre Dame 87-68 two weeks ago, and we lost to State tonight by 113-87. Notre Dame is a very fine team, but there is no doubt that State is the better team. State has more quickness and more bench strength. For instance, Phil Spence, a reserve, is their third leading rebounder and Mark Moeller, their number three guard, is one of the most underrated players in the conference.

"In my opinion, State is one team without a weakness. If they were to play and I had a vote as to which team would win I would vote for State. They're just awesome.

"State's indeed the top-rated team. We did everything we could to win, but they were just too good. State's the best team we've played. David Thompson may be the best player in the country."

"Speaking of Thompson, how do you, being one of the tallest man on the court for Duke, fit into the Alley-Oop defense, Bob Fleischer?"

"Well, I was looking up a lot like I always am when he's playing."

"David, you looked like you might actually be out to prove something tonight. Were you motivated by anything in particular?"

"We just didn't want anybody to sneak up on us now. This team wanted to be Number 1 and being that gave us added incentive tonight. As for me personally, well, I was just in position to get shots. And when I'm open, my teammates get the ball there."

"So, is the Pack peaking at just the right time now with the tournaments just around the corner?"

"We're playing better all the time," offered dapper Norm Sloan. "I wondered if being Number 1 would have a detrimental or positive effect on us. I think it was very positive. We were sharp and alert from the beginning."

"We're running a lot better," analyzed Monte Towe. "We're getting up and down the floor better. Early, we had a tendency to slow down. Also, we're playing better defense than we were."

Tommy Burleson's 7-4 frame slumped on a locker room bench while he munched on a submarine sandwich. "Being Number 1 is added pressure," he confessed. "But it's worth it. We enjoy it."

"How's the muscle pull, Tommy?"
"Oh, it acted up some in the second half, but it'll be okay.

* * * * *

"We can't have any repeats of the last game with these guys," Coach Sloan cautioned them, referring to the two incidents in their first meeting at Reynolds Coliseum. Sloan was wearing a red blazer and a red-and-white tie with the words "Number One" all over it in several languages. He'd worn it for the first time for the Duke game. "I'll admit it's a little hotdoggish," he would tell the press after the game.

"David, you got that?"

"Yes, Coach."

"I mean it now. You got nothing to prove out there with this kid, Reisinger, so let's keep the testosterone in check." Norm couldn't help but laugh as he sputtered: "After all, you did knock him out with one punch last time."

"Okay, Coach. I got it. Okay?" David feigned anger. "I'll let Tommy handle any problem that might come up. He seemed to be real good at dodging the guy's punches." David's face flushed as he broke down laughing.

"Seriously, fellows. We won 19 straight and counting since UCLA. We have won our last 27 ACC conference games. Tonight we can tie Duke's 28 in a row. Therefore, this game is very important to us. If we do this tonight, then we go up against Carolina next week to set a new record for consecutive conference wins. And, we all know how David--and the rest of us--react to Carolina Blue.

"So let's go out there tonight and give our fans back here and the few we might have down there in Littlejohn--something to cheer about!"

"Okay, guys, let's close up and get out of here. We leave for Clemson in about 45 minutes," Assistant Coach Eddie Biedenbach announced. "Managers be sure to secure the area and make sure you've got everything for the trip," Biedenbach concluded as he and Coach Sloan left the locker room to check on their transportation to the airport.

"Hey, Tommy, I'll get this window here, then we'll head out toward the bus, okay?"

"Sure, Phil." He backed up a couple of steps to give his teammate some room.

Spence grabbed the window. "Heck, the chain's stuck."

"Here, let me help."

"No, that's okay. I think I've got it now," Phil responded as he felt the chain that controlled the opening and closing of the window give under the pressure of pushing with his left hand. Suddenly the chain broke loose and the window fell with such force that it shattered when it hit the metal sill, cutting the middle and index fingers of his left hand.

Tommy tried to cover his face and eyes as he realized what was happening but he was too late. He could feel slivers of glass peppering his face and digging into his eyes. He tried not to blink or move his eyeballs any more than he could help. He gathered himself just as he would under the pressure of a game.

"Oh, God!" Phil shouted as he watched his own blood smearing over the shattered glass. Then he quickly looked toward his teammate. "I cut my hand, Tommy!"

"Somebody get Herman down here right away. Phil's hand is cut and I've got glass in my eyes!"

That night in Littlejohn, the home court of the Clemson Tigers, hours after frantic trainers and doctors cleaned glass out of Tommy's eyes and sewed up Phil's hand, Clemson had just reclaimed the lead at 31-26 with less than nine minutes remaining in the first half. They had outscored State 9-0 over a three-minute period.

State surged back with seven straight points to regain the lead 33-31.

After Clemson tied again at 33-33 with 5:14 to go in the half, State hit another streak with Thompson leading the way with 11 of the Pack's 20 points during the last six minutes. The biggest Pack lead had been only four points until they built a 46-40 lead with 1:35 left in the first half.

State held the ball for the final minute of the opening half against a tough 3-2 collapsing zone defense. Greg Hawkins started moving toward the basket with six seconds left, but he passed off to Rivers. Rivers quick-passed to Towe who shoveled it right back to Rivers. Mo forced up the jumper with one second remaining but the shot sailed over the rim as the horn sounded ending the half at 46-40 in favor of State.

"Both teams shot well in the first half: State at 55.5% and Clemson with 54.8%. Thompson had 17 and Burleson 11," Wally Ausley commented at half time just before he went to a commercial break.

In the beginning of the second half, State established its largest lead, 48-40, then, 50-42, but Clemson hung tough, mostly on the play of burly Wayne Croft (6-9, 225).

The Wolfpack was down by one, 75-74, with just 1:49 to play, while they continued to employ the "tease" offense called by their coach. Burleson, harassed constantly by Clemson's sagging 3-2 zone defense, finally broke loose, took the chest pass from Monte, and rolled in an underhanded, off-balance lay-up with 1:26 left. State led 76-75.

Clemson brought the ball down. Mo Rivers anticipated Croft's pass and intercepted it. He charged down court but missed the lay-up under defensive pressure. Thompson followed down the lane and laid the rebound in for a 78-75 Wolfpack lead.

In the last few seconds, Rivers made good on two free throws to establish the final 80-75 score.

"This victory ups State's ACC record to 10-0 and runs the Pack's winning streak over ACC opponents to 28, matching the record set by the Duke Blue Devils in 1964," Ausley announced. "Thompson was, once again, the man State went to down the stretch. He finished with 35 points. Most importantly, Number 44 scored 14 of his points in the last 12 minutes of the game.

"Burleson hauled down 10 rebounds and scored 19 points.

"Tim Stoddard started at the forward post opposite Thompson and played the entire game except for brief rest periods. Normally, he and Phil Spence alternate, but Spence cut his hand in a locker room accident this morning. The cuts to his middle and index fingers on the left hand required about 15 stitches. That left the position up to Stoddard."

Post-Game Press

"I'm kind of glad in a way that the game was close. We needed a game like this to help us get ready for the tournament," Norm Sloan explained. "The Number 1 ranking is secondary to the game. I was thinking only of the conference and a win to help us get the bye.

"Everyone played with real effort. I congratulate our players for having the true will to win and showing that tonight. One real good example was near the end when we came down court, made a turnover, then a great save, and David got a key basket.

"Playing without Phil Spence really hurt us against a team that's as physical on the boards as Clemson. But Timmy and Steve Nuce came through."

* * * * *

"We usually use the zone press only about a quarter of the time, but we used it about half the time in this game," Dean Smith explained about his team's 94-61 runaway victory over Virginia. "I thought our defense in the first half of the Virginia game was the best it's been all year."

"State's increased scoring recently is attributed by many to *their* improved defense. What about that Norm?"

"We've been getting more points on our quick break," Sloan responded. "We're playing the best we've played all year."

This was their final home game. This was also the game that could break the Duke record of 28 consecutive ACC wins set in 1963-64. Fitting that it should be with Carolina. This would be the season's final litmus test unless they met in the tournament. Moreover, this would be Tommy Burleson's final home game. He just knew he'd saved his best for last.

"They might try and convince you that this is just another game, but seniors Tommy Burleson, Steve Nuce, and Greg Hawkins would like nothing better than to finish their home schedule and their last game as seniors on their home court with a victory over their arch rival Carolina.

"As the old Wolfpack saying goes, Jim, 'nothing could be finer than beating Carolina, or something like that.'"

"And, Billy, as if any State-Carolina match-up needed any additional hype, there's a lot riding on the game. Coach Sloan's Wolfpack can conclude a second straight undefeated home season, clinch the Atlantic Coast Conference regular season championship, capture the first round bye, set a new record for consecutive victories against conference teams, and, maybe most important of all, get their seventh straight over Dean Smith and his Tar Heels.

"For Carolina, there is still the outside chance of tying State for the championship and, of course, the chance to stop the nation's Number 1 team and their number one rival and nemesis."

"It will be extremely tough to beat the number one team on their home court," Dean Smith opined. "I really think we have everything to gain and nothing to lose, although it's certainly a game we don't want to lose."

Carolina came to play. Although State led for the first 15 minutes, they never led by more than six points. Suddenly Thompson broke loose for the Alley-Oop from Stoddard and scored. Whistles blew. Hank Nichols waved off the basket. "No basket! No basket!!" Nichols caught the eye of his fellow official John Moreau. This was their third State-Carolina game this season, but calling them never got any easier. "Forty-four violated the cylinder! No basket!" The crowd began to yell and boo Nichols. They didn't see David Thompson's hands following through on the basket rather than pulling his hands back at the last second like he normally did to avoid a dunk. Nevertheless, Hank Nichols saw it, and Hank Nichols called it.

With the score 28-22, the Tar Heels rattled off nine straight points, six of them by Davis, while State went 5:40 without a score.

A three-point play by Mark Moeller gave the Pack a short-lived 32-31 lead with six seconds left. Then, Elston converted a three-point play for a 34-32 half time lead.

"The Tar Heels out defended and out boarded the Wolfpack during the opening half, holding State to its lowest first half point total of the season, 32 points. State was unable to get inside very often as Jones did a great job on Thompson and Mitch Kupchak nullified Burleson. That left Mo Rivers' long distance jump shooting as the primary weapon for the Pack. Carolina also had its problems penetrating the State defense. They had to settle for medium range jumpers for most of their scoring," Wally Ausley recapped.

In the early minutes of the second period, Carolina's lead grew to 40-34. The partisan State crowd was restless. Kupchak dribbled toward the basket, pulled up and attempted to put up a jumper. Thompson cut him off with his body and leaped high enough to stuff the jump shot down Kupchak's throat. "Number 44! Block!" Nichols shouted. "Two shots." The crowd jeered and booed again. This time they also showered the floor with paper cups and scraps of paper.

State seized control of the game in the next six minutes, outscoring the Tar Heels 17-2, beginning with a driving basket by Thompson. A tap by Spence tied the score 40-40.

Burleson then took center stage, scoring nine of the next 13 points. He drove and twisted for 19 points in the second half turning a tight battle in State's favor in his final regular season appearance on the Coliseum floor. Suddenly the score was 55-45 and the Tar Heels were wondering what had happened.

One of the plays that sent them reeling was a steal and a free-wheeling drive for a three-point play by Burleson that opened the gap to seven. He put some extra zing in that move as he did on several in the second half.

They had been "Burlesoned" to the max.

With a ten-point lead, State had few problems the rest of the way. Carolina very briefly cut the margin to six, but the Wolfpack controlled the last seven minutes with a spread offense that succeeded in breaks to the basket or drawing fouls.

After the game was over, television cameras recorded images of Coach Sloan talking with one of the officials but no sound. After a few moments, the referee looked around, spotted a basketball on the scorer's table, and scooped it up, handing it to Sloan.

Norman smiled as he accepted the ball and walked away looking for something or someone in the crowd of folks shoving around in the hallway. Then he spotted the head towering above all around him as Tommy Burleson stooped over in order to enter the Wolfpack locker room. He hurried passed fans and reporters and through the entrance. He caught up with the senior center seated on one of the locker room benches taking off his uniform.

"Tommy," Sloan huffed, a little out of breath.

"Yeah, Coach?"

He held the ball out toward the big guy. "This is for you, son. You really deserve it."

Burleson lowered his head a little as he took the ball and rolled it around in his hands. "Thanks, Coach Sloan." His voice cracked a little. "This means a lot to me. Thanks."

"What's this all about with the ball, Coach?" Billy Packer asked, sticking a microphone between the coach and his star player.

"I just gave the game ball to Tommy Burleson," Sloan explained to Billy Packer. "I've never done that before in my entire coaching career, but people should know this guy is one of the finest centers in the country, and I'm sick and tired of hearing people say he couldn't do this or that. We're a different team without him.

"He's been a heckuva player for us. Look at tonight. He scored the most points, 22. He took the most rebounds off the boards, 11. And, he led in assists as well with four.

"I've never said much about him, but we've been undefeated in the conference the last two years, and this guy has been primarily responsible for it.

"Sure, we have David Thompson and Monte Towe, but without the big man it would be awfully tough. I think he just got tired of hearing about the things he couldn't do.

"Right now, there is talk about who is going to make the All-Conference team, and I've heard a lot of people say they didn't see how they could put him on it. I don't see how anybody can be a sportswriter if you didn't vote for Burleson."

"You hear what your coach is saying, Tommy. How do you feel about that?"

"Sure, it's nice to get the ball. It's a real honor. The important thing, though, is that we won the game," the senior from Newland answered quietly. "I figure I've played pretty well all season for our team to be where it is. They got pretty physical in the first half, about as rough as I've seen. And, during half time, I realized I couldn't play any worse in the second half if I tried, so I just went out there and relaxed and things seemed to come easier after that. But, I was definitely displeased with myself for awhile."

"He sure deserves that ball," Phil Spence butted in, "and probably a lot of other game balls too."

"And, Phil, how was your hand out there tonight? It was pretty rough?"

"Yeah, it was so rough out there the first half, I was really scared I'd rip the stitches out. I wanted to play in this game, though. I would've done anything to play.

"At first, you know, I was just trying to protect my hand. After the first half, though, when we were behind, I just forgot about it and tried to play. I like it rough. This was my kind of game."

"But, David, it wasn't your type of game, was it?"

"No, it wasn't," Mo Rivers interrupted. "They were holding and pushing him all night. David's a great player, though, and just works harder to overcome things like that. Nobody could take what he took tonight and still get 21 points but David."

"Bobby Jones played me about like Keith Wilkes," David observed. "They are very similar. They both body check you a lot and give you a lot of little fouls. The fouls really aren't that big, but they are enough to throw you off a little bit. Jones did a real good job on me tonight."

"But," Rivers added, "we never get down on ourselves or lose our confidence and poise. We were down by 15 against Purdue in the second half and came back. Our offense is just so explosive we feel we can come back at any time. We picked up our defense a little and we got the lead back."

"We were not getting back quick enough on defense in the first half," David added. "They were getting down and shooting before we were ready. The second half we corrected that."

"We were not really over-confident," Rivers continued. "But we beat them at Chapel Hill and on a neutral site so we felt we should beat them here with our crowd and all.

"They really had a better attitude coming into the game than we did. At the half, though, we realized it would be a tough game."

The North Carolina Tar Heels retreated to their locker room to get away from the raucous Coliseum crowd whose yells almost shattered their eardrums. Nevertheless, inside the sanctuary of their locker stalls, UNC's players could find little solace. Again, they had tried valiantly, but for the seventh straight time, they could not beat NC State.

"They're a great team," admitted Darrell Elston, echoing the sentiments of his somber teammates. "And tonight they played the best defense we've faced."

"In the second half, they were more active on defense. They wouldn't let us go inside with the ball. And, we like to go inside. That was a big factor in this game."

It was a physical game, all right, two rivals tearing at each other like wolves and tar heels. Elston emerged from the fray with 17 points, however.

Walter Davis added 18 points and eight rebounds in an elegant display of poise and offensive power. However, the precocious freshman wore the look of a man who had seen his sterling work swallowed up by defeat.

"I hate losing so bad," he moaned. "I just can't remember the good things that happened in this game. But, look, I don't want to take anything away from them. They are great, and I like their players tremendously.

"When we were ahead 40-36 in the second half, we made about four straight turnovers and that was a key. State was aggressive on defense the first half as well as the second. And in the second half Tommy Burleson was a different person, too."

In another corner of the quiet UNC dressing room, Bobby Jones talked about guarding David Thompson. Though the State All-American finished with 21 points, everybody admired the Tar Heel's defensive tenacity.

"We just wanted to keep his percentage down (7-17)," explained Jones. "But Walter Davis helped a lot by switching. Still, Thompson is tremendous. He's like 2 1/2 players in one."

A few moments earlier, Dean Smith saluted State with "They're a great basketball team," then talked about his own team.

"We had some good moments, but not enough," he added, sipping on a soft drink. "When we were down 76-70, I still thought we had a chance if we could have gotten the bucket to cut it to four."

"How about the Pack's defensive pressure?"

"They put a lot of pressure on," he answered. "Both teams did. There was a foul on every play out there. But, I'm not criticizing the officials. It was this way for both teams."

"When the Tar Heels built a 40-34 advantage early in the second half, did you consider using the Four Corners, Coach Smith?"

"Sure, the thought always occurs in a situation like that," he responded. "But we were playing well. Also, they are real good at chasing the ball."

Smith added that both teams could play better, then tossed accolades at Bobby Jones and Walter Davis.

"I thought Bobby's defensive job on David was about as good as can be done," he lauded, "and Davis showed amazing poise. He played a sensational basketball game.

"For them, Rivers hurt us early with 12 points in the first half and everybody hurt us in the second half.

"The Wolfpack has a way of ganging up on its opponents."

* * * * *

"Tonight, Billy, with their 72-63 victory over Wake Forest University's Demon Deacons, the indefatigable Wolfpack of North Carolina State University became the first team ever to complete two straight unbeaten seasons in Atlantic Coast Conference competition."

"In the first half, the determined Demon Deacons stayed close behind the shooting of Tony Byers and Skip Brown and battled State even on the boards.

"However, in second half, they lost Lee Foye at 12:47, Cal Stamp at 7:04, and Mike Parrish at 2:24 to fouls. Though trailing 45-35 at intermission, Coach Carl Tacy employed a spread offense and gradually sliced away at State's lead. Defensively they dug in with a 2-3 zone."

"With 3:55 left, sleek Tony Byers swished a long jumper to whittle State's lead to 62-60. The Wake fans filled the building with their enthusiasm, but the Wolfpack, as it has done so often before, responded to the pressure like champions should. In less than two minutes, it outscored Wake 10-0 for a sudden 72-62 advantage and win number 24 on a 25-game schedule.

"In the final 4:17, Burleson scored seven points and climbed all over the defensive boards. Meanwhile, Thompson deftly penetrated Wake's defense three times to feed Tommy for easy baskets.

"By night's end, Jim, Thompson had 21 points and eight rebounds while Burleson added 17 points and 16 rebounds, Mo Rivers 10 points, and Phil Spence 12 points and 7 rebounds."

Post-Game Press

"It surprises me any team can go undefeated in the ACC two years in a row," offered Coach Norm Sloan. "This team has withstood a lot of pressure, and it has always done whatever it took to win.

"We were not sharp tonight, but we didn't expect to be. We've had our mind on the tournament since winning the regular season last Tuesday. That's not being disrespectful to Wake. They played well."

All-ACC Team

First Team

Name		School	Height
David Thompson		NC State (274)	6-4
195	Jr.	Shelby, NC	
Monte Towe		NC State (251)	5-7
145	Jr.	Converse, IN	
John Lucas		Maryland (242)	6-4
170	So.	Durham, NC	
Bobby Jones		UNC (209)	6-9
215	Sr.	Charlotte, NC	
Len Elmore		Maryland (195)	6-9
230	Sr.	Springfield Gardens, NY	

Second Team

Name		School	Height
Tom Burleson		NC State (163)	7-4
235	Sr.	Newland, NC	

Tom McMillen	Maryland (160)	6-11	
215	Sr.	Mansfield, PA	
Darrell Elston	UNC (151)	6-4	
204	Sr.	Tipton, IN	
Gus Gerard	Virginia (128)	6-7	
195	Jr.	Uniontown, PA	
Tony Byers	Wake Forest (71)	6-2	
170	Sr.	Bessemer City, NC	

Atlantic Coast Sports Writers Association voters had to choose three front line players and two back court men from a stunning array of talent. No team had ever placed three men on the first five, yet Maryland and State each had three legitimate candidates.

NC State's David Thompson was a unanimous choice for the All Atlantic Coast Conference Basketball team announced Sunday night by the Atlantic Coast Sports Writers Association.

Thompson's 5-7 teammate Monte Towe, the smallest player ever to win All-Conference honors, came next in the voting. Sophomore John Lucas of Maryland and seniors Bobby Jones of North Carolina and Len Elmore of Maryland followed him.

Notably absent from the first team were Tom Burleson of NC State and Tom McMillen of Maryland. Both seniors played on the U.S. Olympic team and were All-ACC selections for the previous two years. Joining them on the second team were Darrell Elston of North Carolina, Gus Gerard of Virginia, and Tony Byers of Wake Forest.

Thompson was a leading player on the United States team that defeated Russia in the finals of the World University Game this past summer. Some observers rate him the greatest player in the ACC, which annually has some of the strongest teams in the nation.

Towe has proved conclusively there is a place in basketball for the little man. His outside shooting has been remarkable this season, but it is his leadership qualities that have been most important to the Wolfpack as it completed its regular season with a 24-1 record and a 51-1 mark for the past two seasons.

Lucas was a sensation last season as a freshman and has polished his talents in all departments. He has remarkable control at top speed, which usually is too much for the opposition.

Jones is winding up a sensational career for the Tar Heels by being an outstanding defensive player and rebounder in addition to having a career shooting percentage that is one of the best in the country.

Elmore also is closing out his career with his best work at Maryland. He carries heavy defensive and rebounding burdens, which he handles well. He is the leading rebounder in the conference and when he chooses to shoot, he can be very effective.

Thompson UPI All-American

The first All-American in basketball for North Carolina State University was Morris Johnson in 1930. The most recent is David Thompson, named to the UPI All-America first team.

First Team

Bill Walton	UCLA	6-11
Sr.	La Mesa, CA	
David Thompson	NC State	6-4
Jr.	Shelby, NC	
John Shumate	Notre Dame	6-9
Jr.	Elizabeth, NJ	
Keith Wilkes	UCLA	6-7
Sr.	Santa Barbara, CA	
Marvin Barnes	Providence	6-9
Sr.	Providence, RI	

Second Team

Tom McMillen	Maryland
Larry Fogle	Canisus
Bobby Jones	UNC
Len Elmore	Maryland
Tom Burleson	NC State

Thompson Again Named ACC's Player of the Year

Regarded by many as the best ever in the ACC, David Thompson received the ACC Player of the Year award for the second straight year. Over two seasons, he has led the Wolfpack to a 51-1 record. A unanimous choice for All-ACC, voters named Thompson on all but three ballots for Player of the Year. One hundred and forty-two members of the Atlantic Coast Sports Writers Association took part in the balloting. Bobby Jones of the University of North Carolina garnered two votes. Thompson's friend and teammate Monte Towe received one.

Sloan Named ACC Coach of the Year

Norman Sloan, Head Coach at North Carolina State University, was named ACC basketball Coach of the Year. This is the third time in five years Sloan has received the Gerry Gerard Award. Out of 142 ballots, one hundred and twenty-one sports writers named Sloan. Carl Tacy of Wake Forest garnered seven votes. Dean Smith, University of North Carolina, Lefty Driesell, University of Maryland, and Tates Locke of Clemson each received votes.

Sloan won the honor in 1970, 1973, and, now, in 1974. His eight-year record at State is 141-71.

UCLA Picked to Win NCAA

Reno bookmaker North Swanson of the Reno Turf Club installed third-ranked UCLA as a 2-1 favorite to win its eighth consecutive NCAA basketball title. North Carolina State, currently ranked number one in both the AP and UPI polls is a 3-1 choice.

Neither school has yet earned a berth in the tournament.

10
Maryland and The Preacher Man

AP Poll
1. NC State 25 24-1 770
2. Notre Dame 15 24-1 750
3. UCLA 1 22-3 658
4. Maryland 21-4 443
5. Vanderbilt 23-2 424
6. N. Carolina 21-4 410
7. Southern Cal 22-3
8. Providence 25-3 264
9. Long Beach St. 23-2 189
10. S. Carolina 21-4 182

UPI Poll
1. NC State (21) (24-1) 326
2. Notre Dame (8) (24-1) 286
3. UCLA (5) (22-3) 285
4. North Carolina. (21-4) 155
5. Maryland (21-4) 151
6. N. Carolina 21-4
7. Southern Cal (22-3) 108
8. Providence (23-3) 78
9. Marquette (22-4) 50
10. Indiana (19-4) 47

> *"Because only one team, the ACC Tournament champs, advanced to the NCAA playoffs, that kind of pressure, that kind of excitement can only be duplicated today by the NCAA championship game."*
> Tom Burleson

> *"It was like we were playing a mini-NCAA championship. It was do or die, and neither team wanted to die."*
> Tom McMillen

> *"Six of the players on the two rosters were All-Americas. Ten would play in the NBA."*

ACC Tournament Pairings
Thursday, March 7, 1974

Maryland (2) vs. Duke (7)
    1:30
North Carolina (3) vs. Wake Forest (6)
    3:30
Virginia (4) vs. Clemson (5)
    8:00

Friday, March 8, 1974

NC State (1) vs. winner Virginia-Clemson
  7:00
Maryland-Duke winner vs. North Carolina-Wake Forest winner
  9:00

Saturday, March 9, 1974

Championship game
  8:30

    On Wednesday, the day before the tournament began, the Wolfpack raced up and down the practice floor with the kind of well-oiled, coordinated flow expected of the nation's Number 1 basketball team. Fast breaks developed with crisp passes and little or no dribbling, terminating in often dramatic lay-ups. Jokes and laughter peppered practice, that confident kind of laughter that comes from a team that's playing well and winning and believes that they will continue to play well and win. They had come a long way since December. They were Number 1 now, and they felt they deserved it. They didn't care what some bookie in Reno said.
    Through it all, Tommy Burleson was right in step. Last week's ACC Player of the Week twice tore down court and delivered devastating dunks. When the brief workout concluded, he hung around shooting baskets and practicing tips until Norm Sloan chased him in. Tall Tommy was tuning up for his final Atlantic Coast Conference Tournament in earnest.
    "So much is at stake," the Wolfpack senior said later in the dressing room to some of the press still hanging around. "I don't want to get too keyed up and press like I did my sophomore year. I want to keep it in the right perspective. But I don't want to look back and feel I didn't prepare properly either."
    "Does making second-team All-ACC goad you toward an even greater effort than usual at Greensboro?"
    "The voting was tough this year because there were a lot of good players," he responded. "I don't feel any animosity about that. But, yes, it leaves you with a feeling that you haven't completely proven yourself.
    "So this is another chance to show them you are a good player."

"If the 7-4 pivot man hasn't already shown them, then hogs don't love mud. His career marks include an 18.8 scoring average, 12.6 rebounding figure, and 51.4% shooting from the floor. This season, he has made 17.3 points per game and led the board work in 20 of State's 25 games. He's more than a pivot man. He's a pivotal figure and second team UPI All-American," one reporter spoke into his tape recorder.

"Tommy is a constant threat and opponents key on him," offered David Thompson. "He sets good picks for you, making it easy to get open. And when you get trapped with the ball, he's probably the best receiver in the nation."

"I like to play the Marylands and the Carolinas, the key games," Tommy went on. "These are our main rivals. I really want to beat them. I'm more mentally into the game. Against smaller teams, I don't play with the same instinct."

"Tommy Burleson isn't just talking," the reporter continued. "In three collisions with UNC this season, he has collected 58 points and 36 rebounds. But, always, he is a presence the opposition must sweat over. The trip to Greensboro, however, is not primarily a personal pilgrimage to enhance the cage status of Tommy Burleson. It is to enhance the status of the Wolfpack. It is to win the ACC Tournament."

"Mainly, I want to make a big contribution to the team. I'm concentrating on rebounding and making sure my timing is right. I feel this is the area where I can do the most good."

"Last year, Burleson won the ACC tourney's most valuable player award. And with the pressure of another classic building toward a marvelous crescendo, Tom Burleson from Newland, North Carolina is feeling the urge to turn it on again."

Down at press row before the first game between Duke and Maryland, State's coach Norm Sloan, reigning king of the ACC coaches, held court. Norm was especially affable and relaxed, primarily because his Number 1 ranked Wolfpack didn't have to play in the first round. "I'm really going to enjoy this," he smiled. "We don't have to play."

Even touchy subjects didn't shake him. "What about Tommy Burleson not making first team All-ACC?"

"Well, I was pretty upset about it at first," he said. "But then Tommy came up to me and said 'Heck Coach, it really doesn't make that much difference. It's what happens on the court that matters.'

"That made me feel a lot better about it. If he can accept it, I guess I can, too."

Terps Cruise Past Cold Devils 85-66

"The field for this Atlantic Coast Conference Tournament semi-finals could very well be the strongest the country will see this year, including the national finals, Jim."

"The results of yesterday's opening round, Billy, guaranteed that three of the top five teams in the country will play in these semi-finals tonight: Number 1 North Carolina State will play unranked Virginia at 7:00 and Number 4 Maryland meets Number 5 North Carolina at 9:00. The difference will be the team that is able to come up with that little bit of an edge at this time. It doesn't get much better than that even in the NCAA final four."

"Lefty Driesell, Maryland's affable but flappable Head Coach, had a few things to say after the Terrapin victory over his alma mater Duke."

"We believe we're playing as well as we have all season.

"We started off playing well against Duke. Then we slumped a little. Now, I think we're back where we were.

"Since Owen Brown has been starting, we haven't lost a game."

Heels 'Corner' Deacons 76-62

Dean Smith was determined to avoid a repeat of last year's tournament opener when Wake Forest put it all together in a stunning first round upset. So when the two clubs met Thursday in the ACC tourney opener, Dean made sure that his Heels and their famed Four Corner offense worked well in the latter stages of the second half en route to a 76-62 victory over the scraping Deacons.

Leading by eight points with six and a half minutes, Dean ordered his squad into the four-corners. Almost immediately, Bobby Jones converted a three-point play to push the lead to 67-56.

Coach Carl Tacy saw it differently. "I thought that my ordering the spread offense when I did hurt us more than their four-corners. We were only down by four at the time, and I just wanted to create one-on-one opportunities for our guards.

"And we thought it was going to work when Tony Byers and Skip Brown each got baskets quickly. But, then, their defensive pressure simply got to us."

"We just couldn't keep going," Skip Brown muttered as he toweled sweat from his face in the Deacons' dressing room. "For most of the game, we did everything we wanted to, but then their height and depth started telling and we just couldn't do anything about it."

Cav's Top Tigers 68-63
Bill Gibson Planning on Upset

Bill Gibson had, for the past five years, led his Virginia Cavaliers to the semifinals of the Atlantic Coast Conference Tournament. Each time he'd come up with a loss.

"I had a heart-to-heart talk with the players the other day," Gibson said, "and that's one tradition we'd like to break. We want to get to the finals for a change."

"Beating Clemson 68-63 in Thursday's first round was much easier than beating top-ranked NC State in Friday night's semifinals. How are you going to deal with the Pack?"

"It's a big task," Gibson offered. "And I'm not sure how to go about it.

"We held the ball on them one time and didn't do too well. We tried to run with them and didn't do too well. Hell! You reporters see it all. You guys tell me what to do!

"I'll try most anything. A box-and-one, a box-and-two. Maybe even a box-and-three." Coach Gibson paused and smiled. "Other than that, I guess we'll pray a lot.

Gus Gerard, the Cav's standout front courter, who had 30 points against the Tigers, admits he's a bit awed by the Wolfpack. "Tommy Burleson is intimidating on defense and David Thompson is just tremendous. They are really a great team, but I like playing them, because if you do good against them, you know you've played well."

"On the other hand, Gerard awes a few folks himself, with his deft moves, his feathery shooting touch, and his work on the backboards, wouldn't you say, Coach?"

"He's outasight," said Gibson. "I've said it before, so it's a matter of record gentlemen. Next to DT, he's the man."

Gerard, looking frail and boyish in his street clothes and granny glasses, shrugs off that kind of talk about his ability. "I didn't even know I scored 30 points," he said. "Besides, we won and that's the big thing. That's what I'm happy about. We're trying to make Coach Gibson go out a winner."

Clemson's Tates Locke has no plans for moving to a new school like Gibson's move to University of South Florida after the season's over, but he'd still like to try his hand at winning in the ACC Tournament. "It just gets damn tiring, this losing," said the fiery Locke, whose Tigers have lost in the first round 10 straight years.

"We didn't quit, so you can't fault our effort," he said. "They did last year, but not this time.

"Virginia did a good job getting the ball to Gerard and he put on a clinic in there. And, we just couldn't get the ball to go in.

"Then in the second half we didn't get the ball to the big guy [seven foot Tree Rollins] when he was right."

"What kind of preparation will you guys go through for tonight's game against North Carolina State?"

Virginia forward and all-ACC second team Gus Gerard replied very solemnly, "I guess I will pray." On a more serious note, Gerard said that Virginia's most important asset "is that anything can happen here. They have everything to lose and we have nothing to lose.

"If we have any advantage, it's an emotional one."

Cavalier guard Bill Langloh, only a freshman but responsible for many of the key points in the win over Clemson, said, "We'll need an unbelievable shooting night to win.

"We'd need to have our hottest game ever to beat them but that's not impossible. We have some good shooters on this team and if we get going, I think we can stay up with them."

Wally Walker, the sophomore who is, once again, playing up to his highly touted capabilities, took a more positive approach to the problem. "I don't think that beating State would be much more unreasonable than beating Carolina in Chapel Hill, which we did last year with about the same people. It's not impossible. It just takes a certain combination of things, but the great thing about this game is that there's always that possibility.

"Most important, though, as far as we're concerned is that we stay out of foul trouble.

"No doubt we'll play a zone defense, but I think Coach Gibson will order a normal offensive attack.

"We led them most of the first half in Raleigh just playing normal," Walker recalled. "And in our first game, we started out by trying to slow it down and fell behind by 20 points. So, I think we'll go with a routine offense. We won't take any foolish shots, but we won't hold it just to be holding.

"They're an awfully good team," Walker continued, smiling at his teammate Gus Gerard. "So, I guess I might do a little praying myself. We'll need to round up all the help we can get."

It wasn't that the University of Virginia was an afterthought or anything like that. After all, they had a good team and some quality players. Moreover, they had All-Conference Gus Gerard as well as Wally Walker. They played well against Clemson. They *could* beat you. And, if they beat you now, it was all over just like Coach Biedenbach had told them in practice.

"This is really the start of the NCAA Tournament," Eddie Biedenbach cautioned his players. "There's no second life after the ACC Tournament, gentlemen. Just the end of your season if you lose—even once. So, I wouldn't be taking Virginia or anyone else too lightly.

"So let's get out there and take care of business!"

Finally, the Greensboro Coliseum hummed. Thursday's games had been hors d'oeuvres to the real feast, the Number 1 team in the country defending their ACC title and looking to finally represent the conference in the NCAA tournament. It didn't matter all that much who the other team was. Tonight, it happened to be the Virginia Cavaliers. What did matter was that regardless of whom the other team turned out to be, the Pack had to defeat them. This team could not lose again.

As the Wolfpack came onto the floor, the hum of the crowd became a roar as Number 44 scored State's first 10 points in a display of skill that even awed his teammates. The Pack led 21-8 at around the ten-minute mark of the first half. But Virginia suddenly caught fire. Freshman Bill Langloh scored eight points as Virginia scored 12 in a row to trail by only one, 21-20.

Walker fouled Burleson who sank one of two from the line.

Al Drummond came back with a three-point play putting Virginia ahead 23-22.

The Cavaliers also led again at 25-24, but State reclaimed the lead at half time, 29-27.

State quickly increased its lead early in the second half to eight points. Then, David Thompson exploded for eight straight points. Suddenly, the Pack was ahead by 13, not two.

Thompson went on another tear late in the period, scoring 10 points in a row, taking the Wolfpack to an 80-57 advantage and, ultimately an 87-66 victory.

Post-Game Press

"I haven't played against Bill Walton, but Thompson is the best I've ever seen," said the hustling junior Gus Gerard, who scored 12 points Friday after getting 30 points in Virginia's opening win over Clemson.

"I'm sorry the season is over for us, but at least I don't have to play against him again for eleven months," Gus sighed as he entered the Virginia dressing room.

In the State locker room, players were not elated. How could they be? The game victory was expected. They had not won the tournament yet.

"I thought they played pretty good," Monte Towe observed. "They were passing well, cutting and setting picks. We didn't play well in the first half, but we had David, and that was enough."

"Was the team looking ahead to tomorrow night, Monte?"

"I don't know if we were looking ahead or not. It was probably half-and-half, Virginia playing well and us taking awhile to get going.

"And, sure, we played a little conservative. That's the world. But we went hard the first five minutes of the second half, and that's when games are won and lost."

"Were you concerned at half time being only up by one?"

"No, we weren't concerned," Towe smiled. "We were disappointed that we hadn't played better, but we came into the locker room at the half loosey goosey. We just looked each other in the eye and knew we'd win it.

"I think a lot of teams would have gotten worried in a situation like that. Up by only one point and not playing well, but not us. We're pretty cool and confident."

"'Were you guys a little cocky?"

"Well, maybe it seemed like it, a little," he grinned. "But, if this team ever really got cocky, we'd be the first ones to know it. We know each other so well. We know who we were before we came to State and before all this happened. If I get out of line, David will say, 'Hey, Towe, you weren't like that when you got here.' And, if David gets out of line, I'll say the same thing to him.

"This team will win together and if be, lose together, but we don't think about losing. We don't sit around and talk about the UCLA game. That would really be negative thinking. You've got to be positive about everything in life."

Terp Ironmen Rout UNC 105-85

Maryland defeated Carolina more decisively than any team since Carolina lost to Drake in the third place game in the 1969 national finals. Tonight's loss dropped the Heels' record to 22-5, still with a possible National Invitational Tournament bid.

Lefty Driesell played only seven men and the starting five most of the way while Dean Smith substituted in waves. Nevertheless, the Carolina blue waves couldn't drown the iron men in Maryland red.

Excitement and anticipation saturated the Maryland dressing room as if they were steam from the showers.

"We did it, baby!" Mo Howard yelled, pumping his fist in the air as if he were John Carlos at the '68 Olympics.

"And we did it in their own back yard!" Owen Brown shouted.

"When we execute the way we are capable of executing, it's possible for us to do anything," guaranteed Len Elmore who had just scored 17 points and grabbed 13 rebounds and played defense like a mad man.

"So, how do you guys beat State?"

"Stop David Thompson," John Lucas chimed in as he snapped a towel in the air heavy with the odors of sweat and liniment. He had just scored 24 points in Maryland's devastation of Carolina and was feeling pretty darned good.

"How do you do that, John?"

The Durham All-ACC pick grinned. "I don't know. Maybe we can get lucky," he speculated. "State beat us twice during the season, so the edge has to be to them. And, David Thompson, well, has anybody stopped him?"

"I don't know what it is, but this red uniform does something to Thompson," Len Elmore explained, pointing to his jersey. "He's had some fantastic games against us. But, he's had some fantastic games against a lot of people.

"We're not afraid of State. They're great, sure. But, we're not bad either. We realize this is the time to go. This is the end of the season. You win now or never. I know the State players feel the same way. However, if we keep putting it together as we have in the past few weeks, we can go a long way. We will do our best and see what happens."

"Tom, you had a pretty good night against the team you almost played for. Twenty points on eight for 11 from the floor and four for five from the charity stripe, six rebounds, and three assists. How does it feel to beat the Tar Heels and Dean Smith when you, at one point, announced that you would attend Carolina but later changed your mind in favor of Maryland?"

"Oh, sure, I'm really pleased, even proud, of our victory over a great Carolina team. There was a lot of personal competition involved in this game. I guess there always has been because of the way things happened when I was being recruited.

"But, it was never like a personal vendetta or anything like that. I just took extra pleasure in beating them when we were able to do that like tonight.

"I'm certainly not going to brag about it because I really like Coach Smith and all of his players. I always did, but at the same time, I'm happy I made the decision I made. I wouldn't change anything at all."

"What was your frame of mind like going into this semi-final game?"

"Well, we weren't cocky, if that's what you're getting at. But, we were very confident that we could beat them. Everything is perfect for us in this tournament. We're all set mentally and we're playing the best ball we ever have.

"There's not but one step left."

"If the time has ever been right for us to beat State," Coach Lefty Driesell speculated, "this is it! We've won 11 in a row. We're playing our best basketball. We have momentum going. The players feel they can't lose.

"And, the main reason we're playing so well is because of defense. Last year I out smarted myself trying to do a lot of different things. This year we decided to live and die with the man-to-man. It's our best."

"How do you stop David Thompson, Coach?"

"I don't know what to do with him," Lefty drawled, a sly smile growing on his face. "All I do know is nothing we've tried before worked. And," he chuckled," I take it that praying didn't work either since they beat Coach Gibson and Virginia and they said they were gonna pray.

"But, I keep telling myself there has to be a way."

"Maryland looked like a pro team," Coach Dean Smith commented after his team's loss to the Terrapins, 105-85. "I guess that at least five off this team will make it in the pros.

"I can't remember when a team had such a hot hand against us. But, I really thought this team was ready," continued a depressed Smith. "Maybe it was my fault. I guess I tried too hard to get them up. I know I worked harder at it for this game than any I can remember.

"It just goes to show you. You can never tell when a team is ready to play. Sometimes they just sit around and look unenthusiastic and then come out and play a super game.

"There is no way to tell you how much it hurts," he continued. "Losing in our tournament is greater than losing in the NCAA. But, I'll tell you one thing. I've enjoyed this team more than any I've had. They won the games they should have won and won a couple they shouldn't have. They're a great bunch."

"If the Terps play like they did against your team, Coach, can they beat the Wolfpack?"

"It's hard to say. It will be hard for Maryland to play two games like tonight back to back."

* * * * *

A-A-men! A-A-men! A-A-men, A-men, A-men!

Was this *really* the game for the ACC title or the National Championship? The Preacher Man's team was better, now, than The Wizard of Westwood's, even though they lost to them in the season opener. He was sure of that just as he was sure that *his* team was also better than The Wizard's team, now, although they, too, had lost to UCLA early in the season. And, in spite of the fact that his team had beaten The Preacher Man's team twice during the season, Norm Sloan was more concerned about the possibility of losing to them than to anyone else.

Yes, there must be a way. Lefty chuckled under his breath. Freshman year, David couldn't play varsity. Sophomore year, State was on probation, so even if David and State beat you, they couldn't go to the

NCAA tournament. There must be a way to make David ineligible this season as well. But could he figure it out before he got to the dressing room? The two time ACC Coach of the Year and inductee into the Duke and Davidson Sports Halls of Fame didn't want anyone to think he was having too much of a good time here trying to beat the Wolfpack for the ACC Championship and the only ticket to the National Championship tournament, especially not Lefty Driesell. If he was having too good a time, there must be something up. After all, he *was* Doctor of the Psyche Out, right? If he played with you, you knew you'd been played with, right?

Coach Sloan kept telling them every time they played Maryland that they should not pay any attention to what Coach Driesell or any of his players said to the media before, during, or even after the game. "You can't take somebody seriously who was born in Norfolk on Christmas day two years after the stock market crashed," he would joke. "I mean, can you imagine drooling baby Lefty, bald from birth I presume, as your one and only Christmas present?
"Just think of him like that, guys, and his brilliant psyche outs just won't work on you."
The talent on the court alone guaranteed a game of games no matter what pre-game psyche outs Coach Driesell or his players put into play. The Wolfpack could sense that. They could sense something special was about to take place. When it was over, one of their hopes for a national championship would be done. Just like that. No more second chances.
And, if The Preacher Man's boys played like they did last year in the first Super Sunday basketball game, then David realized they would have their work cut out for them just to beat Maryland for the ACC title and keep going. After all, it took a dramatic last-second Alley-Oop basket to beat Maryland 87-85 on Super Sunday, the first basketball game televised before a Super Bowl. That was what his style and leaping ability were all about, wasn't it? To be able to help his team win when it really mattered. That Alley-Oop also had kept them undefeated.

"Jim Thacker, both State and Maryland arrived in Greensboro itching for a rematch with UCLA in the NCAAs. The haughty Bruins, winners of seven consecutive NCAA titles, nipped the Terps 65-64 in the season opener and embarrassed the Pack 84-66 in December in St. Louis.

But, the Bruins have slipped to Number 3 in the polls after a late-season stumble. Carolina has moved to sixth.

"And, when these players walked onto the court tonight, they knew the NCAA Final Four would be played on this same Greensboro Coliseum floor two weeks from now. The State players know the East Regional would be at Reynolds Coliseum giving them what amounts to a home court advantage if they reach the regionals. So just how big is this game?"

"This game tonight, Billy, is as big as they get! It features a convergence of forces: talent, desperation, even a touch of revenge. It matches two highly competitive, combative coaches: Smooth and dapper Norm Sloan and Maryland's foot-stomping Preacher Man, master of the psyche out, Lefty Driesell.

"And at least ten of the players on these two rosters will probably play in the NBA someday. Six are All-Americans. And, State's David Thompson leads the list. Many hail him as the best player ever in the ACC. Even the opposition coach had nothing but good things to say about him."

"He's the best I ever coached against in college. I know we don't have any one player who can guard him," a video clip of Lefty Driesell observed.

"Earlier, I also asked Walter Davis, a freshman who certainly doesn't play like a freshman, who was going to win the State-Maryland game. He winced, acting as though he didn't really want that question, but he responded anyway."

"David Thompson will be playing, and that has to make State the favorite."

When the coliseum lights went down and spotlights illuminated a small part of the floor near the Maryland bench, State was ranked Number 1 in the nation. The Preacher Man had Maryland at Number 4, although many believed that the Terrapins were really Number 2 if not in a dead heat with the Wolfpack for Number 1.

The tap to start what many have called the best college basketball game ever played went to McMillen off Burleson's right hand. He dribbled into the front court and saw Owen Brown open. Brown took the pass from McMillen, dribbled once across the lane and took the jump hook just over Burleson's up-stretched fingertips. Swish. Seething, Burleson hustled to the other end of the court and took position at the edge of the paint under State's basket. Elmore had all but spit in his face verbally, telling the press and everybody that he was the best center in the ACC, implying that Tommy Burleson didn't amount to much. And, on top of that, the ACC sports writers picked the guy over him for first team all-ACC. By God, he'd show Len Elmore! He'd show the ACC sports writers.

Monte scooted a quick bounce pass to him inside. Tommy scooped up the pass. In one elongated motion, he tossed a jump hook over Elmore's raised arms and shot a snarl in his face. The shot kissed the glass and bounded around the rim and into the net. The snarl remained on his lips as the 7-4 Newland Needle turned and headed to the defensive end of the court. There was no big man in college basketball that was going to back him down now. At the end of all this March madness loomed a national championship, and Tommy Burleson was going to make sure that championship belonged to the NC State Wolfpack.

"After nearly two minutes the score is only 4-2 in favor of Maryland. Nobody from either team seems to be able to buy a basket yet, Billy."

"That's true, Jim. However, this match-up between Elmore and Burleson is already developing into something. You can almost feel the animosity and you can certainly see some of it the way they're bodying up on each other and going right at each other."

With 14:30 remaining, the Terps heated up. They hit 12 of their first 14 shots and the Pack trailed 25-12. Then with 9:30 left in the half, State cut the lead back down to 9 at 33-24. Burleson popped a short jumper from the lane. "It's good!" Jim Simpson paused. "As Lucas brings the ball up court, there's 9:05 left in the first half."

Thompson hit a jumper. Then Towe hit one. Next time down, Monte drew a foul. Maryland called time out.

Then a short jumper by Burleson was his twelfth point and there was still more than five minutes left in the first half. Billy Packer announced, "Burleson is having one of the biggest games of his career at NC State, and it couldn't come at a better time for the Wolfpack."

After another time out, Monte went to the line and hit the first one but missed the second, bringing the score to 39-33 with five minutes left.

Burleson pinned Elmore against his left side as he posted up taking the Maryland center deep into the paint. Tommy sensed Elmore shift his weight, attempting to extricate himself from his hold. It was at that point that Tommy hit a quick jump hook from three feet out. That move brought the Pack to within four at 39-35.

Rivers canned a jumper from 18 feet. David skied for an Alley-Oop. The Greensboro Coliseum crowd ooohed and aaahed as he cradled the ball and dropped it through the hoop, pulling his hands back at the last instant so he wouldn't violate the invisible cone above the rim.

McMillen lost the next possession out of bounds. Thompson took the ball back door on the in bounds pass. Owen Brown fouled him hard. It was his third foul. David hit the first and missed the second, but an alert Tim Stoddard made the put back for the lead, 42-41.

Ten seconds later, Lucas hit a medium jumper next time down to give Maryland the lead back at 43-42. Then he stole the ball for a breakaway lay-up. Maryland led 45-42.

Rivers drove the lane hard, taking defensive elbows in the ribs and face. He crumpled to the hardwood, his nose bleeding profusely. Herman Bunch, the State trainer, stopped the bleeding with bandages and pressure and escorted Mo off the court and into the dressing room.

David blocked a shot, but the referee called goal tending. Then he canned a jumper over Tom Roy who had come in for Owen Brown.

Elmore hit inside.

Roy fouled Thompson in the act of shooting. David hit two free throws.

"It's truly amazing, Jim Simpson, but David Thompson has 19 points with those two free throws." Billy Packer paused and shook his head. "It's just hard to believe. It's games like this one that force you to make the comparison between David Thompson and Oscar Robertson who could beat you to death and you hardly even knew he was on the court.

"It's been that way tonight for David Thompson. Tommy Burleson has been the visible big gun so far for the Pack, but DT has come up with 19 points."

"And he's going back to the line again, Billy."

Thompson hit two charity tosses for his 20th and 21st points.

McMillen hit a jumper from the corner.

Towe sank a short jumper after a pass from Thompson as he was about to fall out of bounds.

The half ended with Maryland ahead by five points, 55-50.

State reeled off 16 points to Maryland's six during the first couple of minutes in the second half to give the Wolfpack its biggest lead 66-61.

Maryland reclaimed the lead at 67-66 with 14:32 remaining. Then, Owen Brown committed his fourth foul when he bashed Tom Burleson to the hardwood with a vicious body foul. The Greensboro Coliseum crowd began to boo as the officials called time out. The crowd continued to boo as the teams left the floor. When the teams returned to the floor, Owen Brown was on the bench, again replaced by Tom Roy.

The Pack didn't hesitate. They went directly inside to Burleson, still hurting from the body slam by Brown. He secured the ball, turned his left side toward Roy and flipped a jump hook over his outstretched arms. The 7-4 giant pumped his fist as the ball banked off the glass and into the net. State 68. Maryland 67.

At 9:56, Maryland led 79-76. Len Elmore drove the baseline, but Burleson stepped in and took the very hard charge.

"My goodness, Jim!" Billy Packer exclaimed. "Just look at that Burleson. He's everywhere and doing everything. How many times will you ever see a 7-4 center give up his body like that to take the charge?"

Eighty-nine to 86 at 5:52.

"The pace has just been incredible. It's hard to imagine that both these teams can keep this up for almost another six minutes."

At 97-93 State, Maryland scored successive baskets by Roy and Elmore. At 1:10 remaining, the score was deadlocked at 97-97.

Monte began to dribble down court when the cramp hit his left thigh. He pulled up lame in front of the scorer's table and quickly called time out with 57 seconds left. Trainers began to work on Monte as soon as he sat down, but Coach Sloan had to call another time out because his point guard, his team leader, was not ready. Finally, Norm had to replace Towe with Mark Moeller. McMillen intercepted the reserve guard's first pass. Maryland called time with 25 seconds remaining.

Towe immediately returned to the lineup even though he was still moving with a little bit of a hitch. The Terrapins ran off 16 seconds before calling time out again.

When play resumed, the Pack defense hemmed in Maryland near the left corner. Finally, the ball popped out to Lucas on the outside. With only two seconds left, he launched a 35-footer. The horn sounded. The shot drew iron.

"It's 97-97. We're going to overtime in this unbelievable ACC Tournament Championship game."

With two minutes left in the five-minute overtime, Phil Spence saw a soft spot inside the defense. He shot for the opening just to the right of the basket. Towe spotted him and whipped a no-look pass through the floundering hands of the defense. Spence fielded the pass and in one smooth motion laid the ball up off the glass and in. The score: State 101 and Maryland 100.

Maryland came down and missed. The Pack then controlled the ball until Mo Howard fouled Mo Rivers with 1:21 remaining. Rivers missed the front end of the one-and-one. Maryland rebounded and sprinted down court, but they were cautious. Maybe, too cautious because they nearly lost the ball, then the Wolfpack tied them up. Maryland's John Lucas recovered the tap but threw a wild pass that ended up out of bounds with 23 seconds left.

Rivers and Towe then ran the clock down until Billy Hahn fouled Monte. With six seconds left, Monte Towe went to the line. In his usual rapid-fire fashion, he quickly rattled home both charity shots to put State further ahead 103-100.

The horn sounded. The final score, in overtime. NC State 103 and Maryland 100.

The Maryland team fought their way through a sea of fans and press to their bench where they had to await the presentation of tournament trophies. Many in the coliseum crowd began to sing:

"A-a-men. A-a-men. A-a-men. A-men. A-men."

The jubilant NC State team raised David Thompson to their shoulders. He snipped away at the net.

"A-a-men. A-a-men. A-a-men. A-men. A-men."

Then Monte Towe . . . .

"A-a-men. A-a-men. A-a-men. A-men. A-men."

. . . . and Tom Burleson . . . .

"A-a-men. A-a-men. A-a-men. A-men. A-men."

and, finally, Coach Norman Sloan. He shook his fist in the air, then twirled the net around over his head in a gesture of victory.

"A-a-men. A-a-men. A-a-men. A-men. A-men."

"Listen to that, Billy. And look at those Maryland Terps."

"They are not very happy campers, are they, Jim?"

"No, they sure aren't, Billy."

"As we listen to strains of the Maryland victory song being sung by the Wolfpack fans in the coliseum, we must ponder this question: How is it possible for a basketball team to shoot 61 percent from the floor and lose?" Wally Ausley paused. "Well, it happened to Lefty Driesell and his Maryland Terps tonight in a game that a lot of people are already saying may have been the best ever."

"This one goes down in the record books as the highest scoring game in ACC history. It's also the Wolfpack's 32nd straight over ACC competition and upped its record to 26-1," he announced.

"Thompson scored 21 of his 29 points in the first half as the Pack closed to 55-50. But the 7-foot-4 Burleson would be the key to victory, with a career-high 38 points, many on hooks and soft bank shots over Elmore."

"It reminded me a lot of the '54 ACC championship, an 82-80 Wolfpack overtime win over Wake Forest in Reynolds Coliseum in Raleigh. Both games had great individual confrontations."

"Speak up a little, Skeeter, if you would. It's hard to hear over the A-men's still being sung while we await the trophy presentations.

"Sure, Wally. The '54 game had Dickie Hemric of Wake—26 points and 16 rebounds—against Mel Thompson—29 points—and Ron Shavlik—18 points and 17 rebounds—for State. Tonight it was David, Towe, and Burleson against McMillen, Lucas, and Elmore. But the Wolfpack had David Thompson, and that made all the difference."

"Thank you, Squire of the ACC Marvin "Skeeter" Francis, former Sports Information Director for Wake Forest University and, for the past six years, spokesman for the ACC. And, sports fans, Thompson *did* score 29 points tonight. Despite the Terps super 47 of 77 from the field, David Thompson and the Wolfpack beat them on the free-throw line, where Thompson converted nine of 11 shots after drawing fouls from what seemed to be half of the Maryland bench.

"But, it was the remarkable play of Wolfpack center Tommy Burleson—38 points and 21 rebounds—that made it *impossible* for Maryland to win this game tonight. Bottom line is that neither of these teams deserves to stay home when the NCAA tournament begins next week. But, Maryland and Coach Lefty Driesell will stay at home."

"Jim, can you tell what's going on over there on the Maryland bench? It looks like Lefty's getting his guys up and leaving the floor."

"Billy, I believe you're right. Yes. There they go, off toward the exit to the dressing rooms."

"Now Lefty seems to be talking to some people, I think they are Maryland officials."

"One of them looks like Jim Kehoe, the Maryland Athletic Director."

"Now the team is coming back to the bench. The players are taking their seats once again."

"Unbelievable. Lefty was going to take his team off the court before the trophies were presented. What a break in ACC tournament tradition that would have been."

"That's the greatest game I've ever seen a big man play." Lefty tossed the compliment at Tom Burleson like a lob pass as he wandered through the Wolfpack dressing room offering congratulatory handshakes all around. "That was one heck of an effort, Tommy. You go on now and win that whole thing!" As the Preacher Man continued around the dressing room, he hoped that, at least, the sermon his team preached tonight would resonate with the NCAA as it should have long before now. His team was too good to be sitting home come tournament time. A lot of other really good teams like Carolina were also good enough not to sit at home during tournament time. He knew it. The Wolfpack knew it. The other coaches knew it. The other teams knew it. And, most important, the NCAA knew it. So, The Preacher Man prayed to the basketball gods to impart at least enough wisdom to the NCAA to effect a change in the rules of their existence so that his flock could finally ascend the tournament mountain.

A-A-men! A-A-men! A-A-men, A-men, A-men!

All-ACC Tournament Team

First Team

David Thompson	NC State	unanimous choice.
Tom Burleson	NC State	Tournament MVP
John Lucas	Maryland	
Mo Howard	Maryland	
Tom McMillen	Maryland	

Second Team

Len Elmore	Maryland
Owen Brown	Maryland
Monte Towe	NC State
Gus Gerard	Virginia
Billy Langloh	Virginia

Post Tournament Press

"I can't make any apologies for the way our team played tonight. This was the best game ever played by one of my teams. To lose with that kind of effort is really tough, especially when you know there's no tomorrow left in this season."

"What was all that about after the game was over when you and your team seemed to be leaving the court before the trophies were presented?"

"I just got tired of waiting, but we were told to go back to the bench. I just think it's the most ridiculous thing in the world. I've sat and watched it three years in a row, and they got kind of carried away out there today. It took them twenty-five minutes to set up."

Tom McMillen: "It was like we were playing a mini-NCAA championship out there. It was do or die, and neither team wanted to die, and then we had to sit there and wait and wait with the crowd hassling us and singing. It was hard to take, that's for sure."

"Tom Burleson." Billy Packer had to look up at nearly a 180-degree angle to see the young center's face. "You were first-team All-ACC in your sophomore and junior years, only to be edged out this year by Maryland center Len Elmore. On top of that, Elmore made some caustic remarks after the Terps' 80-74 loss to you guys at Reynolds Coliseum on Son of Super Sunday. I believe he said something like, 'Go tell that dude I'm the Number 1 center in the league.'

"How did you react to all that coming into tonight's ACC championship game?"

"Both those things really fired me up, so I was out to prove something tonight. It was a championship game, and it was a grudge game."

"How does winning this game make you feel?"

"Winning this game is like getting a 1,000-pound gorilla off your shoulders."

"Why is that, Tommy?"

"Because, if we had lost tonight, we'd be done. Only one team, the ACC Tournament Champs, advances to the NCAA playoffs. Now, we're the ACC Champs again, and unlike last year, this time we get to go to the NCAA tournament."

David Thompson: "This ACC Tournament had as much talent as any Final Four. We had three of the top six teams in the country in this tournament. Not often do you get that many in the Final Four."

Coach Norman Sloan: "If that wasn't the greatest college game ever played, I'd like to see the one that was. It was unbelievable the things those players did out there tonight. The emotion, the play, was fantastic. We played a great team that played a great game. It was one of the few times I had cotton in my mouth. I was terrified, scared to death.

"But can you believe these guys? You just can't win 32 games in a row against conference teams. You just can't keep doing what these guys do," he enthused. "I told this team before the season started it could be one of the greatest college teams of all time. And, I think it's beginning to show some of those traits.

"I have to say," he continued, wagging his head, "that this was one of the greatest college games that has ever been played. And, I think we beat the second best team in the nation tonight. What a beautiful finish of a beautiful tournament for a beautiful team."

The front-page headlines in the Raleigh *News and Observer* of Sunday, March 10, 1974 would read:

> **Seven Plead Not Guilty in Cover-up**
> **SLA: Patricia Is Okay**
> **Arab Division Seen On Oil Diplomacy**
> **Burleson Leads Pack to Title in Overtime**

Only one of those headlines would matter to Len Elmore. For the moment on this Saturday night, however, the serious, thoughtful student of Lefty Driesell's psyche-out U could only stare ahead blankly, his well-known and highly touted composure having nearly deserted him. He focused on a large metal tray of orange halves on a table just a few feet away. For two days now that table had been a rallying point for their team celebrations. That was where the players set up their tape system to play loud rock and soul music, where they had slapped hands, and where they had vowed to keep on winning no matter what.

Tonight there was no music, no slapping hands, no vows to keep on winning. There was only orange slices on a metal tray and the knowledge that they had lost. The loudest noises were the muffled tones of players talking among themselves or giving interviews because they had committed themselves to doing so.

Bodies brushed Elmore's shoulder, his elbow, his knee. His body seemed to simply roll with the pressure and pop back into his hunched, blank stare position. He had been "Burlesoned" big time, and he knew it. He felt the psychological welts from the switching as keenly as he felt the soreness in his muscles and the bruises on his body.

He had told everyone that he was better than Burleson, that he deserved to be first team all-ACC, not Tommy. Finally, after two seasons, they believed him. He made the first team this year. Tears welled in the defensive master's dark eyes. His huge hands seemed to wipe the tears from his cheeks of their own accord. He looked upright, his eyes clear once again. "It's a damn shame that my defense would collapse at this time--when everything was on the line. It doesn't seem fair."

He stood up and pushed his way through the growing throng of reporters toward the metal tray containing the orange halves that now seemed yards, rather than inches, away. After snapping up several halves and returning to his bench seat, he sucked briefly on one slice, then discarded them behind his feet under the bench. Then the beaten center continued to take questions.

"Was it unfair to your team to be playing here in North Carolina?"

"I couldn't stop him."

"You mean Tommy Burleson?"

"Yeah. I just couldn't stop him."

"Do you think some of your remarks in the past about being better than him could have made a difference in his play tonight?"

"I don't know. I have never seen him like that before. I still can't believe it happened. I have enough confidence and pride in my defense to know I can stop anybody, but Burleson was a different person tonight. I can't figure out what happened.

"No one has ever done anything like that to me," he muttered, still in disbelief. "I've been playing almost all of my life and no one has ever made me look bad--not Bill Walton or anybody else.

"You know, I keep thinking that I would block one or he would throw up an air ball and it would end, but it didn't. He was shooting his hook shot perfect, and he was facing me and then going to the basket, things like those that he hadn't tried before.

"At half time, he already had 14 points, so I really tried to get myself together. I thought, if I could go back out there and block his first shot, he'd back off. But, the first time he got it in the second half, I was out of position and he hit a lay up. Then he got inside of me for another one and it kept getting worse."

Len bent over to untie his shoes letting the reporters know that this interview was over. Just at that moment, Jim Kehoe, Maryland Athletic Director, shoved his way through the knot of newsmen and warmly thumped his star center on the back. "You're still the best, Lennie," Kehoe insisted. "You are still the best!"

"Thanks, Mr. Kehoe," Elmore barely acknowledged. "But tonight he was."

11

"Nobody can stop me!"

AP Poll	UPI Poll
1.NC State 24 26-1 792	1.NC State (17) (26-1) 313
2.UCLA 17 23-3 748	2.UCLA (13) (23-3) 286
3.Notre Dame 25-2 652	3.Notre Dame (3) (25-2) 260
4.Maryland 23-5 503	4. Maryland (23-5)184
5.Providence 27-3 411	5.Marquette (23-4)134
6.Vanderbilt 23-3 353	6.Providence (24-3)114
7.Marquette 22-5 327	7.Vanderbilt (23-3)104
8.N. Carolina 23-4 303	8.North Carolina (22-5) 99
9.Long Beach St. 23-2 284	9.Indiana (20-4) 82
10.Indiana 20-4 241	10.Kansas (21-5) 39

    The bold black letters of Marvin Barnes's quote almost seemed to leap out from the bulletin board in the Wolfpack's dressing room as if they had a life of their own. Coach Sloan had thumb tacked copies of two articles beneath the enlarged quote. Every player had noticed them when they came through the door to dress for practice yesterday. Now, every player would have to notice the words when they came in on this Thursday to dress for their game against Providence College and their superstar Marvin Barnes.

    Outside the door in the Coliseum hallway, Phil Spence paused outside the dressing room to answer a few questions. "Phil, you've guarded Tom McMillen of Maryland and Virginia's Gus Gerard so close they seemed handcuffed. How do you feel about going up against Providence's Marvin Barnes, especially in light of the remarks attributed to him? Are you worried?"

    "It's gonna be a great challenge, but I'm looking forward to it. I know he should be good, but I'm not such a bad player myself.

    "He says he can't be stopped, but we'll see. If he can't, then I'll go tell him afterwards that he's right--that he can't be stopped, at least not by me."

    "So, you're not afraid of Marvin Barnes?"

    "No, I'm not afraid. You don't go out on the court afraid. You go out and play hard and enjoy yourself, and may the best guy win."

"How do you plan to play him?"

"I'll try not to let him get the ball, but if he gets it, I hope to keep him away from the basket. It'll be me and him chest-to-chest.

"On the boards, I guess we'll just go up together. I'd like to out rebound him. You know he's Number 1 in the nation.

"Look, fellows, I'm just a small frog in a big pond whose gotta go get dressed for the game."

"Thanks, Phil, and good luck tonight."

Phil Spence closed the door behind him, when he entered the Wolfpack dressing room. He stopped directly in front of the bulletin board, dropped his athletic bag to the floor, and glared in silence at the large black letters that formed Marvin Barnes' words. His fingertips touched the copies as if they were basketballs.

Barnes Livens Up Tonight's Regional
Roy Brown, *News and Observer*,
Staff Writer

Providence star Marvin Barnes, who seems to relish the limelight, has stolen the show again. With his penchant for telling it the way he thinks it is, Marvelous Marv has almost made us forget that Furman plays Pittsburgh in the opening game (7:05 p.m.) of tonight's Eastern Regional at Reynolds Coliseum. And if NC State's Wolfpack didn't happen to be the host team and ranked number 1 in the country, we might even be asking: "David who?"

Barnes has almost single-handedly turned the 9:10 p.m. bout between top-ranked State and fifth-ranked Providence into a nail-biter. Before he hit town, everyone figured State would cruise to the regional crown and into next week's national championships at Greensboro--especially considering the way the Wolfpack won the ACC championship.

Nevertheless, Marvin has folks thinking the Friars have a chance. Before he arrived in Raleigh, the media quoted Marvin saying that he "couldn't be stopped when I'm right." That was later labeled a misquote, but questions remained.

Then, Coach Dave Gavitt reportedly said he plans to put the 6-9 Barnes on Wolfpack All-American David Thompson, which seems unlikely. Moreover, while Gavitt prefers to let everyone keep guessing about his defensive plans, Barnes has gone along with the report--although he's not making any foolish statements. "I don't think anybody can stop Thompson, except himself," Barnes says of his World University Games teammate. "He's probably the best around. All I can do is go out and play him the best I can.

"And I don't think Keith Wilkes of UCLA stopped him when they played either. He just had a bad day. He didn't have any trouble shooting over Wilkes, but his shots just weren't dropping."

Don't get the idea Barnes is giving up. That's the furthest thing from his mind. "I hope both Dave and Tommy have good games," he says. "I just hope they lose.

"We gotta play good," says Barnes, the nation's leading rebounder and a 20-point plus scorer. "We have to get our running game going, play tough defense, and shoot well. If we play at only 80 percent, we're liable to lose."

Providence comes into this game with a 26-3 mark and an 11-game winning streak. The Friars also have more than Marvin. Guard Kevin Stacom is a classy shooter and 5-11 Cary Bello an adept playmaker. Also making big contributions are freshman Bob Cooper and sophomore Mark McAndrew. While Barnes and Stacom have supplied most of the stability in this season's success, Gavitt feels the others are fitting in better with each passing game.

"The kids are taking the cue from Barnes and Stacom," the coach says. "They've worked hard, developed a rapport. They have a feeling that they can't lose. It all fell together a lot better than I anticipated at the beginning."
NC State's Norm Sloan, meanwhile, contends he's not worried about any match-ups. The Wolfpack, he says, will play its usual run-and-gun game.

"Right now this technical stuff--the offense and defense--is automatic," he says. "Attitude is what counts most now. It just depends on which team wants it the most."

Providence official says Barnes victim of misquote
Tim Stevens
Times sports writer

Marvin Barnes is sorry--and mad. So is Providence coach Dave Gavitt and everyone else who hopes the Friars can upset No. 1-ranked North Carolina State Thursday at 9:10 p.m. in the Eastern Regionals here.

The cause of concern is a story carried by one of the major wire services following Providence's easy 84-69 victory over Penn Saturday night.

The story quoted Barnes as saying, "When I get going, there's nothing I can't do on the court and no one who can stop me."

From there, it got even more far-fetched. It further quoted Barnes as saying he could stop State's All-American forward David Thompson.

The story was filled with the type of quotes that Coach Norm Sloan has a tendency to make sure his Wolfpack sees--the kind of articles that have been known to fire a team up.

"There's going to be a correction run" noted Providence's sports information director Mike Tranghese. "The quotes were distorted and all messed up."

"He was asked if he could play against Thompson," said Tranghese. "Marvin said, 'Sure, anybody can play against him, but stopping him is something else.'

"Then they asked Marvin if he could stop Thompson," said Tranghese. "He said something like, 'Can anyone stop Bill Walton? I can try.'"

Barnes, a 6-foot-9 first team United Press International All-American, is averaging 22.5 points and 18.8 rebounds per game for the 27-3 Friars.

"David and Billy (Walton of UCLA) are by far the best I've ever been up against," Barnes said. "They are both just really super."

"It is no exaggeration or stretch of the truth to say NC State has far and away the best team Providence has played this year," Gavitt said.

Providence is basically a man-for-man defensive club but has employed zones in several games.

"We're capable of giving State a good game though," noted Tranghese. "We're playing our best ball of the year right now and we seem to be peaking at the right time.

"I just wish that story hadn't gotten out. I heard Marvin when he gave the interview and he sure didn't say what he was quoted as saying."

"Bull!" Phil muttered. So, this was his man tonight! "Lefty didn't psyche me, and neither will you," he half-whispered to no one in particular or, maybe, it was the apparition of Marvelous Marvin Barnes who was at this moment talking to the press in front of his locker room . . . but only after they interviewed Phil Spence, he chuckled to himself. Finally, he picked up his bag and moved off toward his locker. The look in his eyes was one of absolute concentration and determination. "Well, Marvin Barnes, I'm gonna give it all I've got, man," he muttered. "I can promise you that."

David shook his head as he watched his teammate react to the quote that Coach had posted before yesterday's practice. He noticed that Tommy was also staring after Phil. "You know, Tommy, it's really hard for me to believe that Marvin said all those things that the papers reported."

"Yeah," Burleson nodded. "I just never thought about him being full of himself like that, you know, when we were all playing together in the World University Games."

"Just doesn't fit with him, with the guy who used to hang out with me and Quinn Buckner while we worked on my Alley-Oop shot back then." David paused, incredulous. "Naw, I don't believe it. I've got to believe that retraction story, but if it helps Phil get up for the game, that's great."

"Yeah, he's the one who'll be guarding him." Tommy Burleson looked down at his superstar teammate from the other side of the aisle between lockers. "And he sure looks ready."

"Yeah, he's got that same look he had in the championship game with Maryland when he shut McMillen down cold."

"Yeah, what was that Coach said? 'Don't let him breathe?"

"Something like that. And he didn't."

Outside the Providence dressing room, Marvin Barnes, in the flesh, talked with reporters before dressing for the biggest game of his career, a contest that had the ironic tinge of being played against friends.

"NC State deserves to be Number 1," he was reiterating. "Anytime a team can go through the Atlantic Coast Conference undefeated, they deserve it—and State's done that twice."

"What about all the controversy about your comments earlier in the week?"

"What about them?" Marvin Barnes shrugged his huge shoulders. "The paper printed a retraction, man." He paused, a little unsure as to whether to go further or not. "Look, we're all friends. David and Tommy and Coach Sloan and me were all together on the World University Games team last summer and we all respect each other."

He grinned. "In fact, I hope Tommy and David have good games tonight. I told them that when we saw each other during the Pitt game. I'm not wishing either one of them personal bad luck. I just hope they lose, that's all. I want them to look good . . . losing."

"Who will you be guarding tonight, Marvin, David Thompson or Tom Burleson?"

"I'm not sure yet. Coach has said maybe David, but Tom is their tallest guy and I'm our tallest guy. Either way, I don't think I'll be able to intimidate them. Tommy's just too tall for that. He'd probably laugh at me or something if I tried. If I guard him, I'll just try to do the best I can from letting him do what he wants. I hope that I'll be able to help persuade him to do things different from what he's used to."

"But what if you do guard Thompson?"

"We called him Superman last summer in Europe. There's nothing he can't do. No one stops him. It's ridiculous to think that a player as good as Thompson will be stopped by one man. If he gets stopped, he does it himself."

"What will it take to win tonight?"

"We can't play like 80 percent and even come close. Each member of this team would have to give his best game for us to win. But we all think that's possible or else we might as well give up now."

"Okay. Thanks, Marvin, and good luck tonight."

"There's a great story about NC State's David Thompson and Providence's Marvin Barnes when they played together last summer on the United States World University Games team. It seems they became good friends during the warm-up games tour." Billy Packer smiled into the television camera as he spoke. Sometimes it was hard to believe that C.D. Chesley and ABC were actually paying him to have so much fun. "One afternoon, the US team walked into the lavish sports complex in Bulgaria to inspect the basketball court for an exhibition that night. Marvin Barnes picked up a basketball and began blasting it through the rim as if he were testing the backboard out for strength. One of the USA team members yelled, 'Hey, Superman, come show this guy how it's done.'

"Norm Sloan, the assistant USA coach, described it earlier."

"Clad in sneakers and blue jeans, David Thompson and Marvin Barnes went one-on-one for 45 minutes. It was unbelievable. I just wish I'd had it on film. The rest of the squad stood on the side and watched them go at it. I've never seen anything like it. They were stuffing each other in the basket.

"And, who won?

"Superman. Well, maybe it was a draw," a sly-smiling Sloan allowed. "But it was the greatest two-man show I ever saw. They almost wore themselves out and caused us to almost lose the game that night."

The tape of Sloan ended. Packer faced the camera again. "That one didn't count." He paused for effect. "But tonight's confrontation between these two All-Americans will be for real as State and Providence meet in the NCAA Eastern Regionals first round in Reynolds Coliseum.

"The Wolfpack-Friars conflict promises to be one of the most interesting games of the NCAA regionals, because of the pitting of these two giants and two of the country's best teams: State, Number 1 and Providence Number 5."

"Providence coach Dave Gavitt had this to say."

"We're looking forward to playing the nation's number one team, but we're not too anxious to play Number 1 in their house.

"I don't think our kids are going to be awed by the people in this building, they're not afraid. But the thing is, State just plays better here."

"Providence is the defending champion of the eastern regionals but Gavitt is reluctant to say this club compares equally to last season's" Packer interjected.

"We came into the regionals last year with a team three years in the making. We come in this time with a team one-year in the making.

"You don't lose the rookie of the year in the pros--Ernie DiGregorio--and two other starters and not feel it. The secret to our success this year has been Marvin Barnes and Kevin Stacom playing great all year and adjusting to new players very well. We've been confident and loose and not fearful of anyone.

"We respect State, but we don't fear them."

"Stacom was Ernie D's running mate last year. And while DiGregorio usually stole the show with his ball handling and passing wizardry, Stacom had two outstanding games in the regionals at Charlotte."

"No, I haven't tried to take Ernie's role," said the soft-spoken Stacom. "I've kept my own style of moving without the ball, trying to create movement, keep something going.

"The team philosophy hasn't changed. We key on Marvin's rebounds, pass and fast break down court. We're not as fancy without Ernie but we've been just as effective."

"Stacom who, along with Barnes, was a teammate of Thompson and Burleson in the World Games last summer, said he was looking forward to tonight's meeting."

"State has to be a great team, but we feel we have a chance. I know how great Thompson and Burleson are and I know that it'll take a lot for us to win."

"Stacom figures he'll get some defensive time on Thompson."

"The only thing you can try to do is deny him the ball."

"Deny Superman?" Packer smiled at the camera again. "That might take the Best of Barnes and Stacom, plus Kryptonite."

"This game has been more like a street fight than a basketball game," Billy Packer opined early in the second half. "The first half was so rough, it appeared that the game might get out of hand. Officials Tom Richards of the Missouri Valley Conference and Buford Goddard of the Big Eight didn't call much of anything, Jim Thacker."

"Yes, Billy, but led by freshman Bob Cooper slashing inside on the bigger Pack, Providence pulled ahead by one, 54-53, early in the second period. But, State quickly regained the lead on buckets by Burleson and Rivers. The Friars matched baskets. The score stands now at 63-62 Providence."

"Okay, men," Coach Sloan addressed his team. "They're hiding their defenses well and mixing it up a lot. We haven't been able to figure any way to deal with it so far, so let's just go play our game. Run our offense, kill them on defense, and to hell with what they're doing."

After the time out, Tommy Burleson put back a rebound for two. Providence missed a jumper from Stacom. Providence fouled Monte Towe on the way down court, and he sank two foul shots. After Providence missed from the floor again, Thompson leaped and glided off the fast break to tap in another rebound off the glass over the top of his World Games teammate, Marvin Barnes.

"The Friars are making one more bid here, Billy, behind Marvin Barnes and Kevin Stacom. They have led a rally to cut the score to 73-69."

Mo Rivers hit the first of a one-and-one. He took a deep breath, bounced the ball a couple of times, and shot. "Left!" he shouted.

Tommy was up and over everyone for the rebound. He passed it out to Monte who glanced toward the bench, then slowed his dribble and waved everyone to spread out.

"And, Jim, it looks like Wolfpack coach Norm Sloan has ordered Monte Towe to start the spread offense here with 7:01 to go and the score 74-69.

Towe passed to Rivers. Mo didn't seem ready for the ball for some reason and Stacom snatched it and headed down court. Sloan plowed his right fist into his left palm. Then, a steal by Thompson to Towe to Burleson. Tommy muscled up against Barnes. As he posted up and backed Marvin underneath the basket, the State center pivoted to his right. His left elbow caught Barnes in the right eye as his jump hook banked home. "Sorry Marv," Burleson whispered as he passed by Barnes on his way back down court. Before the ball crossed the 10-second line, Rivers snatched it from Kevin Stacom and streaked for the easy lay-up. That boosted the margin from six to 10.

The margin mounted steadily on feeds underneath and lay-ups and the game was all but over with four minutes left. The Pack outscored Providence 18-9 after Coach Sloan ordered the tease.

With just seconds remaining, Towe made a blind pass over his head. Thompson snatched the ball above the rim and dropped it through for the final basket of the game.

The coliseum crowd went crazy!

Post-game press

"There he was, flying around, all over the place like Superman," Marvin Barnes moaned to the small group of sports writers clogging the entrance of the Providence dressing room. The menace that usually lurked in his dark eyes, that was his trademark, that had wilted many a mere mortal was faded if not extinguished. "Now you all know why we call him Superman. You just try not to let him get 50."

He shrugged, something he was, unfortunately, getting used to in this Eastern Regionals. "But how do you stop State? I mean you can't leave Tim Stoddard, Tommy Burleson, Mo Rivers, or Monte Towe alone, either.

"I mean, there's Towe, dribbling around two inches off the ground. And there's Thompson flying around--everywhere."

"Do you think you could have made a difference on Thompson?"

"I don't know. I couldn't have stopped him, but I might could have cut down on his backdoor play. I saw it all summer in games and when he and Quinn Buckner from Indiana worked on it in practice.

He shrugged yet again and almost smiled. "But if I had taken Thompson, who would've guarded Burleson? He was so tough. He's going to make a good pro."

In the Wolfpack locker room, a horde of reporters and television cameras surrounded Superman. "David, you had 24 points by intermission. What about that?"

"Everybody was not as sharp as usual in the first half, so I concentrated on getting open more."

"Was this your best game?"

"I think I've played better."

"When?"

"In both regular season Maryland games, I believe."

"Was this game more physical than most?"

"There was a lot of contact. Though Marvin and Kevin are friends, you give your all. And, this is the NCAA Tournament, you know. There was a lot of unavoidable contact."

In another corner of the locker room, Mo Rivers talked about disappointment and defense. "Yeah, I know I was 3 for 16. At the half, it was really on my mind. I knew I missed some wide-open shots. But, the ball just didn't seem to want to drop for anybody.

"So, I tried to apply more defensive pressure in the second half. I think everybody tried to compensate for bad shooting by playing even tougher defense. I know I felt like if I worked real hard on defense hoping get an easier shot. So, when the game got close in the second half, I started looking for the steal. Somebody had to do something at that point. I was lucky to come up with a couple of steals."

"We knew their point guard, Bello, was a real good ball handler. Kevin Stacom is more of a shooter than a dribbler though. We felt that we could make him turn and then trap him."

"What about losing the ball the first time down the court after Coach Sloan called for the 'tease?'"

"I could see it in the papers tomorrow morning," Norm Sloan interrupted as he walked up and put his arm around his shooting guard. "Sloan Orders Tease and Blows Lead."

"Oh, it didn't bother me, Coach. After my turnover, I felt they couldn't get the ball again unless they fouled again. I knew we couldn't change our game plan because of one turnover.

"But it is kinda bad when the shooting guard can't shoot, you know?" He wagged his head almost as if he were still in a state of disbelief that he shot so poorly for an entire game.

"Did the cracked nose you suffered in the ACC finals against Maryland effect your shooting tonight, Mo?"

"It's not slowing me down any. The coaches told me to be a little more careful and try not to hurt it any more this late in the season. I just try to forget it. About the only time it really bothers me is when I try to rebound. The thought that an elbow could dislocate it does come to mind."

"I just hope he has to worry about that nose for another three games," Tim Stoddard chuckled. We want another shot at UCLA. We think we are just as good as they are. Maybe a little better. We want to win this thing. Beat UCLA and win the national title."

"What about your game plan--yours and Phil Spence's--on how to guard Marvin Barnes? Was it a success?"

"The one goal we both had was to play Marvin as tenaciously as possible. I felt we did about as much as we could. We tried not to let him get the ball. We wanted him to take the ball outside. And he scored and rebounded a lot less than his averages."

* * * * *

Friday morning, the Pittsburgh Panthers were hustling through a light workout and practice as a cluster of reporters looked on. "Coach Ridl, the consensus is that NC State will win the regionals tomorrow. How do *you* assess your chances?"

"If we shoot 80 percent and State shoots 10 percent, I think the game will be close," Panther Head Coach Buzz Ridl chuckled as he scooped up a stray ball and tossed it back onto the court.

"When you play a team like State, there's only so much you can cover on defense. There's not much you can do at the height Thompson reaches.

" But, come what may, we're going to stick with basically what got us here. We'll employ our system of changing defenses and use the running offense that helped us get 22 straight wins this season."

As Bill Knight trotted up beside the coach, another reporter shot a question at him. "You sure got your game back with a vengeance yesterday with 34 points against Furman. What do you think about the game with NC State tomorrow?"

"We've got nothing to lose," the 6-7 senior responded immediately with a slight smile. "We were not even supposed to be here. There's everything to gain for us."

"But, to win, you have to somehow stop the Pack. How?"

"Well, for one thing, we can't let Thompson go wild like he did the other night. Of course, he's still going to get his 25 or so.

"Also, the main thing we need to do is stop Tommy Burleson. He can get 40 points and 25 rebounds against us if we don't keep him off the boards. To compensate for their height, we'll have to change our defense and try to keep them from lobbing the ball inside. That Alley-Oop play looks impossible to stop.

"But we'll see," he shot over his shoulder as he headed back onto the floor.

Afternoon practice was over. Wolfpack players wandered around the locker room as if they had nowhere to go, nothing to do but wait for tomorrow's game. Some nursed bruises and bumps from Thursday's brawl with Providence. But, they didn't mind. Rough games were a part of tournament basketball. You just had to live with that reality.

Monte Towe sprawled on a training table. A radiant heat lamp baked away at his aches. "I'm all right," he quipped in response to a reporters query about his injuries. "And, anyway, we've come too far to take anybody lightly. Anybody that gets this far can beat you."

"Coach Sloan," another reporter interjected as Norman Sloan stopped at the table to see how his point guard was doing. "Despite what your bruised and battered point guard says, just about everybody concedes that the Wolfpack will win the Eastern Regionals tomorrow afternoon."

"I'll bet Buzz Ridl hasn't conceded to us yet," Sloan interrupted with a laugh.

"No, he hasn't. But, aren't you concerned about the Wolfpack looking ahead to next week's NCAA finals in Greensboro and, maybe, overlooking the Pittsburgh Panthers?"

Norman smiled patiently. He knew this kind of question was coming. He just didn't understand why the sports writers kept asking him that same kind of question all season long. First, it was "aren't you overlooking your entire opening schedule to focus on UCLA?" Then it was "aren't you overlooking Clemson with Maryland and Super Sunday coming up?" Or, in the ACC tournament, "Do you think your team is looking past Virginia to the semi-finals of the tournament?" Now they were supposedly overlooking the Panthers.

"Well, guys, I don't want to disappoint you or anything like that, but Pitt has one of the finest defenses in the country. They call it their 'amoebae defense.' It is really tough.

"Also, I hear that their All-American, Bill Knight, says that they have nothing to lose because they weren't expected to get this far. That makes the Pittsburgh Panthers very dangerous.

"We're in for the battle of our lives, and we know it. I don't think anybody on our team is looking at anybody but Pitt. If we are, we'll be at home next week watching ***them*** on TV from Greensboro."

12
The Spirit of '76

"Fifteen stitches." Dr. Jim finished off the last stitch. "That was a pretty good gash, David. I'd say it beat the one you gave yourself when you banged your head against your locker by a good margin. Remember that? When you were a freshman after losing the Carolina game?"

"Yeah, Dr. Jim. I do remember that. Coach Sloan got all upset when he heard about it."

"Yep. He was scared he'd lost you before he ever really got you, you know?"

David nodded.

Nurse Kelly cleaned up and dressed the wound, then wrapped a white bandage around his head.

"Well, it's still a strange scene here at William Neal Reynolds Coliseum. The fans just don't seem to know how to act. Everyone is worried about David Thompson, the All-Everything Junior forward for North Carolina State. So the typical cheering on of a crowd favorite like State seems very subdued, hesitant, almost as if the fans feel it would be somehow irreverent to cheer too loudly or for too long."

"That's you Ausley's talking about, young man."

"Yes, sir. I know."

"You feeling okay, though?"

"Yes, Doctor Jim."

"You're sure?"

"Yes, sir."

"Dr. Hara says you seem to be fine, hard as it is to believe, only a mild concussion." Dr. Manley wagged his salt-and-peppering head. "He says you want to go back to the game. Is that right?"

"Yes, sir!"

"Why?"

"It's good for the fans, and the team to see I'm really okay, and . . . ."

"Yes? And?"

"And I'd really like to see the rest of the game, Dr. Jim, you know?"

"Yes, I know. So would I, David. So would I," Doctor Jim chuckled. "Okay, giant-slayer. Let's take it easy getting up and walking to the ambulance. I'll escort you back to the bench personally," he winked, "just so there's no foul up."

"Thanks, Dr. Jim. Thanks a lot."

"Okay, David. Let's go tell your Mom and Dad. They're worried sick about you."

* * * * *

" Burleson's at the free throw line. There's a time out called by the officials. The score is 78-57 as the teams walk off the floor with 6:51 left in the second half. This is Wally Ausley for the Wolfpack Sports Network. We'll be right back."

With a white bandage wrapped around his head, a single swatch of blood visible, David looked like the fife player in *The Spirit of '76*. A fan spotted David and stood clapping her hands over her head, tears gushing down her flushed freckled cheeks, shouting "David! David! David!" as Dr. Jim ushered him into full view of the Coliseum crowd.

"See what I told you, Dr. Jim." David pointed toward the scoreboard hanging from the coliseum ceiling and winked at his doctor as they entered the arena just beyond press row on the sideline. "The guys are creaming Pittsburgh!"

As more fans became aware of him, they followed the first woman's lead and began to stand and applaud and weep until everyone in the building was standing and applauding and crying, stamping their feet and shouting "David! David! David!" David wept openly while Dr. Jim led him onto the court and across to the bench. He embraced Monte, then Tim and, finally, Phil.

"I'm so sorry, man. So sorry. I didn't mean . . . ."

David looked at Phil Spence's face contorted with fear and guilt and relief all at the same time. "It wasn't your fault Phil. It wasn't anybody's fault, unless, maybe, it was mine." Coach Sloan put his arm around David's shoulders and sat down next to him on the bench.

With 1:32 left, Phil left the game for good. He and David embraced again. Again, the Coliseum crowd thundered to its feet in another standing ovation. The game ended with David and Phil on the bench cheering their teammates on to a 100-72 mauling of Pittsburgh.

Atop the sturdy shoulders of Tim Stoddard and Phil Spence, one from Indiana and one from Raleigh, David cut down the net at the end of the court where, earlier, he had fallen. Sure, they had cut down the nets in Greensboro, but they hadn't cut down the nets here, at home, in the House that Everett Case Built.

And, how appropriate their celebration was since cutting down the nets was an Old Gray Fox tradition. During his tenure at Frankfort, Indiana high school, the Old Gray Fox had been the first to dramatize pre-game introductions by darkening the arena and shining a spotlight on the players as they were announced. He was, also, the first to have his players cut down the nets in celebration of an important victory the same way his teams at Frankfort High School had done after winning state championships in 1925, 1929, 1936 & 1939.

David stared at the spot where his head had struck just hours before when he fell to the Coliseum floor in The House that Case Built. Draped around his neck was the net he had cut down from the hoop over where he had fallen because of a tradition that Case built.

Now, after two seasons of happiness and heartbreak and because of a tradition of winning and of excellence that the Old Gray Fox had instilled in North Carolina State University starting way back in 1946, Monte, then Tommy, and finally Coach Sloan were lifted up by the team to snip at the nets.

Hey! They were finally Eastern Regional Champs!

NC State Statistics
Eastern Regionals 1974

PLAYER	G	FG	FT	RB	PF	PTS
David Thompson	2	19-33	10-13	12	2	48
Tommy Burleson	2	16-38	10-13	36	7	42
Monte Towe	2	11-31	12-13	8	5	34
Morris Rivers	2	11-28	6-10	11	5	28
Phil Spence	2	5-12	2-3	16	5	12
Greg Hawkins	1	1-4	5-6	1	2	7
Steve Nuce	2	2-6	6-6	6	4	10
Tim Stoddard	2	4-15	1-2	9	7	9
Bill Lake	1	0-0	2-2	0	0	2
Mark Moeller	2	0-0	0-0	2	0	0
Dwight Johnson	1	0-0	0-0	0	0	0
Craig Kuszmaul	2	0-0	0-0	0	0	0
Bruce Dayhuff	2	0-0	0-0	0	0	0
Mike Buurma	2	0-0	0-0	0	0	0
TOTALS: NCSU	2	69-167	54-68	118	55	192

NCSU	OPPONENT	High Scorer	Top Rebounder	Attendance
92	Providence 78	Thompson 40	Burleson 24	12,400
100	Pittsburgh 72	Burleson 26	Spence 14	12,400

ALL-TOURNAMENT TEAM
David Thompson, NC State (Unanimous)
Tommy Burleson, NC State (Unanimous)
Bill Knight, Pittsburgh
Monte Towe, NC State
Bruce Grimm, Furman

OUTSTANDING PLAYER: (tie)   David Thompson, NC State
                                 Tommy Burleson, NC State

[71 members of the media voting]

Post Game Press

"Mrs. Thompson. Nick Pond. WRAL-TV Sports. Would you mind taking a few minutes with us?"

Ida Thompson looked up at the tall dark-haired man. He was big enough that he probably was a basketball player like her David. He had a nice smile. She recognized him from the television. She'd talk to him, but just for a minute. "Okay, young man. Vellie, come over here. This young man wants to talk to us about David."

Vellie shuffled to his wife's side, squinting in the glare of the television lights. The tall dark-haired man with the microphone shook his hand.

"Mr. Thompson. Nick Pond. WRAL-TV Sports. Good to see you, sir."

"Thank you."

"What went through your mind, Mr. Thompson when your youngest son's head hit the coliseum floor during the game today?"

"It ran through my mind that his neck might be broken. He hit so hard and just lay there on the floor unconscious."

"Has David ever been hurt like this before?"

"No. This is, by far, the most serious injury David has ever suffered on the basketball floor or anywhere else for that matter. It was pretty scary."

"It sure scared me to death."

"What were you thinking, Mrs. Thompson?"

"I thought he was hurt badly. I was afraid he was, maybe dead."

"And him coming back like he did. And, the way the crowd here at the coliseum reacted to his return. Wasn't that something special?"

"Oh, yes, it was. I remember David said in the ambulance that he didn't even want to go to the hospital. He asked me what happened because he couldn't remember. I told him he jumped up high and fell."

"Is David really all right, Mrs. Thompson?"
"Yes. I believe he is. Don't you, Vellie?"
"I do. And, the doctors say he is."
"But, he's scheduled to be checked by the doctors again in the morning before he starts back to classes on Monday."
"And he's already been given permission to return to practice."
"And what about the big game against UCLA next Saturday?"
"Right now he has the green light to play Saturday against UCLA in the national semi-finals."
"Thank you, Vellie and Ida Thompson. The concerned parents of the great David Thompson who suffered a horrific fall earlier today during the Pack's rout of Pittsburgh. According to his parents, Vellie and Ida Thompson, their son is fine now and will likely play against Walton and the Bruin clan on Saturday.
"This is Nick Pond reporting for WRAL-TV from William Neal Reynolds Coliseum in Raleigh."

* * * * *

Thirty-three turnovers. If anyone had told him that his team would have 33 turnovers in one tournament game, he wouldn't have believed them. Not be able to hit a shot. Okay. They'd done that. Lazy defense. Yes. They'd done that. Poor free throw shooting. Sure, they'd done that too. But, this team usually took care of the ball. So, the Tar Heels would fly back to Chapel Hill tonight. Purdue, the Wizard of Westwood's old school, would continue in the NIT.

Several fans' radios interrupted Dean Smith's thoughts, blaring out the news of David Thompson's miracle recovery and his return to a tearful and thundering standing ovation just as Dean and his defeated Tar Heels left the Madison Square Garden court.

He could hear one announcer saying that it was the most touching moment he had ever experienced in all his years of covering sports. He believed the announcer had actually used the word poignant much to his surprise.

Dean could well imagine the emotion that must have swept through William Neal Reynolds Coliseum. David was revered there and around the world. He had been since his recruiting days. Ah, but now, to come back after such a spectacular fall with little injury and your team still carry the day. It must have been nothing short of magnificent, he mused. Simple sports moment perfection.

To accomplish such miracles was quintessential David Thompson. Dean chuckled to himself as he entered the gloomy Tar Heel locker room in Madison Square Garden. It was hard to be light when you'd lost, but, somehow, it seemed okay to laugh a little once he knew David was going to be okay.

13
A Fresh Start, Man

FINAL UPI "National Championship" Poll

1	North Carolina St. (17) 26–1	Norm Sloan
2	UCLA (13) 23–3	John Wooden
3	Notre Dame (3) 25–2	Digger Phelps
4	Maryland 23–5	Lefty Driesell
5	Marquette 23–4	Al McGuire
6	Providence 26–3	Dave Gavitt
7	Vanderbilt 23–3	Johnny Orr
8	North Carolina 22-5	Dean Smith
9	Indiana 20–4	Bobby Knight
10	Kansas 21–5	Ted Owens

"I'd watch David Thompson on TV and say, 'Oh man, there'll never be another player like that.' "

Michael Jordan

Wednesday, March 20, 1974. David, dressed in his practice uniform, stood alone in the semi-darkness of William Neal Reynolds Coliseum just before the doors were to be opened for the fans to come in and watch practice. None of the overhead lights was on yet. He stared at the basketball floor where he fell. Surprisingly, nothing seemed to be going through his head. His mind seemed to be like a blank just the way his memory of the fall was a blank. He recalled being undercut and the refs not calling it. He remembered sprinting off down the court chasing after his man. He remembered leaping into the air and suddenly lurching. Then, nothing. But, he knew it had happened. His parents, Coach, the doctors had all told him about it. So had his teammates. But, he still couldn't seem to recall anything about it on his own, even after sneaking a look at the replay of the fall last night with Monte.

"They're expecting a mob to see you work out today, to see if you're really all right."

David nearly did one of his 42-inch vertical leaps out of his sneakers at the unexpected sound of Monte's voice behind him. It echoed off the ceiling and walls of the empty coliseum even though he spoke quietly.

"Yeah, the fans are going to want to see, I guess."

"Yeah, everybody wants to know: How's David? That's the question on everyone's mind, you know? Nobody's believing you could take that kind of fall—you saw it—and end up with just a minor concussion and a few stitches."

The overhead lights glared, suddenly erasing the semi-darkness. People began filing into the coliseum seats. Teammates appeared one by one on the floor, tossing basketballs and launching shots at the opposite basket giving him and Monte some space.

"Yes. But, David, you can make a statement today, with this practice." Monte continued. "I mean look at all these people coming in now. Reminds me of our first year when all the kids used to come out to see us play. Remember? These stands would be full by tip off time of our freshman games."

"Now, the seats are filling up just to watch us practice."

"And to see that you're okay. So, you've got to show them the answer to their question: 'How is David?' because they do really care about you as a person, not just David Thompson the basketball player."

"Yeah. I guess I knew that when I walked back in here Saturday with Dr. Jim and everybody stood up. I was so . . . ."

"Overwhelmed?"

"Yeah, that's it. Overwhelmed. I just knew then that we'd accomplished something, Monte. Something special."

"You're right, David. And, it all started that first day our freshman year. Remember?"

"How could I forget?" David stopped, then began to laugh. "I guess it was pretty simple to start with, wasn't it?"

"Yeah. You thought I was somebody's little brother or something."

"Then you just came up to me and said . . . ."

"Yeah, I said, 'Hi, I'm Monte Towe.'"

"And I said, 'David Thompson.'"

"We shook hands."

"And, as they say, the rest is history," David chuckled.

"Yeah. And, I guess it's lucky that I didn't focus only on baseball and you didn't decide to become the next Bob Hayes."

Forty-five minutes later, Coach Sloan barked, "Okay, guys, hit the showers!" As the players trotted off the floor, David suddenly realized that he still had a ball in his hands. He remembered what his friend Monte had said earlier. The fans just wanted to see that he was okay. They'd been putting on dunk drills all afternoon, hadn't they? So? He smiled. What did he have to lose? He turned and lofted a jumper from mid-court. The ball arched for the basket. Nothing but net.

The 5,000 plus fans committed pandemonium.

David winked at Monte. "A fresh start, man."

Fans poured out of the practice session screaming about David's swish from half-court. They had already forgotten about the half dozen or so acrobatic dunks during the practice, all just a few days after the injury against Pittsburgh.

"That half-court shot was just so David!"

"He's definitely back and ready to play."

"Too bad they don't have instant replays of practice."

So, tomorrow they would be on their way to Greensboro, a team that was being called a "circus team with a midget, a giant and a high-wire artist." Burleson, the "Newland Needle," was the 7-foot-4 "giant" center from the mountains. Thompson, 6-4, was the acrobat and "high wire artist." The standing joke was that he could leap, grab a quarter off the top of a backboard, and leave change. And, Towe, the 5-7 "midget" point guard from Indiana, was the team's glue.

The Pack, which had gone 55-1 over two seasons, was going to run head-on into the Walton Gang, once again—the UCLA team of center Bill Walton and forwards Keith Wilkes and David Myers, the team that represented that one loss in two years. This time it would be in Greensboro. This time they had to do something about that.

That night the team would normally have crowded into 206 Sullivan—David's and Biff Nicholls' room—to watch TV and just hang out together. Placed neatly on the door of their dorm room were campaign buttons from elections in which David played a role of some sort. There were also color photos of his favorite athletes (Larry Brown, Vida Blue, Rollie Fingers, Gus Johnson, and Dave DeBusschere) and other photos of Sly and the Family Stone, the Temptations, and the Isley Brothers. At the top of the door, however, was a headline clipping out of the campus newspaper, the "Technician" that read:

STATE PLACED ON PROBATION FOR RECRUITING VIOLATIONS.

Instead, tonight, they crowded into a motel room under a very tight curfew watching a special on the NCAA tournament.

"We felt humiliated about the first UCLA game." Monte's voice reverberated from the television.

"We are the best team in the country," David's voice followed. "We love each other as people and respect each other as ballplayers."

"The Wolfpack was on probation last year for NCAA recruiting violations," the television announcer continued. "Jerry Hunt, a Freshman from the same hometown as you, David—Shelby, North Carolina—and one of your closest personal friends, said that you 'were troubled by it all' since the news first came out in October of 1972, but at the same time you were 'unaltered by the heat of conflict.' Jerry further stated: that 'If you didn't know him like I know him, you would never have known the difference.'

"What do you have to say about your friend's comments?"

"Jerry's probably right about all that. There were sure times when I even wondered if my coming here was worth it all. I guess if I had to do it over again, though, I would make the same decision and without much reservation."

"Here comes David's dorm room door thing, guys," Monte chuckled.

On the screen, David was speaking to the camera. "Even now I have the headline taped on my dorm room door that says: STATE PLACED ON PROBATION FOR RECRUITING VIOLATIONS. Every time I walk through that door it is a reminder for me to play that much harder every time I take the court. I owe that to the fans and to my teammates."

Next, John Wooden glowered straight into the camera as he spoke. "I want North Carolina State to remember that 18 points from last time. Let them think about who has the psychological advantage."

"Yeah, right!" Monte shouted. They all laughed at the old guy on the television screen trying to play with their minds. "He only wishes."

"Yeah," Tim chuckled. "And we've had Lefty trying to play with our minds and he's the greatest at that stuff."

"Wooden could use a few of The Preacher Man's sermons," Phil added.

"That's right. I want North Carolina State to remember that we beat them by 18 on a neutral court," Wooden reiterated. "I want them to remember that Walton was ready for them last time, and he'll be ready for them this time. That's something for them to think about."

"Sure. We're shaking here," Tim belly-laughed as he poked Monte, who slumped next to him on the couch, in the ribs.

"We were too anxious in that first game. We're more versatile than UCLA," Sloan said to the television audience. "We're playing at maximum efficiency. We have something left to prove. And, we still have Thompson. I like the odds."

Now, there were just three other teams left. Marquette. Kansas. And, UCLA. Along with the Pack, they comprised the Final Four. The guys in the motel room substitute for 206 Sullivan all looked at each other and yelled with their thumbs up. They liked the odds too.

14
David & Goliath

"A month ago North Carolina State got my vote to end the dynasty, to render it senseless. Nothing has changed since then. The Wolfpack to win it all."
Larry Donald, The Basketball Weekly,
March 27, 1974

"UCLA because even a team as blasé as the Bruins have become can get up for national championship games. Whoever plays in the championship game against them will not have much chance. In this case the NC State-UCLA game will be the championship match."
Rob Sieb, The Basketball Weekly, March 27, 1974

"Emotionally I would go with North Carolina State. The injury to David Thompson is a major factor of the emotion. How UCLA would really act in North Carolina Country will be a real test of its championship ability. A slim vote for North Carolina State."
Jim Haughton, The Basketball Weekly, March 27, 1974

"UCLA to win. The Bruins will be ready to play this key game against North Carolina State. Bill Walton is the main factor to their games. His knowledge that he has only two college games left will provide the incentive for a superb effort. He doesn't want to end his career without a championship. The availability of David Thompson is still in doubt, and UCLA is a better balanced team. UCLA will play Marquette in the finals and win."
Tim Staudt, The Basketball Weekly, March 27, 1974

"At any rate, all four teams have a chance at the title, a refreshing situation for the NCAA in recent years. But UCLA is UCLA and the team's incentive for victory may be even greater than normal. After all, the Wizard my be coming down off the mountain."
Barry McDermott, Sports Illustrated, March 25, 1974

"I won't believe it. It just doesn't fit into history."
Andre McCarter discussing possibility of UCLA's losing to N. C. State

The guys had left. Sitting in the motel room alone, David Thompson knew that the David in the *Bible* didn't get a second shot at Goliath. Then, again, he didn't need one. His slingshot had worked right the first time, during the regular season so to speak, and there was no championship tournament to be played later. That David saved Israel from the domination of the Philistines.

However, NC State's Goliath was of a different sort. He, too, was a giant: a 6'11" center, towering over most players on the basketball court. David could have a second shot at this red haired Goliath from UCLA although his own slingshot didn't perform so well the first time during the regular season. Why did he get a second chance? Because there *was* a championship tournament to be played later, and this *was* it. What happened during the regular season didn't matter anymore—whether you beat a particular team or you didn't—because it was the way of the NCAA college basketball tournament that as long as you win, you get to keep on playing until, finally, there is one team left: the NCAA Champion.

They were just two games away from that championship now, and David was determined that his team would be the one team left standing at the end. He could not let them down again like he had done in that first game against Carolina when they were freshmen and again when they played UCLA last December. This would be the third strike, and he wasn't going to strike out. He was determined that his slingshot was going to work just fine this time, and he would slay that Goliath from UCLA and save the championship for his team, for his fans who were no longer just from Wolfpack and ACC country but, hard as it was for him to understand, from all over the world.

* * * * *

North Carolina Governor Jim Holshouser proclaimed Saturday, March 23, 1974 to be "Wolfpack basketball day."

* * * * *

"Coach Sloan, the Bruins' Tommy Curtis called your first meeting 'A real whippin'.' But, what's even more unusual is John Wooden and his comments. He's sounding more like The Preacherman than the Wizard, isn't he?"

In between sneaking almost motherly glances at David's patched head, Coach Sloan responded somewhat offhandedly: "I have to say that I am really surprised at some of John's 'un-Woodenlike' remarks such as: 'I want State to dwell on that 18-point margin.' I mean, really?"

State Forward Tim Stoddard was more to the point as he yelled over his coach's shoulder. "Yeah, that's not too smart, you know. We know they aren't 18 points better than us," he said, "but what's more important is that *they* know it, too!"

Television Announcer: "The magnitude of the UCLA-North Carolina State rematch has not gone undetected by Marquette's Al McGuire or Ted Owens of Kansas, the antagonists in the *other* semifinal game today. At a small party on Friday evening attended by all the competing coaches except Sloan, who was off somewhere undoubtedly selecting his wardrobe for today's game, McGuire said he was just glad to play in the 'B class division' while Owens expressed pleasure at coaching in the 'preliminary.'

"The main attraction semifinal will be a game for the history books. Not only does it bring together the Number 1 and Number 2 teams in the land, but its main match-ups include four of the finest players in the sport—Burleson vs. Walton and Thompson vs. Keith Wilkes—and there is no hiding the bad blood that remains from their first meeting back in the snows of St. Louis when UCLA blew out NC State 84-66."

You could almost hear strains of The Band's song *The Weight* in the background as Bill "Big Red" Walton stepped off the plane in Greensboro with sandals on his feet and a bag of fruit in his hand. Goliath and his teammates, the LA Philistines, headed immediately and without comment to check into their hotel and, later, to hold a practice behind closed doors.

"Bill Walton is friendly, funny, thoughtful, intelligent, talkative, concerned, altruistic, sincere, open, idealistic. Bill Walton is moody, secretive, confused, uncommunicative, introverted, naïve, immature.

"These are some of the words used to describe Walton, the man. On Walton, the athlete, there's no such disparity. UCLA's gangling, red-haired center is a non-pareil. At 21, he possesses skills so fair that in the pros he'd be 'The Franchise' anywhere. Soon, he must decide whether to accept a professional offer likely to make him several times a millionaire. The oddity is that he isn't sure he'll say yes. Friends say he's truly undecided.

He prefers the simply life.

"What will you do when you graduate next month?"

"I'm gonna put on my backpack and go. I don't know where, but I have to think about things," he told an interviewer in a rare interview opportunity. "I want to play, because I like basketball a lot. But I won't play in cold weather cities, and I'll only play as long as it's still fun."

Walton has at times downgraded the importance of his game. "What do I do that's so important, put a round ball in a basket?" Or "Let's face it, on a world scale, basketball doesn't mean much."

How does he rationalize such comments in the light of the probability he will make the game his occupation?

"I suppose if I look at it logically, I can't. I suppose it's B.S. I'll probably play because the pros play the best basketball, and because basketball's maybe the thing I do best.

"I'm not sure it will make me happy, though."

He has said money means little to him. He turned down millions of dollars when he was a junior. "If they pay me what they're talking about, it's obvious I'm going to become a millionaire. Hell, I couldn't spend that much money in a lifetime. I'll tell you one thing. I won't invest it in United Fruit Company.

"I'm a socialist, and I believe wealth should be spread around. I don't have a specific program yet but I'm going to put it where it can do some good . . . do something important."

"What is important to Bill Walton?"

"Having fun. Enjoying life. Helping others. Being myself. Time, that's so important. That's why when the season's over I have to get away. That's why I sometimes wish I'd been blessed in something other than basketball. That's why I may not turn pro at all."

"What then?"

"I don't know. Maybe work on a teaching credential. I'd love to teach. Or maybe put out forest fires. That would be worthwhile."

Walton has had three years as the most publicized player on the most publicized team in college sports. He's won the Sullivan Award and a trunk full of others. He's a sure three-time all-American.

"But, throughout, he has been a reluctant superstar. He has recoiled from the limelight, actively avoided public contact for reasons beyond modesty. First, he genuinely prized his privacy. Second, though it may be an aberration to hold that average players should get as much attention as great players, he sincerely believes they should and ducks publicity on grounds it should be shared equally among his peers.

Thus, interviews with Walton have been rare, this year more than ever, even though friends say that with maturity Walton is taking a more balanced view of the world. He's a history major with a B average. He likes geography, too, and reads a lot about it at his apartment near the campus. It is one large room, a kitchen and a bath.

There he does "some cooking and not too much cleaning."

Last summer he went to school at Sonoma State College, bicycling the 500 or so miles. The summer before that he hitchhiked through the U.S. and Canada. He's an outdoorsy person. "I like to learn from school, but I don't like being cooped up.

"That's why I'm glad school's almost over for me. I had a good time, learned a little about a lot of different things, and I'm sorry to see it end. But it's time to move on."

After the J.D. Salingers of college sport slipped into their usual isolation act for the remainder of the weekend, Andre McCarter did emerge at one point on Sunday afternoon to talk to the press. In responding to a question about the possibility of UCLA's losing, he said, "I won't believe it. It just doesn't fit into history."

Eighty miles away the Wolfpack worked out on its home court in Raleigh before a crowd of 6,000 and then retired to their motel for the night.

As Sly & the Family Stone put it: "Different strokes for different folks."

2 UCLA v # 1 NCSU
March 23, 1974

With all the interest focused on the UCLA-NC State match-up, the other semifinalists received very limited attention. Marquette and Kansas had struggled to win the Mideast and Midwest regionals, respectively, but their meeting provoked mostly yawns in North Carolina and around the country. Kansas coach Ted Owens jokingly referred to the first semifinal as the "preliminary" game.

And after his Marquette team, which he personally rated only seventh best in the country, had scored a humdrum 64-51 victory over the Jayhawks, Warriors coach Al McGuire decided not to waste either his or the media's time.

"We'll answer a few questions," Al McGuire announced, "and then you guys can go watch the championship game between UCLA and North Carolina State."

The UCLA vs. NCSU game for the right to play in the finals against Marquette was, more importantly, the grudge game for the Walton gang and Thompson and company. This time it was for the money, so to speak.

David twirled the basketball between his hands, hands that seemed so delicate to be so large and so strong. He put the ball on the floor for one dribble and lofted a fade away jumper toward the rim.

Everyone told him, all his life, that when he went up to the plate he was just supposed to meet the ball solidly and try to get a base hit. Never was he to go to the plate thinking "home run." The reality, however, was quite the opposite as David had found out through experience.

The ball scorched the bottom of the net. Chip Sloan tossed it back to him. David began to move with the ball toward the baseline. He saw that the area was clear of players. Suddenly he launched toward the basket.

It was only those who could go up to the plate when a home run was needed and know that he had to hit a home run and then hit a home run that would ever be great. That was what it all boiled down to, being able to go to the free throw line knowing that you have to make both of them to win the game. No more mind games, trying to convince yourself that these free throws are no different for all the other free throws you've ever had. These free throws are *not* just like any other free throws. These free throws are for all the marbles. You win or lose with them and you accept that. Just like going up to bat knowing that the only way you can assure a win is with a home run.

David kissed the ball off the glass and into the basket without violating the cone. Just like not being able to dunk, you accepted your reality. You used that personal pressure to up your level of play. You hit the home run. You sank the two free throws. You found the telephone booth. That was what it was all about, wasn't it? Meeting the challenge face to face, recognizing it, and overcoming it. Molding the destiny of the game with big plays at important times during the contest.

Oh, but a lot of responsibility went along with that kind of thinking. If you felt personally that you should make the difference, then what happened when you couldn't pull it off? You felt guilty, like you let the team down, let you coach down, let your family and friends down, let yourself down. That's hard to take. It was much easier to just shake it off and blame the loss or the failure on the team or the officiating or something, but people like him knew that wasn't it at all. David realized with a certain angst that when the team lost it was because he was unable to find a telephone booth to change in when the Wolfpack needed their Superman.

The first time he played against Carolina, his freshmen team lost. Then, they lost to UCLA last December ending a 29-game winning streak, 30 if you counted the Athletes in Action game, 56 if you counted the rest of his freshman year, and 78 including all of the World University Games contests. The only two losses he'd suffered during his college career. Both times, he had let his team lose. He would not let that happen again. He would step it up when and where it was necessary for him to do so. He would do what he was supposed to do, what he'd been recruited to do. He would find a telephone booth in time.

"The first time the ACC and UCLA tangled was in 1962," Billy Packer commented. "Wake Forest was 22-9, and they went on to win the ACC and the eastern regionals. In the final four, Wake took third with a win over UCLA.

"In 1968, with a 26-6 record, Carolina won the ACC, a second regional, and reached the national finals, losing to UCLA.

"Last December, Lefty Driesell's Maryland Terrapins lost by just one point to John Wooden's UCLA Bruins.

"And, finally, NC State lost to UCLA also in December in St. Louis."

"So, thus far, the only ACC team to beat UCLA is your alma mater, Billy, and UCLA's record against the ACC is 3 to 1."

The Wizard's magic sliver cross nestled in the left trouser pocket of his green suit, and UCLA rushed to a 49-38 lead early in the second half. School certainly seemed to be out again for NC State when they missed yet another shot. Walton controlled the defensive rebound, held it high overhead, and looked up court.

Then, from behind, his 7'4" rival Tom Burleson darted in front of him and plucked the ball out of Walton's hands. Burleson quickly dropped it in the basket for two. As Walton ran back on offense he snarled at Burleson, swearing vengeance.

UCLA pushed ahead to yet another big margin, 57-46, with 11 minutes to go. But State was not through this time, either. As Towe cracked the whip, tearing down the lane or firing football-type passes from midcourt, the Pack came back. Scoring 10 straight points, it closed to 57-56, then to 61-60, and grabbed the lead at 63-61 when Thompson vanished into the rafters again with still another Alley-Oop. He sank a free throw for a three-point play.

With 51 seconds remaining and the score tied at 65, Walton missed a hook and Burleson rebounded. After a State delay offense, the burly Stoddard missed an open corner shot with five seconds left that would have won the game in regulation.

In the overtime, it was State's game to win after Stoddard stole a pass from Greg Lee, enabling the Wolfpack to hold the ball once more. Thompson drove for the payoff with 10 seconds to go. Instead of shooting himself, however, he passed off to Burleson whose short spin toss bounced off the rim.

"Doesn't anybody want to win this thing?" Billy Packer questioned, shaking his head.

"If it comes to that situation again, either me or you have got to take that shot," Monte yelled into David's ear.

David laughed it off.

Monte didn't. With a third chance to win, he would make sure that David had the ball and took the shot.

UCLA took over in the second overtime, after Walton and Wilkes canned baskets that put the Bruins into a 74-67 lead with 3:27 remaining.

The Pack pressed tighter, opening up the floor and forcing turnovers. They scored and got every offensive rebound they needed to score some more. Just like that, UCLA's lead was down to one.

After Meyers missed a critical one-and-one with 1:16 on the clock, David drove the lane. Looking desperately for that phone booth he knew he needed now, Number 44 leaped high into the air and banked in a jump shot from the left side over Wilkes. The Wolfpack led 76-75.

The basketball world held its breath.

Moments later, Lee forced a long one-hander and missed. In the fight underneath for the rebound, Wilkes pushed Thompson. A whistle blew.

David realized this was the final test. These were not your usual free throws. He knew that making both of them meant victory over Goliath and a chance to play for the national championship. Number 44 had one more Superman act for this game. He calmly went to the line and made both free throws, widening the lead to 78-75.

With 27 seconds to go, Burleson stole Lee's pass to Walton and rifled a pass to Monte Towe. Curtis fouled Towe, and the little man made both his shots for 80-75.

Walton loped down the floor after—fittingly enough—scoring UCLA's last basket. He nodded to his comrade Lee as if to say, "It's okay." Now it was over for sure. He came to play, as always, but this time somebody played even better, and that was life. That was okay.

After the teams exited the floor for their respective locker rooms, the same NC State fan, who had asked the UCLA pep band leader in St. Louis if they played their fight song while the UCLA pom-pom girls danced even if the basketball team lost, observed that the pep band was not playing the Bruin fight song. The UCLA pom-pom girls were not dancing to the music with abandon. He smiled. Now, he had his answer.

Bill Walton sat naked in the dressing room refusing to talk to the press as usual. Grinning like a Cheshire cat and gnawing on a banana, he dressed in silence. Everything was okay. Even in defeat, Bill Walton knew who he was.

Once dressed, he shoved his uniform into a bag and left to sign autographs for some children. He stopped at the Coliseum exit when a man in overalls grabbed his arm. "Mr. Walton," the man said, "I work here, and I just want to shake your hand."

"Thanks," the player said. "And thanks for all you've done for us." As always, he had come to play. That was his standard. At the end, Bill Walton didn't even need to win.

"The year is 1974, and a team led by a high-flying forward named David has challenged the sport's last dynasty—a Goliath from UCLA, clad in light almost-Carolina-blue—in Greensboro. When Norman Sloan's NC State Wolfpack met Coach John Wooden's Bruins in these semifinals, UCLA owned a string of seven straight NCAA titles and had beaten the Pack soundly in a regular-season meeting in St. Louis.

"But, the giants fell today, and how State finally succeeded was simple enough, Jim. The Wolfpack forced the Bruins to start their offense farther out than they like, and State stopped the back door plays as Thompson held his former nemesis, Wilkes, to five baskets in 17 attempts while scoring 28 points himself. Towe buzzed around the UCLA guards until they finally got tired of swatting and started tripping over him, and Burleson prevented Walton from dominating though Big Red had the edge in points and rebounds, 29-20 and 18-14, Tall Tom actually prevailed on more big plays.

"The Pack rallied from an 11-point deficit in regulation and then came back from a seven-point deficit with about two minutes left in overtime to win, signaling the beginning of the age of parity in college basketball.

"The contest was a hard fought two-overtime battle between two great teams. But David Thompson hung over the hardwood longer and better than anyone else on this Saturday afternoon of March Madness when the chips were finally down for keeps," Packer concluded.

Post Game Press

The Wizard had long since lost his grip on the lucky silver cross buried in the left slacks pocket of his dark green suit. He seemed to be lost as he wandered toward the first NCAA Tournament press conference in 12 years he had ever attended as a loser.

"Sorry," he mumbled as he nearly walked into the NC State dressing room. There was only red and white in that locker room, he realized and released the door, ambling off again in the direction of where he thought the press conference was being held.

When he arrived at the press conference, Norm Sloan was still speaking, so John Wooden, the Wizard of Westwood, settled in a metal folding chair in that back hallway of the Greensboro Coliseum, flanked by barrels of floor wax, stripper, and cleaner as well as buckets and mops and various other maintenance equipment.

"We've had a great run," he began when he finally took the podium. "We've had outstanding basketball teams, and we've had a lot of things break right for us. But, they didn't break right for us today. So, we're out.

"In my entire coaching career, this is the game I am most disappointed with," Wooden explained. "Some people won't believe me. They still think the loss at Notre Dame to end the winning streak was the most disappointing, but it was no worse than any other non-conference loss. We had already broken the record by 27 games, and that game had nothing to do with our getting into the tournament. This loss puts us out of the NCAA tournament championship."

"The aura of invincibility and the mystique of a program that produced Lew Alcindor, Bill Walton, Henry Bibby, and Gail Goodrich made the Bruins the perennial favorites to win it all is no more," Jim Simpson whispered into the microphone just yards from where Wooden was speaking.

"That reliability went out the window this afternoon. It has been a year that saw the American presidency nearly crumble and the UCLA dynasty finally crumble. Billy, you just can't seem to count on anything anymore."

"You are so right, Jim," Bill Packer responded. "The Bruins' record 88-game was snapped in January at Notre Dame. UCLA then lost two more winning streak games in February and fell out of its familiar top spot in the national rankings."

"The Walton Gang was considered the favorite, though, as the NCAA tournament began."

"That's true, but North Carolina State, led by David Thompson, had revenge on its mind. The Bruins had routed the Wolfpack in December in a regular-season game at a neutral site. This time, State had a decided advantage. The Final Four was played in Greensboro, N.C."

"Obviously, playing in our home state and getting the fan support was important," said Thompson. "It was helpful, but it certainly wasn't a deciding factor.

"They had beaten us and we were looking for redemption. I think we were somewhat in awe of them the first time around. We panicked and lost the first game. Beating them in the tournament and breaking their championship streak was very important to us."

"The game certainly proved to be different from the December meeting. A give-and-take first half ended in a 35-35 tie after UCLA's Dave Meyers sank a buzzer-beater. Thompson was playing better than he had in the regular-season game, when he scored 17 points, and 7-foot-4 center Tom Burleson took Walton's best shots and remained standing."

"So, Jim, it was surprising to see the Bruins ahead, 57-46, with just under 11 minutes remaining in regulation."

"Yes. But, the Wolfpack came back. Turnovers by UCLA and another of Thompson's 'Skywalker' moves let the Bruins know the Pack wouldn't go quietly. Thompson took a lob pass from forward Tim Stoddard and slammed the ball home on the Alley-Oop, drawing a foul. He made the ensuing free throw and NC State had a 63-61 lead with just over two minutes remaining."

Meanwhile in the winner's locker room, David smiled at the announcer in that boyish way he smiled most of the time. "We've kind of popularized that Alley-Oop thing," David explained. "Since we aren't allowed to dunk the ball, we had to figure something out. Spectacular plays like that can be keys for me and the team."

"UCLA tied the score, 65-65, and the teams dragged through the first overtime, ending the extra session at 67-67. Walton and All-America forward Keith Wilkes gave the Bruins a quick 74-67 lead in the second overtime, and the UCLA faithful began waving their "Eight is Great" banners.

"But the Pack wasn't ready to despair and disband just yet. Monty Towe hit some free throws and the Bruins went into a turnover frenzy, just as they had late in regulation. Just as quickly as the lead had grown, it was gone.

"Thompson hit a jumper with just under a minute remaining to give NC State a 76-75 lead. Thirty seconds later he hit a pair of free throws to close out his game-high 28 points. Towe's free throws sealed the victory."

"They had their chance when we went down by seven in the second overtime," Thompson said. "But our team never gave up. We kept fighting and Coach Sloan kept telling us to make something happen. So, we did.

"We denied Walton from getting his third title. I think it'll be awhile before he gets over that.

"Right now I just want to be happy in what I'm doing. Sure, I'd like to make money doing what I love, playing basketball, but I think if I get the opportunity to play pro ball I will be happy no matter how much I make. Right now my focus is on our team and our fans and finally winning our National Championship."

"What about you, big guy? Ladies and Gentlemen, Tommy Burleson, the Wolfpack's All-American Center, has just joined us. There were some real Burleson moments out there today. What was the best one for you?

"Yes, sir. Well, the best was when Walton seemed to lose his composure in the last two minutes of overtime. He cocked the ball above his head; I stole it and laid it in. He came down the court expressing his middle finger at the back of my head on national TV. That was not indicative of someone with his class and character. I knew we had them then."

"You two have had a very intense individual rivalry, haven't you Tommy?"

"At first it was basically West Coast against East Coast. They've had such a dynasty. Seven straight titles." Tom Burleson smiled. "But not number eight."

"So when did it get personal?"

"I guess after he started saying stuff like he was a dominant center and that he got a better game in practice from Ralph Drollinger and Swen Nater than he did from me in St. Louis."

"And you sure proved that wrong today as well. Tommy Burleson. David Thompson. You guys'll be celebrating tonight? Right?"

"Well, sure, the team will celebrate a little. We'll probably get together in one of the guys' rooms and listen to music or watch TV."

"Yeah, I agree with Tommy. We can only celebrate a little, because as big as this win over UCLA is to all of us, the game that's for the championship is coming up on Monday night with Marquette. If we don't win that one, then we don't win anything."

* * * * *

The celebration in Raleigh began a little after five o'clock on Saturday evening as if the Pack had already won the title. Spontaneous caravans of vehicles clogged the streets. Students and fans began to fill the area around the NC State Bell Tower. Soon they were spilling into Hillsborough Street obstructing traffic flow on one of the major streets in the West Raleigh area. Suddenly, two male streakers emerged from the throng. They sprinted across Hillsborough Street and around the corner onto Oberlin Road where they raced through the Players' Retreat tavern. On the run, they scoffed down free beers offered by cheering customers.

A short while later, police charged one youth that they identified as "one of the streakers," with indecent exposure, blocking traffic, and resisting arrest. As the police car bearing the streaker pulled away taking him to the Wake County Magistrate's Office still in the nude, several young women began stripping atop cars.

"Alright, young man," the plainclothes detective shouted at the teenager in front of him dressed in jeans and an NC State sweatshirt, ogling the strippers, and puffing as hard as he could on a large joint. "You're under arrest for possession of a controlled substance, in this case marijuana."

"Oh, come on, man. Why me? This is just getting good, man. Smell the air, man. It's everywhere, man."

Police units in riot gear arrived in the campus area for the first time about 10 p.m. They formed a one-abreast line with riot sticks extended and forced the crowd off Hillsborough Street onto less-traveled Oberlin Road.

"Leave us alone!"

"We beat UCLA! Let us have our fun!"

After the game in Greensboro, NC State University Chancellor John T. Caldwell returned to his home on the campus about 10 p.m. He was listening to the jubilation of his students on radio when he suddenly detected a change in the tone of the crowd. "There's something wrong over there," he mumbled to his wife. "I guess I better go over there and see what I can do."

"If you think so, John. Go on ahead. Just be careful."

He left immediately for the celebration area.

"Chance" Caldwell, as his students knew him, arrived on the scene shortly after 10 p.m. He urged the crowd to go home or move onto the campus from the street.

"We don't want to spoil a great day," Caldwell repeated again and again to the crowd almost as if it were a prayer.

"Hey, Chance, you can get the police to leave, can't you?" yelled one student. "We're not breaking any windows or anything."

"Yeah, all we want to do is celebrate," shouted another.

Caldwell palavered with Chief of Police Goodwin protected from a sudden light shower as they huddled under a police umbrella.

"Chief. We've always had a good relationship with the police department. You've always been judicious and cautious in your use of force. I'm just real concerned about this confrontation here."

"Chancellor Caldwell, we entered the situation only when it appeared to be getting out of hand. We have received numerous complaints of the crowd beating on cars, blocking traffic, disturbing neighborhood property owners, and streaking. One couple even complained that they had been dragged from their car."

"Well, perhaps we can just back things up and let things cool off a bit. What do you think, Chief Goodwin?"

A few minutes later the police left as Chance Caldwell moved among the subdued crowd.

Another hour passed. Suddenly, a youth jumped into the midst of crawling traffic line on Hillsborough Street and dropped his trousers in front of one car's headlights. The crowd jeered and cheered.

Chance Caldwell darted into the street after him. He tugged on the youth's pants, trying to get them up. "Come on, now, son. Let's get you out of the middle of Hillsborough Street before the cops come back and arrest you."

"Okay, Chance," the young man acquiesced, grinning sheepishly, his head down and red as a NC State Wolf. Once the student hitched his jeans up, he and Chance Caldwell led a march toward the campus, chanting: "We're Number 1! We're Number 1! We're Number 1!"

The short march seemed to clear part of the area temporarily and calmed the students and others, Chance Caldwell returned home to monitor the activities on the radio with his wife. The celebration continued, ebbing and flowing with the intermittent rain.

When police returned shortly before 1 a.m., traffic snarled for several blocks on Hillsborough Street on either side of Oberlin Road. "We've got a lot of traffic congestion and citizen complaints are continuing to pour into headquarters, so we felt we had to come out again with our riot officers."

By about 1:20 a.m. light traffic moved freely onto side streets with the main streets still blocked off. "There are about 90 uniformed officers and plainclothes policemen here in the area right now," Captain Atkins announced over a bullhorn. "This assembly is unlawful, so anyone refusing to disperse will be arrested, and if this crowd doesn't scatter right away, we will employ tear gas."

The crowd didn't budge. After about five minutes, they hadn't scattered at all. If anything, their numbers had grown. Chief Goodwin and Captain Atkins assessed the situation and ordered a one-abreast line of uniformed and helmeted officers into action. They marched from Woodburn Road down Hillsborough Street, dodging beer bottles and other debris as they sprayed gas from pepper-fog machines.

A beer bottle struck one officer on the forehead, knocking him unconscious for several minutes. Another uniformed officer fell for no apparent reason and had to be dragged to the sidewalk.

Police continued their sweep up Oberlin Road with tear gas canisters and spraying machines. The students took refuge in a bank parking lot, but the police flanked them with a pincer movement of officers in the street and others moving in from an alley-driveway.

Except for scattered passersby and a last-minute news interview, the streets were clear by 2:30 a.m.

"I think the exuberance and enthusiasm of victory were aided by a few more beers than usual, and with the addition of the police to the scene, we had a rightly touchy situation there for awhile."

"Do you think the police should have intervened, Chancellor Caldwell?"

"A lot of things are matters of judgment. It is not up to me to make that judgment. A lot had already happened before I ever arrived on the scene."

"The police can't win in a situation like this," Goodwin added. "We just try to lose as gracefully as possible."

"The confrontation marks the first time in about 10 or 15 years that police have had to use crowd control measures as strong as tear gas in the State area. Other incidents "a long time back" involved panty raids to girls' campuses," Goodwin said.

"We have worked with the campus people for years," he continued, "and, frankly, we've been proud of the relationship that has built up over the years. We don't want to threaten anybody, but we must keep the peace."

Caldwell also pointed to the relationship between police and campus. "The main thing I deplore is this stand off between police and the crowd," he said. "I don't like to see this develop."

Thirty-one persons were arrested in the Hillsborough Street area near the NC State Bell Tower between 5:30 p.m. Saturday and 3:00 a.m. Sunday according to Wake County magistrate's Office records. Nine were NC State students. Most of the arrests came after midnight on charges of disorderly conduct or unlawful assembly when police blocked off the area to clear clogged traffic, then to disperse the celebrants with riots sticks and tear gas.

Authorities released most of those arrested on bonds ranging from $25 to $300 by daylight Sunday morning. Five spent the night in jail. One was still in jail Sunday night.

Flying beer bottles or other missiles injured at least seven city police officers, Police Captain Charles Atkins said. Three required medical treatment. None was hospitalized.

Police reported minor injuries among the crowd estimated at between 1,000 and 3,000.

Spokesmen for the NC State Infirmary, Rex Hospital, and Wake Memorial Hospital reported no patients treated as a result of the confrontation between police and students/fans.

No estimates of property damage were available late Sunday. Most of the damage appeared to be to police cars—smashed blue lights, missing antennas, and slashed tires.

By 3 a.m. Sunday, streets in the area were still littered with broken beer bottles and other debris.

* * * * *

In Greensboro, fans mobbed Vellie and Ida Thompson as they entered the lobby of the Albert Pick Motor Inn shouting, "The king is dead! The king is dead!" Fame and commotion seemed not to have affected David's parents too much. But, all this fuss was difficult to ignore.

"I don't think it's changed us much. We still don't have anything to boast about. We're just thankful for the opportunity," Mr. Thompson said to a sports reporter as he and his wife stood to the side of the lobby and shyly accepted the plaudits heaped upon them.

The sports reporter thought the Thompsons seemed too small to have produced their six-foot-four, 195-pound superstar son.

Each time a fan approached, stuck out a hand, and started into an effusive congratulations, the parents of Number 44 accepted it with a soft "thank you" and a smile that lit the room.

Those extending congratulations were among jubilant, well-dressed, mostly white fans that jammed the motel lobby. Receiving them were a slight, black textile worker and his wife.

There was little in the Thompsons background of hard, honest work in a Piedmont textile manufacturing center that would have thrust them into the setting. Except that their last son became possibly the best basketball player the Atlantic Coast Conference has ever seen.

Later, back in their motel room, the Thompsons finally got a chance to relax.

"We expected State to win. We knew if they all had a good night they wouldn't lose. Dave told us after the first UCLA game that the team would get back and take UCLA the next time," Thompson said. "Today our dream came true."

Both of the Thompsons planned not to go to work Monday. Instead they will drive back here from Shelby to catch the NCAA championship contest between State and Marquette if they can get through the snow that is being predicted.

"We've tried to get up to Raleigh for all the big games since he's been at State, even out to St. Louis for the first game with UCLA, but we haven't always made it," he said.

"People have been pretty nice to us. We don't feel like we deserve it, but we're glad it's coming our way. We just give thanks to the Lord for all that's happened."

"Both Thompsons work in Shelby, where they raised David and his 10 older brothers and sisters. They don't think their youngest had any problems adjusting when he moved to Raleigh in 1971."

"He's always been the type to make friends in a hurry, so at State he didn't have any problems. But he enjoyed living in Shelby with us too," Mrs. Thompson said.

"How did David get interested in basketball?"

"Well, I guess he's been interested about all his life—he used to watch it on television a lot, seeing Wilt Chamberlain and Charlie Scott. One day I brought home a surplus basketball net and put it up," Thompson said.

"The senior Thompson used to work at a military surplus store in Shelby before taking his job in a textile factory. And one of his jobs was to travel to Ft. Bragg to pick up surplus equipment, including basketball nets."

"I gave it to David because he's the baby.

"He tried a lot of different sports, but basketball has always been the one he came back to. In high school he was playing some football, but not much, and running some track. The coach told him it was a lot better for him to stick to basketball," he said.

"The Thompsons are obviously proud of their son—very proud—but it's a quiet emotion."

"He's always been the same kind of boy that he is today. He never got in trouble and always got along so well with his friends," Mrs. Thompson reflected, leaning back on their bed.

"He was always trying to do something for them—helping them with basketball and anything else he could," she said.

"David is a junior at State, but he's only 19 years old."

"We sent him to school at five. We were working in the fields so we just sent him to school with the others. He grew fast so they didn't ask his age," Mrs. Thompson said.

"The family thinks David will stay on at State for his senior year rather than turning to professional basketball and a quick fortune."

"But we haven't talked about it and we're leaving the decision up to him," Thompson said.

"Last week, when David took the fall heard round the world in the quarter-finals against Pittsburgh only 10 minutes into the game, his parents suddenly developed extra concern about the future."

"Our hearts kind of stopped. I could just see his career all over, but it was great the way he got along after the fall. The doctor said he didn't even have a headache," Mrs. Thompson said.

"He's just got a real strong constitution," her husband added.

"Both parents think that David's conduct on and off the court will help bring black people an additional measure of acceptance in the state."

"This could be a turning point in North Carolina. People recognize his ability and the way he carries himself. I think he's been a real help to all of us," his father said.

"But most of all they're just glad to have such a talented son."

Thompson paused, sipped on a soft drink and looked down at the red "Wolfpack Club" cap he wore during the game, then he looked at his wife, dressed in a red and white dress and a big white corsage.

"You know, I felt bad after that first UCLA loss (where David had one of his worst games ever and State took a 84-66 (drubbing) but not as bad as I would have felt if they lost tonight," he smiled.

Inside one of the team rooms at the Albert Pick, Coach Norm Sloan was trying to keep his Wolfpack focused, "Okay men, We have crossed this UCLA dynasty hurdle. In a lot of ways, it was our biggest hurdle. Hell, I've already heard from people from all over the country who told me where they were, what they were doing, where they watched the game on TV or listened on the radio. I had one fan call from Hong Kong to tell me that he was on a boat in the Hong Kong harbor when people heard the score of our game. Then horns started going off in the boats all over the harbor.

"Now, I know the fans think it's a given that we're going to beat Marquette. But, we haven't finished this race yet, and don't you forget it. If you want to be National Champions, you've got to go out there on Monday night and complete the mission."

"Hey, Coach," Nick Pond hurled at Sloan like a sharp pass as he walked through the motel lobby into the parking lot. Nick was also a former Everett Case player. He, too, knew how important this victory had been for that legacy. He, too, knew how much the Old Gray Fox would have loved breaking UCLA's hold on the National Championship. "Do you think this is the beginning of a dynasty, Norm?"

"Just the opposite, Nick," Norm threw back at him with no hesitation at all. "Just the opposite. The era of one-team domination is over in NCAA basketball, Nick. That's what this game was all about today."

THE SEMIFINALS
UCLA (77) v NCSU (80)

UCLA Game Statistics

Player	FG	FT	RB	PF	TP
Meyers	6-9	0-1	8	4	12
Wilkes	5-17	5-5	7	5	15
Walton	13-21	3-3	18	2	29
Curtis	4-8	3-4	5	5	11
Lee	4-11	0-0	4	2	8
Johnson	0-3	0-0	0	0	0
McCarter	1-2	0-0	0	0	2
TOTALS	33-71	11-13	44	18	77

NCSU Game Statistics

Player	FG	FT	RB	PF	TP
Stoddard	4-11	1-2	9	5	9
Thompson	12-25	4-6	10	3	28
Burleson	9-20	2-6	14	4	20
Rivers	3-8	1-2	2	3	7
Towe	4-10	4-4	2	4	12
Spence	2-3	0-0	5	0	4
Hawkins	0-0	0-0	0	0	0
TOTALS	34-77	12-20	44	19	80

UCLA	35	30	2	10	77
NCSU	35	30	2	13	80

Official Attendance: 15,829
Officials: Rick Weller (Big 10), Paul Galvin (SW)

15
Beyond Giants and Wizards

"The Marquette game was the one in which I panicked. We were one game away from the championship, and we knew we should win it, and all of a sudden I tightened up."

Norm Sloan

New York City native Al McGuire signed on as Head Basketball Coach with the Marquette Warriors in April, 1964, not quite ten years after David Thompson was born and about seven years before he accepted a grant-in-aid from NC State. It almost seemed as if they were somehow star-crossed to meet in this NCAA Finals on Monday, March 25, 1974 in the Greensboro Coliseum.

McGuire was also a player. He began his basketball career at St. John's Prep in Brooklyn where he also played football. At New York's St. John's University, he teamed with his brother Dick, a future hall-of-fame player, for the Redmen's 1948-49 season. During McGuire's years at St. John's, the university's team earned three National Invitation Tournament bids and one NCAA bid.

He received his bachelor's degree from St. John's in 1951.

His NBA career began with the New York Knicks where he again teamed with his brother for the 1951-52 team. Al continued with the Knicks through the 1954 season.

Dartmouth College named McGuire as an assistant coach in 1954. In 1957, at the recommendation of another McGuire, Frank, Belmont Abbey College in Belmont, N.C. selected him as its Head Coach. In his seven years there, he led the Crusaders to 5 small college post-season tournaments and a 109-64 record.

He began his tenure as Head Coach at the close of a 5-21 season, the worst in university history. His first Marquette team, in 1964-65, posted 8 wins and 18 defeats, then turned in a winning season in 1965-66 with a 14-12 record. The next year marked a major advance for McGuire's team, as it placed second in the 1967 NIT and finished the season 21-9. The NIT appearance was the first of 11 consecutive years of post-season play for McGuire's teams. By the end of the 1967-68 season, United Press International rated the team as the 10th best team in the nation.

Coach McGuire led the team to the 1970 NIT championship, and in 1971 was named Coach of the Year by the Associated Press, United Press International, Sporting News, and The U.S. Basketball Writers' Association.

He won Coach of the Year honors again in 1974 from the National Association of Basketball Coaches.

Pundits assumed that State would whip Marquette, but Sloan wasn't taking it for granted. He knew Marquette had a fine team and a lot of pride. And, he knew Al McGuire. Al McGuire was a winner. They never doubted that this was what it was all about. UCLA was just another scalp on the way that meant a helluva lot, but that victory only got State to the title game. Beating Marquette for the title . . . . Well, winning the NCAA championship was what it had been all about since Norm, himself, was a freshman under Coach Case.

And, the Pack players were determined to complete the task just like Coach had told them to do on Saturday night at the Albert Pick Motor Inn after they'd finally beaten the Big Red Head and his clan of bears. They all knew that without a win on Monday night there would be no championship and without a championship there would be no sense of final accomplishment. As far as the team was concerned, they decided the championship game right there in that motel room. All that remained for them to do now was go out there on Monday and play like the champions they knew they finally were.

"Coming into this game NC State has a playoff record of 11 and 8 in its eight appearances in the NCAA tournament, Jim Simpson."

The Warriors fell behind 10-2 in the first four minutes but rallied to tie the score at 12-12 at the end of eight minutes. Then, they began taking control of the game tempo. Lucas and Ellis, the Marquette 6-9 twin pivots, out positioned the Wolfpack repeatedly for rebounds. Earl Tatum stuck to David like a skin graft, and guards Marcus Washington and Lloyd Walton held up the Pack fast break and forced a number of turnovers.

Late in the first half an official whistled Marcus Washington for charging into Thompson after his driving score put the Warriors ahead 28-27. Coach Al McGuire came off the bench and onto the floor screeching—too loudly for the officials—and was hit with a technical foul.

Thompson drilled home three free throws. At 2:48 on the clock, Towe tossed the in bounds pass to Burleson who twisted in for a lay-up to make the score 32-28 State.

Less than a minute later, Marquette threw the ball away. Mo Rivers spotted Burleson open underneath. He scorched a bounce pass inside. Tommy scored again. The Warrior's lost the ball again. Towe brought the ball down and immediately spotted Phil Spence breaking underneath. He shot a pass up toward the glass. Spence leaped, snagging the ball and muscling it by Maurice Lucas for the basket. Lucas slapped the ball off the rim. A whistle blew.

"Goal-tending," the referee yelled as he waved his hand downward. "Basket is good!"

McGuire leaped off the Marquette bench and onto the court again.

Zap, another T on McGuire. Marquette went to the locker room down 39-30.

Thompson scored a baseline lay up and a follow-up free throw to open the second half. Burleson hit one of two free throws. Towe swished a twenty-five footer. The score was 45-30. The Pack continued to light it up during the first five minutes of the second half, outscoring the Warriors 12-2 and building a 19-point lead. At that point, however, State Coach Norman Sloan ordered one of the most explosive college basketball teams in history into his "tease" or "delay" offense. Sloan's reasons remained his own, but one could not help but speculate that he had decided that, with a 19 point lead and his growing fears of a Marquette comeback, the Wolfpack should play "not to lose" rather than "playing to win."

However, while the Pack offense bogged down in the "tease," Marquette cut the deficit to nine points with 10 minutes remaining. Their next shot missed. Unfortunately for the Warriors, coming from that far behind left little gas in their tanks, and the Marquette players were still staring up toward the rafters fearing another attack from Number 44. While the Warriors looked toward the rafters, Monte Towe and Mo Rivers continually slipped beneath their radar to keep the Warriors from getting any closer.

With 2:10 remaining, State led 69-56 despite the tease offense Coach Sloan had initiated with just a little over five minutes gone in the second half. Almost as if because of some signal, Monte Towe began to dribble around between the top of the key and the midcourt line, dodging around guards Marcus Washington and Lloyd Walton, finally splitting their attempted double team.

"Monte seems to be daring the Marquette players to try and take the ball away from him, Billy."

"And listen to that crowd, Jim."

"We're Number 1! We're Number 1! We're Number 1!" the Greensboro Coliseum crowd chanted for the first time.

Monte dribbled.

The crowd continued to scream the words that had taken an entire season to realize. "We're Number 1! We're Number 1! We're Number 1!"

With twenty-four seconds left on the game clock and Monte putting on another dribbling exhibition, Coach Al McGuire—St. John's and New York Knicks star and College Coach of the Year—slipped down court to the Wolfpack bench. He grinned at Norm Sloan's startled face when he looked up and saw his rival coach standing there with his hand stuck out. "Congratulations, Norm. You guys did a helluva job tonight. You deserve the championship."

Once Norm found his voice he answered. "Thanks, Al. I really appreciate that."

Then, Al McGuire was gone, leaving Norman Sloan to wonder if he had ever even been there. Monte stopped dribbling the basketball. The horn sounded.

The final score: NC State 76 – Marquette 64.

The crowd cheered: "We're Number 1! We're Number 1! We're Number 1!"

THE FINALS
Marquette (64) v NCSU (76)

Marquette Game Statistics

Player	FG	FT	RB	PF	TP
Ellis	6-16	0-0	11	5	12
Tatum	2-7	0-0	3	4	4
Lucas	7-13	7-9	13	4	21
Walton	4-10	0-0	2	2	8
Washington	3-13	5-8	4	3	11
Delsman	0-0	0-0	0	2	0
Daniels	1-3	1-2	0	3	3
Campbell	2-3	0-0	1	3	4
Homan	0-4	1-2	6	2	1
Brennan	0-0	0-0	0	0	2
TOTALS	25-69	14-21	43	29	64

NCSU Game Statistics

Player	FG	FT	RB	PF	TP
Stoddard	3-4	2-2	7	5	8
Thompson	7-12	7-8	7	3	21
Burleson	6-9	2-6	11	4	14
Rivers	4-9	6-9	2	2	14
Towe	5-10	6-7	3	1	16
Spence	1-2	1-2	3	2	3
Moeller	0-0	0-0	0	0	0
TOTALS	26-46	24-34	34	17	76

Technicals: McGuire (2)
Marquette 30 34 64
NCSU 39 37 76

Official Attendance: 15,792
Officials: Jim Howell, Irv Brown (SW)

16
At Last, The Ring!

Norman Sloan cut the last strand of the net as he straddled the shoulders of his Everett Case prototype team, THE team. He could almost sense the Old Gray Fox's presence even in the Greensboro Coliseum eighty miles away from his final resting place overlooking US Highway 70 as it made its way west toward Durham, Burlington, and ultimately Greensboro. It had been a long and winding road since 1946 when Coach Case had arrived from Indiana nearly unnoticed with nothing more than his duffel bag full of coaching tricks and his dream of creating the best college basketball in the world. And, he had actually done it, even though he hadn't lived to see the results of those fabulous seeds he'd sown all those years ago when even the great visionary that was Everett Case couldn't have foreseen a David Thompson or a Tom Burleson or even what the prototype team would ultimately look like. The shoulders beneath Coach Sloan parted carefully. Arms reached up and helped guide him back down to the hardwood as he waved the net over his head. Finally, they were the national champs in the true Everett Case tradition.

"Ladies and gentlemen, may I draw your attention to center court where we are about to introduce to you the 1974 Final Four All-Tournament team.

"And here they are: Tommy Burleson, NC State. Monte Towe, NC State. Maurice Lucas, Marquette. Bill Walton, UCLA. Player of the Year, David Thompson, Most Outstanding Player, NC State.

"And, now, it is my pleasure to present your 1974 NCAA national basketball champions, the Wolfpack of North Carolina State University and their coach Norman Sloan.

"We're Number 1!" the crowd cheered as the Wolfpack followed their coach onto the hardwood one last time as a team, as NCAA Champions. "We're Number 1! We're Number 1!"

The cheers of delirious fans had barely subsided when Lefty Driesell screamed at the Wolfpack team bus as it pulled out of the parking lot. "You guys are great!"

David, Monte, Tommy, Tim, Mo, and Phil clapped and waved through the bus windows at the coach of that super Maryland team of Len Elmore, Tom McMillen, and John Lucas. In some ways, that ACC final had really been the game for the national championship as far as they were concerned.

"I'm going to go home and work my butt off and do the same thing!" Lefty hollered and waved as he walked across the parking lot into the glare of scattered headlights from cars still leaving after the game.

This Wolfpack team had been required to overcome every kind of adversity. The lack of a freshman eligibility rule had stopped them their first year. The no dunk rule they overcame by inventing the Alley-Oop. Their probation last year for violations during the recruiting of David and Tommy that had been so unfair that even the media thought they had been treated badly. Certainly, no one expected a ban on their eligibility for the NCAA championship. Third year. They lost to UCLA. They got down by 15 to Purdue. They almost lost the ACC championship to Maryland. David fell during the Pitt game, and they thought all was lost. They came back to beat UCLA in the final four. And, they finally did it. They beat Marquette for the national championship.

Yes. It also had been a long and winding road since 1949 and that first game against Washington & Lee in William Neal Reynolds Coliseum, the House that Case Built. It was a real shame that Coach Case hadn't lived long enough to help cut down these nets celebrating his North Carolina State Wolfpack's first National Championship coached by one of his own originals.

Now, here they were, basking in the glory of final victory with their fans and friends. Tim Stoddard, Monte Towe, David Thompson, Tommy Burleson, Phil Spence, Mo Rivers, and the rest of the Wolfpack stood in front of the thousands of cheering students basking in the transitory moment called glory. A huge white banner with "NC State Number 1" painted in red on it fluttered behind them.

"We're Number 1! We're Number 1! We're Number 1!"

"Wow, how cool!" Monte screamed out over the noisy mass of students. "We're national champs!"

"We're Number 1!" the crowd answered. "We're Number 1!"

With a NCAA National Basketball Championship banner hanging from its rafters, William Neal Reynolds Coliseum would be complete now just as David's room in his family's house finally had a solid wall rather than a plastic covering.

The House That Case Built and The House that Vellie Built. That these two houses came together in their completions had been no small thing.

Acknowledgments

I relied upon some of the following materials in great detail. Other sources I hardly used, if at all. Yet, I have made every effort to ensure that all materials relied upon, no matter how minor the reliance, are properly credited under these acknowledgments. No improper or plagiaristic use of these or any other materials is intended in any way, and I apologize for any oversights.

I would also like to acknowledge the continued support of my wife, Lana, for her belief that someday my writing would amount to something other than keeping Champion Paper Company in business. Further, I want to thank my dear friend and fellow NC State alumnus James E. Maynard, Jr. [Jim] for his invaluable assistance and support. Our many discussions on the subject of this book eventually led me to realize that I was writing more than a book about the 1973-74 team. I was writing a book that really dealt with the culmination of nearly thirty years of effort from the beginnings of the Everett Case era at State and the ACC era in southern basketball. I came to understand that without the Old Gray Fox and William Neal Reynolds Coliseum, The Dixie Classic, and the ACC tournament, Dads would not have erected basketball goals in practically every backyard or driveway in North Carolina in the fifties and sixties. Without those goals, David Thompson, Tommy Burleson, Michael Jordan and many others might never have existed. And, we would all be the poorer for it.

I also would like to acknowledge interviews with the late Nick Pond, Dr. James Manley, and Norman Sloan, as well as with Monte Towe and Eddie Biedenbach. These interviews took place within a few years of the Wolfpack's national championship run.

Finally, I want to extend a most profound thanks to one of the all-time great college basketball centers and one heck of a person, Tommy Burleson for his willingness to read the manuscript and make comments.

1. "NC State," *The News & Observer*, Chip Alexander, November 24, 1991.
2. "It's your call: DT or Laettner," *The News & Observer*, Caulton Tudor, Staff writer, March 31, 1992.
3. "'74 Wolfpack slew the giant," *The News & Observer*, Chip Alexander, Staff Writer, November 15, 1998.
4. "THE ENVELOPE PLEASE," *The News & Observer*, Caulton Tudor, Staff Writer, November 14, 1993.

5. "ACC FLASHBACKS: It seems like only yesterday," *The News & Observer*, Chip Alexander, Staff Writer, March 9, 1993.
6. "Memories are made of these," *The News & Observer*, Caulton Tudor, Staff Writer, March 5, 1998.
7. "PACK TO PLAY A PART IN FREAKY FRIDAY: A drive down madness lane," *The News & Observer*, Charles Salter Jr., Staff Writer, March 8, 1996.
8. "David Thompson, the greatest," *The News & Observer*, Chip Alexander, Staff Writer, August 22, 1999.
9. "Thompson the winner in landslide," *The News & Observer* April 4, 1992.
10. "Thompson tells story of new faith," *The News & Observer* By David Justice, Staff Writer, December 31, 1996.
11. "All-Time ACC Media Guide," *The News & Observer*, November 14, 1993.
12. "Holiday tournament to salute Thompson Ex-Pack great to speak to FCA," *The News & Observer* By Tim Stevens, Staff Writer, December 11, 1996.
13. "When last we visited" *The News & Observer* By Bill Woodward, Staff Writer, April 1, 1994.
14. "Goaltending from the sidelines: Francis remembers it all," *The News & Observer* By Caulton Tudor, Staff Writer, November 24, 1991.
15. "In game for the ages, it was do or die," *The News & Observer* By Chip Alexander, Staff Writer, March 4, 1999.
16. "End of an era: NC State's '74 stopped UCLA's reign in a dramatic semifinal, a harbinger of parity in college basketball ," *The News & Observer*, Bill Woodward, Staff Writer, December 26, 1993.
17. "Generations apart, linked by the game," *The News & Observer*, Tim Stevens, Staff Writer, November 24, 1999.
18. "Uplifting remembrance of Thompson's fall," *The News & Observer*, Al Myatt, Staff Writer, March 16, 1999.
19. "Century shapers," *The News & Observer* By Dane Huffman; Staff Writer December 28, 1999.
20. "READER'S VIEWS OF DAVID THOMPSON," *The News & Observer* February 7, 1996.
21. "Thompson takes spot in Hall," *The News & Observer* By The Associated Press May 7, 1996.
22. "Humble Thompson brought people together," *The News & Observer* By Tim Stevens; Staff Writer February 11, 1996.
23. "Chasing victories with life on line," *The News & Observer* By Al Myatt, Correspondent, March 4, 1991.
24. "NC State Tags David 'Super Star,'" *The Basketball News*, By Frank Dascenzo, Associate Editor VOL X, NO 23, MAY, 1972.
25. "State Frosh Sensation In Two Sports," *Durham Morning Herald*, Chuck Lewis, Sports Writer April 2, 1972.
26. "The Burden of David Thompson," *Charlotte News*, Ronald Green, Sports Editor November 24, 1972.
27. "Thompson's fame spreads to the Hall," *The News & Observer* By Chip Alexander; Staff Writer February 6, 1996.
28. "Michael Jordan, changed the game - and the marketplace," *The News & Observer* By Caulton Tudor; Staff Writer August 22, 1999.
29. NCAA FINAL FOUR: CHAMPIONSHIP RESULTS Sunday, March 14, 1999, 14:26 ET© Copyright 1999 NCAA®, Host communications, and Total Sports All rights reserved worldwide.
30. "Everyone got caught up in the team," *The News & Observer* By Chip Alexander, Staff writer December 29, 1999.
31. "'A beautiful basketball player' Thompson poised to join game's greats," *The News & Observer* By Chip Alexander and Dane Huffman; Staff Writers February 5, 1996.
32. "ECU's still got sand in its shoes," *The News & Observer* By Caulton Tudor, March 14, 1991.
33. "State does a number on old stars," *The News & Observer* By A. Sherrod Blakely; Staff Writer, February 25, 1999.
34. "This memory can't be broken," *The News & Observer* By Bruce Phillips February 16, 1991.

35. "Monroe is just a big game away from legend's record," *The News & Observer* By Dane Huffman, February 11, 1991.
36. "It was David Thompson's day but Rodney Monroe's show," *The News & Observer* By Dane Huffman, Staff Writer, January 14, 1991.
37. "50 Years of Thrills," *The News & Observer*, November 8, 1998.
38. "Cornerstone of a conference," *The News & Observer* By Chip Alexander; Staff Writer, February 24, 1999.
39. "Remembering Reynolds Coliseum," *The News & Observer*, February 24, 1999.
40. "Wooden's worst day," *The Bergen Record*, By Kevin T. Czerwinski, Staff Writer, Feb. 11, 1996.
41. "SI hasn't forgotten soaring Thompson," *The News & Observer* By A.J. Carr; Staff Writer, December 22, 1999.
42. "Memories of '74 championship team special, Sloan says," *The News & Observer* By Bill Woodward, Staff Writer, December 26, 1993.
43. "The UCLA streak ends," *The Sporting News* By Joe Gergen, 2000.
44. "World University Games—1973," *The News and Observer*, Friday, August 17, 1973.
45. "World University Games—1973," *Greensboro Daily News* By Bill Hass, Staff Sports Writer, August 28, 1973.
46. "David Thompson Comes Home" By Ken Dingler, 1973.
47. "Nothing Could Be Finer," *Sports Illustrated*, by Curry Kirkpatrick, April 1, 1974.
48. READER'S VIEWS OF DAVID THOMPSON *The News & Observer* February 7, 1996.
49. "All-Century" lists ESPN.COM Chat room   Sunday, Sep. 5 11:11am ET.
50. "A Towering Twosome: No other pair in the college game is at the level of Sam Perkins and Michael," CNN/SI, Curry Kirkpatrick, Issue date: November 28, 1983.
51. "All Bases," *Charleston Daily Mail*, Bill Smith, Sports Editor, February 6, 1974.
52. "Wolves and Bears," *Time*, December 24, 1973.
53. "Half of Big Red is Too Much," *Sports Illustrated*, Curry Kirkpatrick, December 12, 1973.
54. "All-American's Mother Speaks," *Shelby Daily Star*, David Camp, Staff Writer, December 14, 1973.
55. "Would You Believe David Thompson at East High," *Forest City This Week*, Jock Lauterer, June 19, 1974.
56. "Boys' World to Open," *Forest City This Week*, April 17, 1974.
57. "Superstar's Family Plays It Cool," *Charlotte Observer*, Bob Whitely, Sports Writer, October 14, 1973.
58. "David! David! David!" *Durham Herald*, Joe Gergen, Post-Times Service, December 8, 1974.
59. "The Littlest Giant," *Charlotte News*, Ronald Green, Sports Editor, 1974.
60. "Thompson: The Best," *Charlotte News*, Ronald Green, Sports Editor, 1974.
61. "Leader of the Pack," *Newsweek*, January 8, 1973.
62. "Pack's Most Popular Personality," *Durham Herald*, Chuck Lewis, Sports Editor, 1973.
63. "David Thompson named Christmas Seal Chrmn." *Belmont Banner*, December 11, 1974.
64. "David Thompson Files," North Carolina State University Athletic Department.
65. "1973-74 Films," North Carolina State University Library.
66. "North Carolina State Wolfpack Basketball," Department of Athletics, NC State University, 1971-72, 1972-73, 1973-74, 1974 75 editions.
67. "Super Thompson and Monty Towe," *The Hickory News*, Charles H. Deal, June 20, 1974.
68. "Everybody Amazed, Even Sloan," *Greensboro Daily News*, August 28, 1973.
69. "U.S. Cagers Open With Win As University Play Begins," *The News and Observer*, August 17, 1973.
70. "David Goes After Goliath," *Sports Illustrated*, Curry Kirkpatrick, November 26, 1973.
71. "That Championship Season," *The News and Observer*, John Coit, Staff Writer, February 18, 1973.
72. "David Thompson: 11th Child Special," *Charlotte News*, January 23, 1973.
73. *Baltimore Evening Sun*, Bob Ibach, 1974.

74. "David's Parents Shy, Proud," *Raleigh Times*, Michael J. Hall, Staff Writer, March 19, 1974.
75. "'Oh Lord, It Scared me to Death,'", *Shelby Daily Star*, Eddie Southards, Sports Writer, March 18, 1974.
76. "Superstar's Family Plays It Cool, *The Charlotte Observer*, Bob Whitely, Sports Writer, October 14, 1973.
77. "Wolfpack by a Fang," *Sports Illustrated*, Barry McDermott, March 18, 1974.
78. "David Thompson Voices His Views on Basketball," *The News and Observer*, December 1, 1974.
79. "A Lesson for the Preacher Man," *Sports Illustrated*, Barry McDermott, January 22, 1973.
80. "Thompson's Legend Grows Each Week," *Greensboro Daily News*, Alfred Hamilton, January, 1974.
81. "Man behind the hoopla," *The News & Observer*, Chip Alexander, Staff Writer, December 31, 1999,
82. "Cornerstone of a conference," *The News & Observer*, Chip Alexander, Staff Writer, February 24, 1999.
83. "ECU's still got sand in its shoes," Caulton Tudor, *The News & Observer*, March 14, 1991.
84. *Fayetteville Observer-Times*, "Bones knew how to live, how to laugh," Jim Pettit, Assistant sports editor, May 18, 1997.
85. "Wooden, John," Microsoft® Encarta® Online Encyclopedia 2000, http://encarta.msn.com © 1997-2000 Microsoft Corporation. All rights reserved.

ACC Basketball History Through 1974 in a Nutshell

1954: First season of the new Atlantic Coast Conference. No team ranked. NC State won the ACC tournament and had a 26-7 record. Duke was 21-6 and Maryland 23-7. State placed third in the Eastern Regionals.
1955: State ranked fourth in AP and sixth in UPI polls. Coach Everett Case's Wolfpack, starring guard Vic Molodet and center Ronnie Shavlik, finished the regular season 28-4, but was ineligible for the NCAA. Duke 20-8 lost in the first round of the NCAA playoffs.
1956: State ranked Number 2 in both polls with a 24-4 record. The Pack won the ACC title for the third straight time but lost a memorable four-overtime NCAA playoff game to Canisius.
1957: Carolina went undefeated in 32 games and was Number 1 in both polls. Coach Frank McGuire's Tar Heels, starring Lennie Rosenbluth, beat Michigan State (3 overtimes) and Kansas (also 3 overtimes) for the national title.
1958: Maryland finished fourth in regular season but won the ACC tournament and was ranked Number 6 in both polls. Coach Bud Millikan's Terps, featuring Nick Davis, AL Bunge, and Charlie McNeil, had a 22-7 record and placed third in the regionals.
1959: AP ranked State sixth and Carolina ninth. UPI ranked State fifth and Carolina sixth. State won the title but could not go to NCAA, so the Tar Heels went, losing in first round. State was 22-4 and Carolina was 20-5. McGuire pulled his starters early, basically throwing the game because they didn't need to win it since State was on probation.
1960: No team rated in polls. Wake Forest (21-7) and Carolina (18-6) tied for the regular season title but Duke, fourth, won the tournament and placed second in regionals.
1961: Three ACC teams ranked in UPI's top ten: Carolina sixth, Duke ninth, and Wake Forest tenth. AP rated Carolina fifth and Duke tenth. Carolina could not play in the NCAA and did not enter the tournament. Wake, with Coach Bones McKinney and ACC player of the year Len Chappell, won the tournament and placed second in the regionals. The Deacs were 19-11 for the year. Duke 22-6 and Carolina 19-4.

1962: UPI picked Wake Forest seventh. AP listed Duke tenth. Wake went on to win the ACC, the regionals, and took third in the nationals (over UCLA). Wake Forest was 22-9 and Duke 20-5.
1963: Duke finished second in both polls, went 14-0 in conference, won the regionals, and beat Oregon State for third place in the nationals. Vic Bubas was the coach, Art Heyman and Jeff Mullins the stars of the 27-3 team.
1964: TEN-YEAR CONFERENCE ANNIVERSARY. Duke placed third in AP, fourth in UPI. The Blue Devils won the ACC, finished second to UCLA in the finals. Mullins led the 26-5 team.
1965: Duke placed ninth in UPI, tenth in AP. With a 20-5 record, the Blue Devils lost to State in the ACC tournament, with the Wolfpack placing third in the regionals.
1966: Duke ranked Number 2 in both polls. Coach Bubas now had Jack Marin, Bob Verga, and Steve Vacendak and placed third in the nationals. 26-4 record.
1967: Carolina, coached by Dean Smith, ranked third in AP, fourth in UPI. The Tar Heels, starring Larry Miller, won the ACC and posted a 26-6 record, finishing fourth in the nationals.
1968: AP picked Carolina fourth and Duke tenth. UPI rated the Tar Heels third. With a 26-6 record, Carolina won the ACC, a second regional, and reached the national finals, losing to UCLA. Larry Miller and Charlie Scott were the leaders.
1969: Carolina rated second in the UPI poll and fourth in the AP. The Tar Heels won an unprecedented third straight regional, placed fourth in the nationals with Dick Grubar injured. Scott and Bill Bunting shone on this 27-5 squad.
1970: AP rated South Carolina sixth and State tenth. UPI listed the Gamecocks sixth. South Carolina had a 25-3 record but lost to State in the ACC tournament. Coach Norm Sloan's Wolfpack, starring Vann Williford, was 23-7 and placed third in the regionals.
1971: South Carolina was rated sixth in both polls with a 23-6 record. Coach Frank McGuire's team, spearheaded by John Roche, won the ACC and placed fourth in the regionals. Carolina 26-6 won the NIT.
1972: Carolina was ranked No. 2 in both polls with a 26-5 mark. The Heels placed third in the NCAA finals. Maryland, 27-5, won the NIT.
1973: State went 27-0 and won the ACC tournament but was ineligible for the NCAA for the third time. Maryland placed second in the regionals. Carolina placed third in the NIT.

1974: TWENTY-YEAR CONFERENCE ANNIVERSARY.
[Adapted from "ACC Basketball Brief History," Bruce Phillips, *News and Observer,* February 13, 1974]

To contact Timothy Brannan or order copies of his other works: *Into the Elephant Grass: A Viet-Nam Fable*, *TEACH*, *Manhattan Spiritual*, *Adventures in Another Paradise*, and *'74: A Basketball Story* please shop, write, or e-mail as follows:

www.amazon.com

Gemini Publishing
2828 N. Atlantic Avenue, Apt. 502
Daytona Beach, Florida 32118

tbrannan@cfl.rr.com

www.ingramcontent.com/pod-product-compliance
Lightning Source LLC
Chambersburg PA
CBHW061321040426
42444CB00011B/2721